OUT OF
CHAOS

"Powerfully honest memoir…couched in clear, spare prose with well-crafted, believable dialogue. A broad range of readers will relate to…Mott's sincere and deep reflection on complicated family and relationship dynamics. And they'll surely be inspired by the effort she displayed to regain control of a life badly derailed."

BlueInk Review

"*Out of Chaos* is a work of pure courage—a story hard to tell about a life that's been even harder to live… Elle Mott cuts herself no slack in sharing her mistakes along with her achievements…this book is a true gift to the reader."

Pamela Whissel
American Atheist Editor-in-Chief

"Captivating, thrilling, this book kept me turning pages late into the night…punk rock, rebellion, and the raw substance of what it means to be human in an ever-changing world. Elle Mott's chaotic journey makes one appreciate who we have in life and how we get through both trials and victories."

Emily Bolte
Public Library Worker, Cincinnati, Ohio

"Compulsively readable and compelling. *Out of Chaos* is the real deal. It is the story of one woman's struggle to overcome family rejection, physical handicaps, alcoholism, abusive relationships, and homelessness. It's a narrative few in that situation would be able to tell so eloquently. Read this book!"

Gary Reed
Author of *Things Could Get Ugly*

"Elle Mott is like Marilyn Monroe, men want to rescue her and women want to be her friend. This book turns you into an Elle Mott fan, a big one, and you want her to win. And it's not because she's a victim of all the rotten cards she's been dealt. The honesty of *Out of Chaos* kicks like judo. It smacks of the truth and it shows you this is one brave writer, the kind that doesn't come around very often, and when it does, you're lucky to read it."

Richard DeVall
Author of *Old Letters and New Demons*

OUT OF CHAOS

A MEMOIR

ELLE MOTT

Boyle
&
Dalton

Publisher's Cataloging-In-Publication Data
(Prepared by The Donohue Group, Inc.)

Names: Mott, Elle.
Title: Out of chaos : a memoir / Elle Mott.
Description: [Zanesville, Ohio] : Boyle & Dalton, [2018]
Identifiers: ISBN 9781633372061 (print) | ISBN 9781633372078 (ebook)
Subjects: LCSH: Mott, Elle. | Homeless persons--United States--
Biography. | Women authors--United States--Biography. | Female
offenders--United States--Biography. | LCGFT: Autobiographies.
Classification: LCC HV4505 .M68 2018 (print) | LCC HV4505
(ebook) | DDC 305.5692092 B--dc23

Book Design & Production
Columbus Publishing Lab
www.ColumbusPublishingLab.com

Copyright © 2018 by Elle Mott
LCCN 2018946062

Print ISBN: 978-1-63337-206-1
E-book ISBN: 978-1-63337-207-8

Printed in the United States of America

1 3 5 7 9 10 8 6 4 2

People, pets, places, and events described in this book are real. Most names have not been changed. Some names were changed out of memory lapse, to eliminate redundancy, and in a few cases, to protect privacy. Conversations are at times presented word-for-word, and at other times, as the closest approximation possible while staying true to the story.

Encouraged by others to write my story, my heart goes out to those left behind: Kris, Steve, Jim, and Richard (aka Josh). My heart goes out to the families of Bud and Mike, both of whom have since died from their own chaos.

I wrote my story to show that no matter what mistakes we made, what wrongs we did, or what hardships we endured, we can make a right-about face. A change of heart and action makes it possible to become a contributing member in society. This change gives us peace, a sense of belonging, purpose, and meaning.

Inspired by memoir, focused on life today.

Written in memory of my maternal great-grandmother, Marie. I dedicate this debut book to my late father, Bob Wells, whom I came to know and love only after he died.

❖

PART ONE

CHAPTER 1

WHO AM I?

B urnt orange rays flatline on the horizon. Like the setting sun, I'm tired and ready to rest. We wait, standing on the sidewalk at an intersection for the crosswalk light to change. Traffic passes by on this balmy evening in April 1993, somewhere deep in Midwest America. Makes no difference where exactly we are. As usual, we'll be back out here, on the interstate on-ramp pushing us farther from the place we once called home.

I tug at the straps on my backpack, adjusting the weight, but have no room to complain. His pack is a lot heavier, with a full frame. He has our bedroll and a plastic gallon of water tied to it with bungee cords. His pack carries our hygiene kits, flashlights, a little food, and other things we need. My pack has our few clean T-shirts, dry socks, tobacco, and a deck of cards. He also keeps his weathered childhood family photos pocketed deep in his pack, lest he forget where he came from. I have no pictures, no heirlooms, and no keys to the past.

Eighteen-wheelers force their way in and out of a truck stop, spilling billowy exhaust. Their horns blare and their Jake brakes screech. A suit-and-tie guy in a sports car races to the on-ramp with his convertible top down. A station wagon with a back seat full of kids exits the interstate and drives out of sight.

The crosswalk light changes, giving us the go-ahead. "Ready?" he asks me.

Pushing matted hair off my sunbaked cheeks, I step off the curb and keep close to him. My old life is abandoned, given up in favor of trusting him completely with how my existence unfolds. Dependent on him, I'm locked into his best judgment for our well-being. I turn my head to see his familiar nod of reassurance.

Our backpacks make our walk across the intersection cumbersome. He's bouncing, same as me in our gait to the nearby underpass. *Just a few more steps*, I tell myself.

Breathing heavily, we lumber up a steep incline to a leveled three-foot-wide space. Its length spans the distance of the overpass above. I drop my pack to the cement ground. After helping him maneuver out of his pack, he releases the bungee cords, unrolling our sleeping bag, and lays it out flat. Our packs will work fine as pillows at the wall behind us.

I sit, letting my lower legs relax with the concrete's slanted decline. This is how we'll have to sleep tonight, but I'm used to that. The night before, we slept on a tree-lined hillside, pinecones and all.

He sits down next to me and lets out a breath of relief. Removing his ball cap, which he always wears backward, he takes the rubber band out of his hair. His curls fall freely from the released ponytail.

After shaking his head side to side, he puts on a knit hat and then puts his ball cap back on over that. He leans into me with a hug and says, "Put another sweater on so you don't get cold. The temperature is dropping."

His hug alone could keep me warm, all 250 pounds of him. Me, I'm scrawny at little more than one hundred pounds. The foundation under me reverberates as a semitruck drives overhead.

Rifling through his pack to find some sort of dinner makings, he first pulls out a bottle of rotgut sweet wine. He takes a sip, then passes me the bottle. We'll need its warmth to keep from waking up shivering cold in the middle of the night. It isn't cold out yet, only a little chilly, but I thirst for the escape to be found in its fruity potency—an acquired taste. Two quick gulps are all it takes for me to feel a warm buzz.

Although sheltered from the wind, I feel my melancholy mood blow away as I stare off into the distance. My heavyset confidante sits beside me, busying himself. I'm okay with letting him lead, but anxious to discover where I—not we—where I will end up.

My childhood place, with Nana's guidance, had come when my family elders were at a loss for where I was supposed to land. And my childhood landing place was only the first of many cycles of my transiency, some gone and some yet to be played out. When I was a child, Nana taught me to have a reason behind my choices, and to persevere.

Back then I had relied on her approval and praises. When a little older, I ran with her ideas. My choices, though, had hurt myself and others, causing havoc. Those choices are now in the past, along with the notoriety that came with them. So, too, is my family in the past, a family who doesn't want me for what I did.

I gulp another swallow of wine and follow his hand directions to help. No words are needed between us over dinner, which leaves me to my own thoughts. I feel like a seaman who has gone overboard from a fishing boat, arguing with gravity against the weight of the water, battling my fears through sharp waves. At a quarter-century old, navigational skills are a must if I'm going to find my place in this big country.

"Are you listening to me?" he asks in a tone as if repeating himself.

I push my memories aside. "I'm sorry, no. What did you say?"

"I was asking you about your birthday next month and where we..."

CHAPTER 2

KIMBERLY LOUISE

I'm riding high on Grandpa's shoulders on his nightly walk down the long driveway to lock up Nana's antique shop. Ahead, the old red barn towers high into the sky, void of any goats or horses or haylofts. It was our routine, one of many we shared. Those were my first memories, filled with adoration for my best friend who filled the fatherly role in my early years.

Pastures and farmland were once the norm, replaced by ranch-style family homes. Nestled in the northwest corner of Oregon, 1970s Salem stretched its arms outward from the city center with family neighborhoods. My nana's shop, Polly's Barn Antiques, fit neatly in this arm stretch, away from bustling inner-city malls.

Grandpa's weathered pale white hands gripped my bare legs as they peeked out from my dress to rest against his warm flannel shirt. The sun hadn't set yet and the early evening was chilly. I turned my head. We were too close to the end of our walk. A big walnut tree shaded the grassy yard beside us and was laden with nuts, many of which lay on the grass below. Unlike the walnuts, fallen from their tree, Grandpa held onto me tightly.

He wasn't actually my grandpa, but my step great-grandfather from my mother's side of the family. With a limited grasp to understand life and where I came from, I had no real concept of a father or a father's side of the family. I had no awareness that I even had a father.

People knew my grandpa as Art, or as Mr. Schmidt, and he assumed his role in my life through his marriage to Nana as her third husband. She was the all-wise one to look to for guidance, even when I thought I could do just fine without someone telling me what to do.

My time with Nana was usually spent as I practiced my ABCs or sang off-tune while she played her piano. It was during those moments that Grandpa retreated to his workshop to make doll furniture and other toys I later found under our Christmas tree, often too big to bother with wrapping paper. A doorbell intercom system alerted us to any customer arrivals to Nana's shop, abruptly interrupting us. She'd dart out the door on cue, leaving me alone. Soon after, Grandpa would come in from his workshop and make my world better. My fondest childhood memories were when I played with my Raggedy Ann doll while Grandpa played Raggedy Andy.

Dinnertime is an equally vivid memory. Grandpa and I shared one plate on a TV tray, as he sat opposite me in his blue wingback chair. Steak was routine, cooked juicy rare and cut into bite-sized pieces for me. Nana preferred a light meal of tomato soup and a bread roll at the round oak table with a view out the kitchen window.

One morning I woke up to an unusual influx of people rushing about the house. Some people I knew. Some I didn't. My mother was there, and my great aunt Peg, and my aunt Vickey, too. I looked up at everyone in my fervent search for Grandpa.

In my childlike mind at only five and a half years old, I didn't have long to take in that scene before Aunt Vickey scooped me up into her arms. I'd rather have been with Grandpa, but I intuited the seriousness of the situation. And serious times came hand in hand with Nana, so it made sense to me that Aunt Vickey took me into Nana's bedroom. With the door shut behind us, we played quietly with the doll I had dragged along to help search.

Later, Nana came in and shut the door behind her. She sat in her chair at her dressing table, but faced me and not the mirror. Pulling me in close to her, she said, "Kim, Grandpa went to sleep last night but he didn't wake up this morning. He went to Heaven."

Nana always called me Kim, even when others called me Kimmy. After all, my birth name was Kimberly Louise, with my first name spelled the traditional way, K-i-m-b-e-r-l-y. I let go of my doll and grabbed onto Nana's forearms for leverage. Her eyes looked back at me piercingly as I asked, "Where's Heaven?"

"With Jesus and the angels. Remember, at night when we say our prayers to Jesus?"

Uh huh, I thought as I nodded.

Nana explained, "That's where he is now—with Jesus and the angels."

I had to look to Nana for truth. Loss and emptiness engulfed me. Life became different from that day forward. The one thing I knew for sure was I missed Grandpa so much it made my child-sized heart ache. My best friend was gone. My rock in this world was gone.

As the days ensued, it didn't help that Nana tried to erase Grandpa and his things. For starters, construction workers knocked out the back wall to Grandpa's bedroom. Nana ordered a sliding glass door. From there, a back porch was built. The familiar sight of Grandpa's bed and green wool blankets was gone, but the room no longer belonged to him. It became the family room, used to watch TV, to listen to records, and to play cards. An added bookshelf became a place for Nana's scrapbook display.

As if the change to one room, Grandpa's bedroom of all places, wasn't enough change to tug at me, I watched in horror as Grandpa's smoking chair was hauled out of our living room by some man I'd never seen before. A white fainting couch from Nana's shop replaced it. The carpet was changed to a low white pile to match the white bricks of the fireplace. The two windows donned ivory panel drapes. Marble tables and Greek statuettes replaced the wooden end tables. New lamps completed the décor without a hint of color.

I wasn't allowed to play in there. Nana needed the room to entertain her formal guests. With my childhood vocabulary, I secretly named Nana's formal living room, "The White Room."

Grandpa was with the angels in Heaven, so through my nightly prayers I went to Heaven to find him. I opened my prayer with, "Dear Jesus, please forgive me if I've done something wrong. I tried to be a good girl today."

Feeling at peace, I next said, "Jesus, please, I'd like to talk to Grandpa now." When assured Grandpa could hear me, I continued, "Grandpa, I miss you so much. I hope you are happy in Heaven."

I held nothing back, pouring my words out loud to Grandpa in our prayer time. "Today I played with Sallie, you know, my favorite doll. And Grandpa, she really likes the rocking chair you made her."

"Grandpa, I miss you. I know Nana loves me a whole lot, but sometimes she's too busy to play with me. Mommy loves me too, but she's never around."

"Today in school we made pictures, and I drew a big picture of you, Grandpa, and colored your shirt blue, your favorite color. I put lots more colors in it. You'd like it."

"Grandpa, Nana is pleased with me because I won a poetry contest. She hung my poem on her bedroom door for everyone to see. Can you see it?"

"Today, Grandpa, some workers knocked out a wall in Nana's bedroom to make it bigger. She wants a big walk-in closet and her own bathroom. She says I'm old enough now to take a bath by myself."

"Grandpa, remember me telling you the other night about Nana's new bathroom? I don't think it's plugged in yet, but there's a telephone on the wall now, right next to her toilet paper."

"Grandpa, today I had a birthday party. I turned seven years old. Cheryl and Lora and lots of other friends were here. I wish you could know my friends, but I didn't meet them until I started school and you were already in Heaven."

I wanted to end my prayers with a, "Thank you, Jesus, for letting me talk to Grandpa. Amen." Instead, I often fell fast asleep before I got that far. I don't remember when I stopped those prayers. It seems my secret talks with Grandpa lasted years.

CHAPTER 3

KIM

"This is my first great-grandchild," Nana said to the saleslady at the cosmetics counter at the Meier and Frank department store as she pulled my chin up, squeezing a smile out of me.

I was too young for lipstick. Nana had chosen a poppy red shade to match a pantsuit she had picked out for her luncheon later that week. Nana never wore dresses. Next on our agenda was our monthly trip to the beauty salon. Oh, how I hated my hair done up in Shirley Temple curls. But to say no to Nana instead of thanking her was unthinkable.

Before our day's end, we stopped at the bank to deposit a few dollars in the savings account Nana had started for my college fund. As we approached the counter the teller smiled and said, "Hello, Mrs. Schmidt. How are you today?"

Nana tightened her grip on my hand and said, "Thank you for asking. I'm good. Have you met my first great-grandchild?"

"Yes, I have." The teller leaned across her counter and bobbed her head downward to see me better. "Would you like a lollipop?"

I nodded. "Yes, please."

The lady handed me one and I thanked her.

The teller's hair was piled high on her head, frozen in place with hairspray. "How was your last bridge game?" she asked Nana.

Nana never missed her Thursday afternoon bridge club, and every day Nana and I raced through double solitaire and enjoyed a few rounds of poker. We each had our own penny jar, which somehow also got filled with nickels. Each time I won a game I got to keep my winnings, but some of it had to go into my savings account.

Our card games were interrupted when customers at Nana's shop rang our intercom doorbell. Puzzles helped me pass this in-between time. My favorite puzzle was big, one piece for each state in the United States, the names of the states printed on the pieces.

I quickly learned the geographical layout of America. By first grade, I already knew basic reading, writing, math, and geography, unlike my six-year-old friends who still had so much to learn.

"Arkansauce," where I was born, was in the middle of my puzzle. Oregon looked awfully far from it, off on the left side. I didn't know the ending "s" in Arkansas was silent. Not daring to say the name of my birth state when in earshot of Nana, she hadn't corrected me. I had learned early she'd scold me if I mentioned where I was born. Nana reinforced that being born to problem parents was not something to be proud of.

But Nana didn't see *me* as the problem. It was my mother who had emotional mental health issues, and my father who, according to my family, was in prison. I'd spent my first Christmas in Arkansas, and my first birthday with my grandmother in California.

I knew little about the beginning of my life. What sparse details I learned came from my aunts and uncles. I was born at 11:30 p.m. on Mother's Day in Little Rock, Arkansas. At six months old, during my first winter, I became deathly ill with pneumonia and was placed in an incubator at the hospital for several days.

Modern for scientific medicine in 1967, incubators were life savers—but not without risks. When I was sick with pneumonia the incubator damaged my left eye. Throughout my childhood I had a routine eye exam every other year with the best-known ophthalmologist nearby, still an hour-long drive away. Each visit we hoped for medical advances, but updates always led to the same news. My blindness in one eye was irreversible.

Every Christmas the whole family showed up at Nana's house. She made sure everyone got a Christmas gift, but the gifts she gave Uncle Randy and me were different from those she gave the others. Uncle Randy was my mother's older brother, and more importantly, Nana's first grandchild.

As I opened my gifts alongside my cousins, I unwrapped collectible Barbie dolls with the pink race car next to their plastic no-name superhero dolls. I got a leather-bound journal with a lock and key versus coloring books, and a pinafore dress and matching parasol from Nordstrom versus a tunic dress with socks from Payless.

We were expected to treat our gifts with respect and appreciation, even when I played beside my cousins who had to make up names for their dolls. In our American culture, religion is often used as the role model to train children in right from wrong and good from bad. Instead, I had Nana and her rules. While many of her rules seemed strange to other family members, Uncle Randy and I understood her reasoning. We understood our place in our family.

Treated differently by Nana, Uncle Randy and I forged a tight bond unlike anyone else in the family. We were the iconic trophies in her showcase of achievements, Randy as the firstborn grandchild, and me as the firstborn great-grandchild.

Nana was the family matriarch. I was firstborn to my mother, Kathi, who had been firstborn daughter to my grandmother Betty, who had been firstborn to my great-grandmother, the woman I knew as Nana. Born Violet Marie Gosney, my nana's friends called her Marie.

As proprietor of Polly's Barn Antiques, named after a pen name she had used when writing an advice column, long before the days of "Dear Abby," Nana personified a can-do business perspective. She demanded a high standard of praise-worthiness, while simultaneously expecting everyone to praise her wisdom. Nana's insight had to be revered. With several careers behind her and two prior marriages before Grandpa, each life-altering event was deemed an achievement.

Following in the footsteps of such a woman, I steadfastly tried to please her, only to feel ashamed when I fell short—as if I knew I could have done better. No matter how hard I tried to hang on to the innocent carefreeness Grandpa had shown me, I instead became driven, near compulsive, and competitive. Above all, I came to rely on Nana's approval, and where due, her congratulatory remarks.

I was special as Nana's favorite and everyone knew it, family and strangers alike, including that lady back at the cosmetics counter and the bank teller. However, my special place in our family lineage didn't come easily. As the best, I was expected to act accordingly. When my cousins were rambunctious or did something wrong, like grab a toy that didn't belong to them, Nana labeled them, speaking out loud. "Your child is incorrigible." Whereas, when I messed up, Nana disciplined me. And try as I might, sometimes I messed up.

Nana was entertaining a friend in her White Room, the room that became hers right after Grandpa died. Her friend's purse was sitting on the hallway mantel. The purse's clasp was open, revealing the contents inside as it lay on its side. I ran my hand over the smooth white leather, prying the purse open wider. Curiosity got the best of me.

When their visit was over, Nana's friend picked up her purse. As she started to shut it, she said, "Marie, I don't understand. My lipstick tube is gone."

Nana flung her hands to her face and shook her head as she asked, "Kim, did you take Hazel's lipstick?"

I couldn't lie to her. That would have been worse than what I'd already done. "Yes. I'm sorry, Nana. I wanted to look pretty too."

"You apologize at once to Hazel. And give the lipstick back to her."

I did as Nana said, but that wasn't the end of it. After her friend left, Nana lectured me well past mid-afternoon. "You are smart and bright, not stupid like the other kids. You know better than to take something that's not yours. You mustn't ever steal again."

Those were only a few of her well-chosen words. I felt sliced open, embarrassment and shame spilling out of me. She was right. I had to be better than other kids.

My choice in friends was subject to Nana's scrutiny. She had to approve, if not outright pick my friends. Nana approved of Cheryl, my best friend from the time we entered elementary school up until age twelve when we started junior high together. She was the daughter of an important man in Salem, and later in our friendship years he became mayor. I'd beam with pride and tell others, "I'm best friends with the mayor's daughter."

Cheryl was never okay with this gloating. I couldn't help it. I was proud that Nana was proud I'd chosen my friends well. Each day without fail for our six years in grade school, Cheryl and I shared the fifteen-minute walk to school together and back home afterward. The walk home was always easier. A steep hill went up to school, then down to home. We didn't see much on our walk besides other kids in our neighborhood.

We lived in the Laurel Heights neighborhood, a deep residential pocket out of sight of businesses or convenience stores. Sloping green lawns edged by camellia trees, rose bushes, and noble firs bordered small estates where important men and their families lived. Politicians, insurance agents, attorneys, a fireman, and doctors, among other elite public figures were the neighbors, and everyone knew each other.

Our neighborhood was far removed from flashy disco bars downtown and liberals who frequented such sordid places. Tucked safely in our dens, the average family in my neighborhood had a fireplace or two, the latest color TV, a crafts table, and a place for us girls to get together after school for our Blue Birds or Camp Fire Girls meetings.

Girls' bedrooms were adorned with canopy beds in soft pastels, collectible dolls on display, Barbie dolls to play with, and a record player to listen to Captain and Tennille, Diana Ross, or my favorite, the Bee Gees. Bookshelves in our bedrooms held the *Nancy Drew* series and the latest in the *Little House on the Prairie* series. Dresser drawers held our plaid bell-bottoms or blue jeans with flower patches, and in the closets hung our many dresses. My Shirley Temple curls gave way to Farrah Fawcett feathered hair.

Cheryl and I did everything together, from horseback riding to roller skating. We trick-or-treated every Halloween in our safe and friendly neighborhood as dusk fell to darkness. The year we were finally too old to go trick-or-treating but went anyway was the year we shouldn't have gone out, or at least we should have done it differently.

In our house-to-house hunt for candy, we giggled when we were supposed to be scary characters. With bags full, we arrived back at Cheryl's house and her mom offered me a ride home. "No thank you," I said to her mom.

"Are you sure?" She waved her arm in the direction of my house, the ice cubes in her glass clinking. "You shouldn't walk home alone."

"Yes, I'm sure, Claudia. I'll be fine."

She'd been drinking cocktails again, and when she drank, which was often, she'd suddenly fall asleep. I didn't want that to happen while I was in the car with her. I also wanted seconds on candy on my walk home.

"Okay, you be safe. Cheryl will see you tomorrow morning," her mom said as she waved goodbye to me.

My walk took me past a few houses to reach the end of her street, Dogwood, then across Madrona Street, catty-corner to my street, Camellia Drive. From there, I had a half block to home. As I crossed Madrona Street, I passed Camellia Drive and instead turned down the next street, Balsam Drive.

Only as I started down Balsam Drive did I realize how late it must have been. Any laughter or shrieks of fun seemed to be far away, and porch lights started to turn off. I had only a short way to go, and so I proceeded, skipping houses with lights off. As I was passing the third dark house in a row, a dark force jumped out from a fat darkened bush, and in an instant, he was practically on top of me with a forceful lunge.

Dressed in all black in an already blackened area of the street, he was tall to my four-foot-one stature. He didn't say anything, but I felt his heavy breath. This tall, dark stranger yanked my bag of candy out of my hand and pushed me. I fell to the sidewalk. Looking up, I saw the back of him disappear into the night as he ran away. "Stop. Bring it back!" I yelled.

My commanding shrills fell on deaf ears. He didn't answer, and no one else seemed to be around to notice us. I was devastated and alone in the dark without my candy.

Other than that fateful Halloween, Cheryl and I had always been inseparable, or so it was while we were in grade school, up through sixth grade. Junior high proved otherwise. Once we moved on to junior high, we were suddenly around kids who came from several other grade schools and other parts of town. That meant more friends to choose from.

Those of us from Candalaria Grade School were pillars of the community, but in seventh grade we walked the halls with kids who had diverse backgrounds, some almost as good as us, and some who were from the trashy side of town. Some had welfare parents, some had brothers who did drugs, and some were destined to be truant dropouts. If only to stay good in Nana's eyes, it was in my best interest not to get mixed up with such outsiders.

I had to stay close to my friends I'd grown up with. It became even more apparent that I needed to stay closer than ever to Cheryl. I believed she'd always be at my side to navigate that great big world called Leslie Junior High. I was gullible. I was heartbroken, lost, and adrift when Cheryl, like a butterfly, fluttered about to make new friends, leaving me behind. Whenever I got close to her, she'd shoo me off.

Seventh grade could have been especially arduous, had it not been for my friends in the Fraternal Order of Job's Daughters, pronounced with a long "o" as in Job, God's messenger.

Job's Daughters met twice monthly at a Masonic Temple for our evening-long Bethel meeting. Each girl held an office or position, serving a six-month term as assigned by our Honored Queen, with duties carried out at our meetings. Meetings were formatted to conduct business, and for initiation of new members.

While each officer performed a ritualistic part, the five messengers had the most to memorize from our Book of Job for recitation. When I served as Fifth Messenger, I stood at my appointed time, hands flat at my sides, and faced the girls during their membership initiation.

I then recited verbatim, "The story of Job is a lesson of life. It has been handed down from generation to generation in the Sacred Writings. Whatever its antiquity, it is as true today as when it was written. The members of this Order are just beginning the warfare of life; the trials of human existence. We are going forth on our pilgrimage filled with ambitions and hope. All the magic of youth and the joy of life are ours and our eyes are filled with wondering interest in the world's affairs. We know not what may be written in our book of destiny. There may come a time when, through adversity, we may be tried for our faith in the Great Creator of Heaven and earth. We may in the years to come be fettered by poverty and toil, yet in our hearts there should forever echo the remembrance of the trials of Job, his steadfastness to God and the reward for his righteousness. The Sacred Book informs us that Job was rewarded by twice as much of the world's goods as he had before, and that other sons and daughters were given to him. But above all he enjoyed the blissful happiness of the commendation of God for his faith. The closing chapter of the Book tells us, *In all the land were no women found so fair as the daughters of Job.* Let it be our purpose so to live that the members of our Order will be known throughout the land as true daughters of Job."

To become Honored Queen, one usually first served as Marshal, then as Guide, then became Junior Princess, and finally Senior Princess. That was how it normally fell into place following elections. Two years into Job's Daughters, our Junior Princess dropped out. That left both Marshal and Guide positions vacant as other girls moved up in rank. I was elected as Guide, with the office of Honored Queen to look forward to in a year and a half.

The Masonic Order also had an organization for the boys, called DeMolay. Twice a year, DeMolay and Job's Daughters had a formal dance. I wasn't interested and didn't attend. My interest wasn't in DeMolay boys, instead preferring friendships among the girls. Liking boys was not an ordinary thing for me. When little I hadn't liked playing with boys, and when older I didn't like to hang out or study with them, let alone meet them at a dance.

I never did have a liking toward boys. I was a girls' girl. Oh, sometimes I pretended to have a crush on a boy so I'd fit in, but had no clue which boys were good-looking, nor what it felt like to have a crush on a boy. My first real stomach-churning, heart-pounding crush would materialize in eighth grade.

Job's Daughters was not going to be enough to get me through my second and last year at junior high. It had sufficed in year one, but I needed more. Then it happened—in week one, I think it was. Kris happened. Kristin Studer was her name. Kristin Catherine Studer. Her family always called her Kristi, and kids at school called her Kristin.

Our teacher had said something about a special project. "Get up from your desks and find a partner."

I was in no hurry to stand up, let alone pick someone I could get through a project with. Kids all around me giggled and grabbed each other's arms. One girl stood by herself. She was in jeans like the rest of us. Her shirt was yellowed, like it used to be white, but wasn't anymore. Her clothes were probably hand-me-downs. I stood still and looked at her. Before I could make out anything more about her, she said, "Kim, I'll be your partner."

That's gutsy, I thought. I mean, I hardly ever talked to anyone, and never anyone I didn't know. Her plain face cocked to the side as if she were using her head to point me her way. I followed her lead by walking to her side. Our teacher proceeded with instructions, telling the class to sit down again, this time at a desk next to our partner.

My partner's heavy bosom towered over her desk. The rest of her was as heavyset as her bosom—not fat, but plump—and her breasts added a natural flow to her shape. Each time we had to work through something new in that project, she took the first move. I didn't mind. I liked her spunkiness and wondered why I hadn't known her before.

She seemed to know what I was thinking. "You knew me. You just didn't want to know me. You came from a school of socs. My family lives on Social Security from my dad being murdered when I was a baby. He was a famous race car driver, you know?"

"Oh, sorry," was about all I could say as she continued.

"We had money too, but when he died, all that changed. I was too young to remember any of that, and now we live off welfare and food stamps, and in a house with a parking lot for a backyard."

I had never overheard her say so much to anyone else. And there she was, as she opened up to me. Of all girls, me. She was different than those socs, and by then, Cheryl had made it clear she was going her own way. My lost friendship with Cheryl had left me feeling rejected, and dejected, and lost, and crapped on, and sad, and with an attitude of, "*Jeez, Louise, what the fuck do I do now?*"

Nana never approved of cursing, but I only said it to myself. It was a phrase I had heard often in the halls. And there was Kris, and we hit it off right away. There was an aura about her, her spunkiness, her bright smile, and her attitude of, *"So—what the fuck,"* as if she had answered my internal question, *"What the fuck?"*

I spent my days on the fence between wanting to spend every moment with Kris and hiding this from Nana. Not only were Cheryl and I no longer friends, but my new best friend came from the wrong side of the tracks.

As far as Nana knew, Cheryl was busy and that's why we weren't together outside of school. I let Nana believe my friends were from Job's Daughters. Besides, I was out of grade school, which meant a bigger school with lots more kids to be around.

Kris's family owned their big two-story house, which was a plus. However, it wasn't on a tree-lined street. Their backyard was not a yard at all. Her yard was part of a downtown city parking lot, exactly as she had told me back on day one. Her home was not professionally cleaned. It fell to neglect from her six older brothers and sisters who partied hard.

Her dad was not a professional businessman, or politician, or government elite as Nana expected my girlfriends' fathers to be. He was dead from a bar fight. Then there was Kris's mother, Lynne. Her mom loved elephants and was an avid hoarder of anything elephant. Lynne didn't work. She lived off royalties and a Social Security payout from her husband's death. Kris's mom's favorite pastime—never mind it was her only pastime—was sitting in front of the tube watching MTV.

In the early '80s when MTV first emerged, it was nearly 24/7 music videos with new wave, punk, pop, rock, romantics, and rockabilly.

And then there were the cats. Their house stunk of litter boxes, the smell overpowering the stench of an unkempt home and drifting pot smoke. None of that ever bothered me. Kris had her own room where we'd always hang with her door shut.

One Saturday, Nana insisted she drive me to Kris's house for my visit, saying, "I know you spend more time with her than you let on. I need to get to know more about your friend."

I knew that idea wasn't going to play out well. To say no to Nana, though, was likewise no easy task. I gritted my teeth and crossed my fingers, hoping above all hopes we'd get through it.

Nana walked me up to their front door and then rang the doorbell as if she expected to meet an idyllic family. Instead, Nana was greeted by Kris's older sister Noreen, who opened the door. Noreen was clad in holey jeans and a white T-shirt with red and black lettering spelling all profanity ever known to mankind. The word "fuck" on her T-shirt was loud and clear.

Nana grabbed the rickety wooden rail beside their porch to brace herself, and with her other arm grabbed my arm as if to pull me back. "Kim, you're going home. You're not staying here with these people. This is not right. You cannot possibly be friends with this new girl with a family like that."

Those were only the beginning remarks of her long-winded reprimand. So much for the fingers I'd kept crossed all the way over there. I had let Nana down. I was humiliated and embarrassed. It hadn't mattered that Noreen was not Kris. Kris may have been a rebel, but she didn't wear "fuck" on her clothes. Kris thought that to curse meant a person was too stupid to talk intelligently. But Noreen was Kris's sister, and according to Nana's infinite wisdom, I was in the wrong crowd. I should know better. I was not raised to be with those kinds of people.

Nana's disapproval didn't kill my relationship with Kris. On the contrary, our bosom friendship blossomed, and we were in love. Or I chose to believe we were in love. Sure, Kris loved me, but we fought over the phrase "in love," only to make up and then make love in the early morning hours behind her closed bedroom door.

One of many shared teenage firsts came when she stole a cigarette from her brother, Jonny. Walking down the sidewalk, she handed me the cigarette and a lighter. I lit the cigarette and blew out foul-tasting smoke. "No, like this," Kris said.

She took the cigarette from me, inhaled, and effortlessly held in the smoke for a few seconds before exhaling. "Here, you try." Kris handed the cigarette back to me.

I inhaled, this time holding it in. A taste much like sour apples wafted in my mouth until I couldn't hold it in anymore, and letting out smoke, I coughed.

The older Nana got, the easier it was for me to get away with mischief. Often I'd tell Nana, "I'm invited to a slumber party," only to go to Portland with Kris. We'd take the Greyhound bus to get there and always stayed with her mom's friend Leif, who was married with kids. Kris's mom, Lynne, had several friends who lived in Portland.

Tagging along with Leif to band practice one day, we got to know some of these friends. Stepping into a house as old and rickety as Kris's house, I saw a group of young guys, probably in their twenties. We didn't have far to go. Inside the front room, a guy with short, cropped hair, spiked on top, looked up from his drum set. He waved his drumstick at Leif and said, "Hey Leif, ol' boy. Just getting warmed up, here. Who you got with you today?"

Leif answered back, "This is Lynne's daughter Kristi." Leif turned to me, and with his hand above my head, pointed his finger down at me. Leif wasn't that tall, not even six feet, but he was taller than me. "And this is her girlfriend, Kim."

"Hi, I'm Duane," said another guy as he passed a beer to another guy, who said, "And I'm Pete." The guy on the drums was smoking a joint. I'd seen Kris's brother smoke joints lots of times.

Leif pointed at the drummer and said, "That's Bruce, and Eccentric wouldn't be a band without him."

"Got that right," Bruce said, controlling his cough. He fanned smoke away from his face.

Leif added, "Girls, take a seat anywhere you'd like. Eccentric has to be ready for a show by next Saturday." We plopped down on a couch. It was the kind with cushions that you sink into. Leif walked over to some sort of equipment in a big black box. Working with some of its wires, he said to his friends, "Guys, no funny business. Lynne will have my hide if you let them have any pot or beer."

I was okay with Leif's order. Vibrations from the drums and an occasional squeak from Pete's microphone was enough excitement. Kris and I didn't need drugs or booze to enjoy their music. It was the first of several trips with Kris to Portland that school year.

Nearing the end of that same school year, my mother told me, "I'm moving to Seattle and you're coming with me."

Anger welled up in my face. Scowling, I asked, "How can I go? I just got elected as Guide in Job's Daughters." I flung my bookbag without caring where it landed. Nana stood by. She didn't scold me. Her look told me she knew I knew better. Lately Nana had been aloof, almost sullen.

I glared at my mother, looked at Nana, then looked back at my mother. Trying to have a conversation with my mother never came easily. I looked out the window, into the yard. "I'm supposed to become Junior Princess. I have school here." *And Kris.*

My mother answered, "I'm sorry, there's nowhere for you to stay but with me."

I looked at Nana. She gave me that sullen look again. I looked at my mother with another glare. I looked out the window. I was fifteen years old and at the mercy of my elders—Nana, who truly was elderly in 1982, and my mother, who truly was my elder. With my look fixated on the camellia bush outside, I asked, "What about Nana?"

CHAPTER 4
KYM, I

Six hours north of the bedroom community I had grown up in, the Seattle suburb of Kirkland was typical of most any small northwestern city. Tall evergreen trees butted heads with an explosive sprawl of chain stores, while apartment buildings invaded besieged homes.

I had been in a few apartments before—Aunt Vickey had once lived in an apartment and Great Aunt Peck lived in an old folks' apartment complex. But here I was not a visitor in someone's apartment home. I was expected to live in a third-floor shoebox with painted lines on the driveway. Even the mailboxes were the kind with a lock and key. *What kind of neighborhood is this that your mail has to be locked up?* I thought.

Two steps inside our apartment entryway, we landed in the kitchen. "Here, let me show you our bedroom," my mother said as she looked my way.

Our room? Don't I get my own room?

While her right hand was on the side wall to the kitchen entrance, her left hand opened a door. "Oh, this is Scott's room," she said.

Scott was my brother, younger than me by almost five years. And of course, he was only my half-brother, since my father's side of the family had long ago been swept under the rug into nonexistence. Disinterested, I turned my head to see a small bathroom straight ahead, likely the only bathroom for all three of us. *Yikes.*

"This is our room," my mother said as she opened the next door. Two twin beds were separated by a window on the back wall, and a dresser of some sort sat under the window sill.

Double yikes.

The first day at my new high school left me confused. Never mind I didn't know anyone, I couldn't even figure out the classroom layout as there were no room numbers. While I may have had History with Mr. Peters at 2nd Period, that's all I knew. I was expected to know where History Hallway was, and from there which classroom was Mr. Peters's. If only I had spoken up and talked to other girls. Nana, I'm sure, was brave when she was a young woman. I lacked ambition to live up to her standards. All I wanted was Kris.

I pulled out my spiral notebook, meant for taking notes and homework, and drew a rainbow, then doodled in some clouds with hearts raining down. I added the words "Kris and Kym Forever."

Although my name was legally spelled K-i-m, I changed the "i" to a "y" everywhere possible. Kris had started that change. I liked it spelled K-y-m. It showed I was not the same as all those other Kims out there. Shoot, back in grade school, I had Kim Bakken and Kim Wycoff to contend with. Kims were everywhere it seemed, but I was Kym.

My need for a high school map didn't last long. My mother soon moved us again, this time to a neighboring suburb called Bothel. It was a different high school, same routine. My desire for friendships floundered. I'd stare into space, missing Job's Daughters and Kris.

One day I pulled a detached prepaid advertisement postcard from a magazine. Those inserts were common back then. I filled in the blanks, and in return received two sample packs of Benson & Hedges cigarettes by mail. With my mother at work, intercepting the mail was easy.

Behind our apartment building, I lit a cigarette. A tingling rush warmed my insides as I inhaled its sweet poison. I let out a breath and watched imperfect smoke rings carry away my pent-up tension. Nana had hated Grandpa's smoking. I inhaled again and looked around, afraid of getting caught. Nana was far away in Salem. I remembered my little-girl climbs onto Grandpa's lap when he had his after-dinner cigarette. I wanted to return to his warm embrace. *That's impossible. He's in the place Nana called Heaven.* I no longer felt deserving of Nana's praise. So, I smoked.

In those days, laws that dictated who could buy cigarettes were quite lax. If there were any age requirements, people weren't automatically carded. When my two sample packs were gone I kept smoking, buying a pack at a little over a dollar every few days.

Each day, as if on autopilot, Scott and I went to school, and my mother went to work. On the weekends, I avoided them. When my mother was in the living room watching TV, I retreated to our bedroom. Mostly she kept to the bedroom, though, sleeping through the weekends.

Before the end of that school year my mother moved us again, back to Oregon, in Gresham, a suburb of Portland. Again, we were in an apartment, and Gresham High School was my fourth high school in two years. Much closer to Salem, I reasoned I'd see Kris soon. And Nana, but Kris was foremost on my mind.

We went on the food stamp program to supplement my mother's income. When I got home from school one afternoon, I went into the kitchen to take my share. Our mother's idea of dinner was to leave us food stamp dollars on the kitchen counter. In those days, the welfare office didn't issue an electronic debit card. Instead, it was blue, pink, and yellow paper money. Scott, who was hanging out in the living room with a friend, had beaten me to it.

"Scott," I said. "Give me some of those."

"Some of what?" he yelled back.

"The food stamps. I get some too."

"You're too late," he said.

I put my bookbag, cigarette pack, and matches on the counter then ran toward him, ready to tackle his scrawny four-foot-five build. Despite his blue-eyed blond looks he was far from sweet.

Scott pushed me aside and ran into the kitchen while waving his fist. "No."

"Scott, please, stop this," I said.

"Oh, what's this?" he asked me, grabbing my matchbook.

Scott's friend stood beside me. I ignored the question.

Scott struck a match, held the flame still, and picked up a piece of paper off the counter. From the pencil markings on the paper it looked like his math homework. He let his homework go up in one flame. The match went out. His homework didn't.

He started to crumple the paper, but as the fire spread through it, he threw it on a junk pile—one of many trash piles—right inside the living room, not far from his friend and me. Instantly, a food wrapper melted. Another crumpled piece of notebook paper, this one already on the floor, reacted to the flame. His friend stomped the fire out. It left a blackened ring on the brown carpet.

That was the first of several fires Scott would go on to set, eventually ending up with an overnight juvie stay for a small fire he started at school. If only he had set our apartment on fire, then maybe that would have been excuse enough to go back to Salem.

My mother didn't seem to care about Scott's crap or our messy house. She had quit talking to us. I saw her in the mornings, but we never exchanged parting words. No "Good morning." No "Have a good day at school," and no "Did you get your homework done?"

From then on, I made sure I got home before Scott, even if it meant skipping my last class. Any change from a food stamp dollar was handed back in real coins. These quarters added up, and I used them at my favorite hangout, the nearby arcade, where I played Ms. Pac Man and smoked in their parking lot.

We were standing around behind the Paramount Theater in Portland, not doing much of anything. It was hours before the dreamy Stray Cats concert. "Quit fussing," Kris said to me.

"I can't help it," I said, tugging at the calves of my black spandex jeans. "I'm still trying to break these in."

"You can never just wear blue jeans like me, huh?" Kris said.

It was a question asked before, and one not worth answering. Kris always wore baggy jeans. I never did. "Hey, look, over there." I darted a look, not daring to point.

Not far from us, a group of guys seemed to be doing the same thing as us, standing around. Kris looked. "I think they're punk rockers," I said.

"No," Kris said, "they don't look like punk rockers. You look like a punk rocker with your pink Converse shoes."

"They aren't heavy metal guys either. That's for sure," I said.

Kris said, "It's just a few wannabes, probably also waiting for the concert. Let's say hi."

We walked up to them. The first thing out of Kris's mouth was, "We're celebrating Kym's sixteenth birthday." Kris put her arm around me and squeezed me once, then let go. She smiled at one of the young guys and added, "I'm still fifteen, even though I look older than her."

The guy she smiled at smiled at both of us. "Aw, happy birthday wishes to you." His thick Australian accent made me blush when I smiled in thanks. After talking, we said our goodbyes and headed off to sightsee downtown. We never did get any of their names. I think my name was the only name that came up when we talked.

Come evening we returned with tickets in hand, and took our seats in the auditorium. Our chairs rocked back and gave little leg room. At first, the long, wide burgundy stage curtain was drawn shut as Kris and I hugged, smiled, and waited anxiously for the Stray Cats. It went up for the opening band, who as it turned out, was the group of guys we had talked with out back earlier that day. They were a band new to the US but popular in Australia, known as INXS.

After the intermission, the stage curtains opened again, revealing strobe lights in oranges and purples. Dressed in pegged jeans and letting their long bright-blond hair flow freely, my Stray Cats danced with their microphones around upside-down trash cans. Their new wave punk style redefined '50s rock.

After the concert, we checked in with Leif. He and Lulu had since broken up, and he was now living in an efficiency penthouse downtown. "Hi girls. How was the concert?" Leif asked us as we melted onto his beige couch, giddy and wired from exhaustion.

"You girls can have my bed tonight. I'll take the couch. Let me call your mom, Kristi, and let her know you made it."

"Thanks, Leif. You're the best," Kris said as she beamed a big smile at him. I could have been jealous but pushed my thoughts aside. She always had a special liking for Leif, but I had to believe it was because he was just close friends with her mom.

If I admired anyone from our group of adult friends, it was Steve. Tall and geeky, it wasn't his looks that grabbed me, but that he had made something of himself. Our other friends were wrapped up in their band stuff, but Steve had a college degree and owned his business.

More than that, Steve believed in the right to practice all freedoms—freedom of speech, sexual freedom, political freedom, freedom to use drugs and drink, freedom to take from the government, and freedom to make one's own riches. His list of freedoms could have gone on ad infinitum, and was against the grain in our Reagan era of that new decade upon us. The 1970s lifestyle was no longer the in-fad, but Steve clung tightly to many of its values.

Kris and I seldom went to Steve's house and never without Leif or another friend. Steve wasn't yet our friend, only a friend of a friend. Leif and the other band guys were in their twenties, but at thirty-two, Steve was twice my age less five months.

"From now on," Leif said, "you two need to find another place to crash when you come to Portland since Lulu and I aren't together anymore. It was different with her and the kids, but as it is now, I can't be letting two teenage girls stay with me in this tiny place."

Any end of a weekend with Kris meant a return to my mother's silence and my brother's chaos. My classmates talked about college plans and who was taking who to what dance. I was far removed from their social circle and had no idea where I was going. Weekends with Kris became far too few, even though Salem wasn't far away.

♦ ❖ ♦

I spent most Saturdays at a strawberry-picking job with migrant workers. I earned a crappy one dollar for each crate of berries, but seven or eight dollars in a day bought my cigarettes for a week.

"Pot, one dollar a joint," I heard one Saturday morning in early June as I was crouched over in my row of strawberries.

I looked up to see a guy walking into the area where I was working. Raising his voice, he said again, "Pot, one dollar a joint."

A guy walked up to him. A few minutes passed as I pondered his offer. Right before he was about to walk off, I approached him with my strawberry-stained dollar. I planned to save the joint for my next visit with Kris.

I had a few weeks to wait until I saw Kris again. Although school was scheduled for summer break soon, I had accepted a real Monday through Friday summer job. So when I arrived home later, I stashed our joint. I made sure I had hidden it well, behind some crap on the top shelf in my bedroom closet.

Kris was no stranger to pot, being born into a hoodlum sort of family, but as the youngest, she was too little to be included when her mom went into her brother Jonny's room and shared bong hits with him. I knew what bong hits were. Kris and I had seen the band members smoke pot, but we had never been included there either. We were treated as teenage girls who hung out while the big boys practiced.

Kris had always been the director, but this time I had made plans, and proudly so. I reasoned if we got stoned, it would calm Kris down. Lately she had been complaining to me that we saw too much of each other. I didn't see how I could be clingy when we didn't even live in the same town.

In my summer break from school, I started my summer job at U.S. Bank helping the tellers with the ATM machine and counting change. It paid $3.35 an hour, which gave me a lot more money than that berry-picking job. Nana was proud of me. She told me, "Oh, so wonderful. I told you, you are smart. This is only the first of many accomplishments you will have."

If only Kris had been as impressed as Nana. More than a month had passed since our concert trip. Our long-distance calls also waned. If we talked, it was when I called, and not the other way around. In her aloofness, Kris explained to me it wasn't normal or right for us to be so close. She wanted to be with boys.

WTF, does she have a thing for one of the band members? I thought.

"No Kym, it's not that," she said as if she had read my thoughts.

Didn't our early morning hours in her bed together while the rest of her family slept count as a testament to our love for each other?

I had no desire for boys, or even another girl. My life was wholly consumed by and wrapped around Kris. So I shushed her, discrediting her tangents. Through twisted angst, I persuaded Kris to meet me again in Portland.

On the Friday evening I planned to bus it to Portland, and from there to Salem to meet her, she called me. "Kym, I can't come up this weekend. My mom needs me."

I didn't need to see her eyes to recognize her deceit. Ignoring her repulsion for cusswords, I exploded, "What the fuck, Kris? You're not doing this to me again."

"I'm sorry," she said. And then, more as an afterthought than anything else, she added, "You know, I love you."

"Well, you sure have a crappy way of showing it."

As if in compromise, she said, "Next weekend, Kym, I promise."

"Damn it, Kris. Since you're not coming to Portland any time soon, I'm coming to you."

"Okay...okay...yeah, okay, that'll be good," she stammered back.

"Fine," I said.

"Fine," she said back.

I set about packing my overnight bag and counted my ones for the Greyhound bus trip to Salem. On the list not to forget was the joint hidden high up in my closet. Finally, we'd try pot together. And it would be our secret.

Shit, it's missing, I thought as I felt around the top of my closet.

"What the fuck?" I shouted out loud. "Scott!"

"What?" he yelled back at me, walking toward my bedroom.

"Have you been in my room?" I asked him as he stood in my open doorway.

Scott answered, "Why? Are you missing something out of your closet?"

I walked to my doorway and stared him down. "Where is it?"

He didn't seem intimidated that he was still shorter than me, too early for any growth spurt. He answered, "You should have hid it better. It's gone now."

"You piece of shit. It wasn't yours to take."

He flipped me off, turned around, and stormed out of the apartment, leaving our front door open. Even though he was outside I could hear him yelling, "I'm gone."

I was home alone with a half-packed bag and no joint. That shit of a brother was only eleven and already into drugs. All I wanted to do was try some pot with my girlfriend—my girlfriend who didn't even know if she wanted to be my girlfriend. I was stuck living in Gresham with that crappy brother and my dysfunctional mother.

If only I had Nana to turn to for guidance, but it had been a long time since I had last talked to her, save for the time I was proud to tell her about my new job. So, that idea seemed a little weird. Even in the times I hadn't told Nana the whole truth and nothing but the truth, I always felt free to probe her. She had been around the block plenty of times. She never had qualms about telling me what she had learned from tough times.

This was more than a tough time for me. It had been nearly a year since I was dragged out of Salem. I missed my life when I had been an achiever and involved in all sorts of neat things like Job's Daughters. If I were still there, I'd be Junior Princess with a purple cape. My life had become nothing but one big catapulted mistake. I had succeeded in landing the bank job, but it was not an adequate replacement for the loss of my life as I had once known it.

I pictured my mother who often had a glass or two of red wine at night to wind down. That's what I needed. I went in the kitchen and opened the cupboard. Not much was in there. Most of our dishes were in the sink, dirty. She always used a wine glass. Several wine glasses with lipstick rings sat on the counter next to the sink.

Several plastic milk glasses sat in the cupboard, not used much. I grabbed the tallest one. Besides, a tall cup could hold more than any wine glass could. Her gallon jug of wine was already open and almost full. It took both hands to lift that jug and pour it without spilling any.

With newfound energy gained from my cup of wine, I set about finishing my packing, which looked more like haphazardly stuffing clothes and other stuff into my backpack. The joint had been the one important thing, and with that gone, it didn't matter much what went in my bag or what stayed. My inebriation gave me courage. I didn't want to lose that courage. I drank another cup of wine. And then another until I had finished off the jug. With the wine gone and my joint gone, I had no reason to stay. I slung my backpack over my shoulder and headed out the door and down the street.

Two teenage girls were walking toward me. I started to pass by, but they were drinking beers, so I stopped them to talk. I had to keep feeding my courage, so one of their cans of beer became my next drink. Ahead was the city bus terminal where I would catch the bus to the Portland Greyhound station to Salem, to Kris. I kept walking toward the bus station.

CHAPTER 5

KYM, II

Early morning sunshine filtered through lace curtains, jarring me awake. A table fan hummed but I was stifling from my tight clothes and a pile of blankets over me. Even my shoelaces were tied as I fidgeted on someone's couch. My head pounded as I looked around the room. Leif's Murphy bed extended to the couch on which I lay. Kris was not with me. I was not at Kris's place. I was on Leif's couch.

Just like I had left those teenage girls with the beers behind, my recollection of everything from that night had been left behind—I had no idea what happened. All I eventually learned about that night, which wasn't much, had to be told to me. Leif was the only person who could provide any facts or revelations. How I got from that moment when I stood with the two girls, to the moment I arrived at Leif's penthouse, has been forever washed away.

I had to use his bathroom. After returning to my place on his couch, Leif poked his blond head up. He sat upright, stretched, exposed his bare chest, and said, "Good morning, Sunburst. How do you feel?"

"Like crap," I answered. Leif yawned and stretched his arms again. I added, "What happened?"

"I don't know," Leif said. "You tell me, Sunburst. You showed up here, crying and babbling about Kristi. You weren't making any sense to me, so I put you to bed."

"Shit, now what?" I asked.

Leif yawned again. "I don't know, you tell me."

"I don't know what to do," I said.

"Well, you can't stay here. You're only sixteen and I'd get in trouble if anyone knew you were here."

"I'm supposed to be with Kris," I said out of embarrassment.

"Kristi is in Salem. This is Portland."

"I know, duh," I replied. I didn't need him to point out the obvious.

"Tell you what, Sunburst," Leif said. "I'll call Steve and see if he can help you. But first I need my morning tea. You want some breakfast?"

Like Nana, my matriarch, Steve was the patriarch in the adult social circle Kris and I had befriended. It made sense to me that Leif suggested Steve had answers, even though part of me wanted to crawl up into a ball under the blanket. After Leif called Steve we waited it out. Leif didn't drive.

We talked, but mostly I listened as he practiced strumming soft melodies on his electric guitar. Leif explained that Eccentric was scheduled for a gig. He had to practice. I didn't mind. I felt too awful to do anything but sit quietly.

Later that day, Steve took me under his wing and helped me recuperate. Steve's home became a haven in my rocky and ever-changing path into adulthood. He set up a bedroom all for me in the three-bedroom house he rented. I never returned to my mother's apartment. Any worldly possessions to take to my new place in this world had already been packed in my overnight bag from my well-intended but failed weekend trip to Kris's place.

Kris and I sort of made up, but only as friends, and lukewarm ones at that. Steve returned home from work each evening with a forty-ounce bottle of Olde English Ale. With a glass of beer in hand, he listened to my babble over her. He always offered me a half glass to sip on while he finished off the rest. I wasn't much of a sipper. I had proven that the first time I drank, only a few days before. I'd gulp my beer as we listened to his Talking Heads and Oingo Boingo records. Soon he was coming home with enough for both of us.

Steve was tall, dark, and handsome—or handsome to me. Before him, I had little inclination to notice anyone other than Kris. My head was no higher than his chest when standing next to him. Steve was also naturally dark from his outdoor work. It wasn't good looks that set him apart from his friends. If anything, he was geeky with rounded glasses and a face full of deep-black curly hair.

Friends liked to drop in, and Steve introduced me to those I hadn't yet met. Not only was I sixteen years old and Steve thirty-two, but I looked even younger. Steve explained my presence to them in phrases like, "Yeah, Kym had problems at home with her mom. I'm kind of watching after her, making sure she's okay. Don't tell anyone."

During one visit, his friend said, "I wondered why you called off your party last weekend."

Steve responded, "There's a band playing at Waterfront Park Sunday afternoon—some new band—they're supposed to be good, I heard. How about we all meet up and do that, since I probably won't have a party this Saturday either?" It was more of a statement than a question.

His words confirmed what I felt in those early days. It wasn't our home. Instead, I thought of it as Steve's house and I lived there with him, clandestinely at that. Laws and penalties in those days weren't as harsh as they are today regarding a teenage girl being with an adult man, but stigma was prevalent in society. My presence in his home had to be shared only on a need-to-know basis. Only those who were tightly woven into the established social circle could know.

That Sunday, Steve and I went to the park where the band was playing and laid out a blanket and sat down. Several friends joined us. Kris showed up too—with Leif. I missed her but knew it wasn't the place to pick a fight. Instead, I stayed close to Steve's side. The river was in front of us, and in between the river and us and a bunch of other people was the makeshift bandstand. The band played popular rockabilly songs like "Goody Two Shoes." The music was good, and when it wasn't too loud to hear over their acoustics, we talked casually. Steve had his thermos with him. He always drank beer, even when he had to hide it.

I was swept up in a conversation with Steve when we returned to his home. Following him into his office, I could feel his upbeat charm. We walked around a hammock, strung from both side walls. Steve said, "And I think I will have a party next weekend. They miss my parties and—"

Steve stopped mid-sentence to push the button on his answering machine in case any business calls had come in. The only message was from a friend. His long desk spanned the width of an open window behind it. A weathered screen on the window let in breezes, cooling our warm day.

His black curls bounced gently on his shoulders from a light breeze behind him, and I caught a whiff of hyacinth bushes. On his desk sat his phone, Rolodex, accounting ledger, and a plexiglass cube with a picture in it. I reached toward the picture. Steve said, "That's Jeff and Phyllis."

We stood close enough to touch but we didn't. He had hugged me several times over the past few days in a friend sort of way. His warm electricity sparked my skin in a way that was not simply a friendship feeling. I felt more. I looked up at his face. Steve explained, "You haven't met them yet—Jeff and Phyllis. They live in Astoria."

He didn't need to say any more, and I had nothing to add. Words didn't seem appropriate. I gazed into his brown eyes to see more of the handsome, strong-boned man who stood close to me. I saw tenderness in him. In compliance with my unspoken wishes, he took his glasses off, setting them on the desk behind him.

He gazed back at me and a warmth filled me. I put my right hand up to his left cheek to feel the glow in his face. When he brought his arm forward from the desk, he firmly put my hand on his chest. I felt his heart beat under his T-shirt. He looked down at me, cupped my head with both hands, and brought his face to mine. I melted into his kiss.

My summer of '83 job at the bank ended. As a high school drop-out, getting another job seemed impossible. So I'd tag along with Steve. It wasn't like he had a boss to report to. He set his own working standards and lived up to his responsibilities.

We'd start our day with coffee and a full breakfast. Then he filled his thermos with Olde English and drank his first cup of beer on our drive to his first client. Sometimes there was a way I could help, like bagging loose leaves. And in a hay field, he taught me to drive a tractor. Other times, all I could do was sit back and watch.

Steve's six-foot-two stature was well-built at about 200 pounds. His skin was naturally bronzed with a look any Caucasian male could be jealous of. Beads of sweet perspiration ran down his face as he pushed his lawnmower up and down row after row of grass. At times, he looked up and smiled at me. It was that ever-quirky goofy smile, but I saw right through it as love. Like a glaze of melted honey, his body glowed.

As warm weather dwindled, so did his long, ten-hour days outside in the sun. Some days he didn't even need to work. On those days, we savored our morning as it stretched to midday. Our hours were filled with hot butter rum and a full-course breakfast while we shared the local newspaper and listened to the latest album.

One day our morning was cut short when he spent time in the basement with a friend. Steve had given me a few dollars to go shopping at a nearby consignment store I liked. When I returned, they were still at it, and I took some coffee downstairs to them. Steve liked his coffee as much as he liked his beer. He thanked me for the coffee, but I got the gist—he didn't want to be interrupted.

In my few minutes downstairs, I saw that they had built a room in the far corner, and I saw his friend carry a handful of small potted plants in. That made sense to me—the potted plants—Steve was a landscaper. *But why the basement?*

I was curious but respected that it was none of my business, retreating to the living room. At the end of their day, after his friend left, Steve sat me down to inform me what they had built. Turns out, it *was* top secret. *Very top secret.*

"We built a room downstairs. It's a grow room and I have fifty juvenile cannabis plants in it under timed lights," Steve explained.

He continued, "The plants will mature in one month and then I'll transfer them to that spare bedroom." He pointed up toward the front of the house. "Their final budding will be under a different set of lights. I still have to cover and seal that window."

I paid attention to him with nothing to add. Lastly, Steve said, "It isn't right for the government to take free enterprise away from people."

Over time, I became familiar with and accepting of his opera-
tion. I even complimented his work, but always saw it as his thing
and not mine. He wasn't a pothead. He only smoked it sometimes,
like at his Saturday night parties or when he had a new buyer.

I had finally tried pot at one of his parties, and then tried it a
second time to find I didn't like it. I liked handling it, though. It
excited me to see the babies grow up to sprout golden brown hairs,
or resin, as Steve informed me, and I came to understand that the
resin was what made it potent. To hold its flowers was like holding
soft broccoli, but there was a beauty about it, unlike with broccoli.

Steve's landscaping business was the perfect cover for his need
for soil and fertilizer. A smooth penny slid into the outdoor meter
box from time to time worked to prevent the utility company from
detecting the increased meter usage. At times, to ease his workload,
I helped with manicure duties as well as weighing and preparing
baggies of pot for sale. I didn't ask him to pay me. I was happy to
help. But he had a business attitude and felt it was only right to pay
me. We agreed that the easiest arrangement was to keep me stocked
with my Lyon's dry vermouth as compensation.

Sometimes while Steve was away, someone would come by,
wanting to buy a baggie of pot. I used discernment, acting dumb
to anyone I didn't know well. I knew selling pot was against the law
and I didn't want to get into trouble. Often I was afraid of the risks
Steve took, both in the illegal pot business and in tweaking his electric meter, but I drowned those fears in my vermouth. I had less of a
fear that I'd be the one to get in trouble. It was Steve who was on the

lease. I was a minor. I couldn't possibly be held responsible should anything go wrong.

I contributed to our homelife when possible, but I also took advantage of my surroundings. Respect for Nana had restrained me, but this was my true coming-of-age time with no real restrictions or limitations imposed. As a forward-thinking woman, Nana was fine with my new home and relationship with Steve, yet I was reserved in sharing more with her.

Although I felt proud to be with someone like Steve, his insistence on keeping our relationship hush-hush kept me at bay. He had a business reputation to uphold, along with a good standing in his social life. Nana harped when she needed to, and so did Steve. No longer was Nana the only one I looked to for wisdom; Steve also filled that role.

Rounding out the serious understanding between us, we immersed ourselves in music. The neighborhood record store was a favorite place. A new wave of upbeat and unconventional punk rock was the new sound. Talking Heads, Oingo Boingo, Violent Femmes, The Clash, U2, and even INXS seemed to always have a new record out that we had to have. Steve had a TV, but we rarely watched anything on it unless it was the latest episode of *Dr. Who*, or maybe once a week, local news.

Friday nights were spent at one of two places. Sometimes we went to *The Rocky Horror Picture Show* at Clinton Street Theater, always with a small group of friends. Other times, friends would meet at our place and we'd walk to a nearby all-ages club for a concert by any one of many local bands. Dark, smoky, and crowded, we'd drink and dance. Although the bands were small-time in their musical careers, they always seemed big to me. To live in the '80s, one had to think big. The '80s was about big ideas, big possibilities, big shopping, big hair, big clothes, big stereos, big bands, big cars, and being big at anything one could be big at.

Every Saturday night was the party at Steve's house. Of course, it was now our house, but the parties had been a long-standing tradition before I entered the picture. His parties were the perfect complement to my experimental age. They included not only drinking, but trying most any recreational drug. Not addictive or scary drugs like heroin, but fun drugs like coke or MDA. Pot was the norm, but since I didn't like it, I'd always forgo my turn at a joint.

Alcohol was by far my mainstay. Although my first drunk had sent me into a blackout, I learned that by having fun when drinking, I was fine. I was no longer living in anger at my mother, hatred toward my brother, or resentment at Kris. That was what had fueled me into that first blackout. Resentments remained, but deeply hidden, far from any surface. Instead, I was happy, in love, and enjoying life to the fullest.

Sunday mornings my head easily felt groggy from the party night, but I found the cure to perk me back up. I listened to a Eurythmics record and cleaned up the party's aftermath, imbibing leftover drinks I found sporadically throughout the entire house.

Sometimes I had to pick out fruit flies or other gunk with a tea-spoon, but I didn't care, and it didn't matter to me who had been drinking what or out of which glass.

Two guys who were regulars at the parties never drank from someone else's glass. They were afraid of catching AIDS. I'd heard a little bit about that disease from the news, but didn't know much more than that I didn't have to worry since I wasn't a gay man.

Steve introduced me to Jeff and Phyllis, the couple I'd seen in the picture on his desk. He knew them from college. Jeff was a land-scape instructor at a residential vocational school called Tongue Point Job Corps in Astoria, where they lived. It was three hours away, westward from Portland, on a peninsula where the Columbia River meets the Pacific Ocean.

I liked Jeff and his older wife right away, but could also sense they were not as easygoing as our other friends. Their visit was almost formal, as if Steve watched his Ps and Qs in his behavior around them. That wasn't like him.

I found out about the place called Job Corps from Jeff. With a good long-standing reputation, Job Corps existed to help disadvantaged teens better themselves in preparation for a career. I was intrigued and needed something worthwhile in my life. With Steve's enthusi-asm for the endless possibilities that such an opportunity could bring me, I filled out the admission application and mailed it in.

Shortly thereafter, I got a letter back with an admission date of early February 1984. The drifter in me had no qualms about going for it. I'd miss Steve, but knew I'd return home when my stay was over. The sooner I completed my vocational training, the sooner I'd return, and we'd have some weekends together. My time in Job's Daughters had given me plenty of self-confidence, and I believed I would successfully achieve my academic pursuits.

We professed our committed love to each other and promised it would withstand our distance. Any risk of disrespect to our relationship only came from my immaturity. I think Steve knew this, but in his wisdom he didn't voice it. He was willing to gamble, trusting that Job Corps was for my good no matter the outcome.

With a bus ticket in hand, paid for by Job Corps, Steve waited with me inside the Greyhound lobby for my departure. We stood, and people watched. I often turned to look up at him, and he'd return a look. No words were needed between us. We had already said our goodbyes.

It was a large bus station and busy for a Monday morning. Nonsensical lines of people in all directions stood and waited and sat and penciled in crossword puzzles. My head bobbed no higher than Steve's chest as we looked out at the crowd. The busy station was loud with people who came and went, but all seemed quiet to us. We tuned everyone out to feel each other's vibes.

Breaking our silence, a chunky black beat cop approached us. In a stern voice, the cop asked, "How are you two?"

Steve answered, "Good, good, we're just fine, sir."

"Are you her father?" the cop asked Steve.

Steve answered, "No, just a friend."

"Are you all right, miss? Is this man bothering you?" the cop asked me, firing two questions at once.

I looked at his fat face. "No, he's my friend. He's waiting with me until I get my bus."

Steve added, "She's leaving for Job Corps in Astoria today. I'm seeing her off."

The cop couldn't seem to take his eyes off me. "May I see your ticket, miss, please?"

I showed him my ticket.

"Okay, thank you and good luck to you," he said, then walked away.

Steve turned to me and said, "A lot of young runaways hang out here and then get caught up in prostitution, so the cop was looking out for you."

I excelled in Job Corps as one of the youngest students, soon earning three-day furloughs twice a month. My first weekend home started a year-long tradition for Steve and me, replacing his Saturday night parties. After I put my weekend bag away, I joined him in the kitchen. He was pulling a hodgepodge of food out of the freezer but stopped to give me a bear hug. "I want you all to myself tonight, Kym."

He smelled like a fresh bubble bath. After hugging, I pulled back, felt his soft cheeks and said, "Thanks, it's good to be home."

"I know it's hard for you to be away for so long, but your decision to go is a good thing," Steve said. He turned to grab a pizza pan. "Here, help me."

We laid out every imaginable processed frozen food item on the pan. Then we topped our French fries, tater tots, chicken nuggets, fish sticks, battered shrimp, mozzarella sticks and battered mushrooms with sliced sharp cheddar cheese. Steve poured two glasses of beer.

When done cooking, we laid our pizza pan and a variety of dips, from ranch to Dijon mustard and everything in between, on the hardwood floor in front of the couch. Sitting with our backs to the couch, we devoured our dinner with the TV tuned to *Dr. Who*. It was like being with Grandpa, but instead of steak and potatoes, we shared a smorgasbord.

On Sunday mornings, two hours shy of going back to Job Corps, we'd lay on the couch together. It was a long avocado-green couch with four firm cushions, plenty of room for Steve to stretch his long legs, but he never took up that much room. In a quiet melancholy, we melted into our last bit of time together, not to make love, but to feel our shared love. If I moved, it was to twirl my fingers in his thick chest hairs as I imagined a tree-lined forest to get lost in.

Christmas break was much like the Christmas before with Steve. We took a trip home to his mom in Fort Rock, Oregon. He had grown up there, graduating in the same month and year that I was born. The road made me feel like a time traveler, far removed from family ties and holiday shopping obligations. I loved it. Radio waves conked out in the mountain pass, which left us to our own devices—talking, laughing, and singing.

The only scenery in Fort Rock was its namesake—a tall rock, naturally made from an ancient crater and frequented by climbers. The town's only businesses were a post office, bar, elementary school, and small market, all in one building. With miles of open land beyond what my one good eye could see, Fort Rock had twenty-five residents in all, and Steve's mom, Genevieve, owned half the land.

In February 1985, I graduated from Job Corps with about twenty other classmates. It had been one full year since I began my vocational training, and I was months ahead of classmates from my prior high schools who would graduate in June. In my green cap and gown, I received my diploma and an award as Business Student of the Month. Steve's eyes welled with tears right alongside the parents of my classmates.

Life at home with Steve resumed and job choices opened wide. My self-confidence peaked at not quite eighteen years old. I began my working career with a temporary employment agency that kept me busy with a variety of typing, filing, and phone reception jobs. The more I proved myself, the more businesses asked for me when calling my agency. Without expectations, I appreciated honing my office skills and enjoyed the accountability, all in the heart of downtown Portland, a place I had come to love, to know well, and feel safe in.

In February 1986, one full year after graduation, I landed a damn good job. It was secretarial-type work with the Social Security Administration. It didn't provide any benefits as a temporary one-year position, but the opportunity was awesome. I grabbed it.

I called Nana to tell her. Pleased, she said, "Oh, Kym, that's wonderful. I'm so proud of you. Don't let anything stop you. You need to always have meaningful work and make something of yourself."

No longer a burgeoning adolescent, I was a young woman at almost nineteen years old. Questioning my future overtook my new reality. Resentment for Kris, Scott, and my mother returned. In the evenings and on weekends I drank to mask my ill feelings of discord, but it made anything I did a mess. Steve had always managed well as a heavy drinker—*why couldn't I?*

And then Delane popped in one Saturday afternoon. I stood next to Steve as he opened the front door and said, "Hi, Del. I wasn't expecting you. Come in."

"Thanks, Steve. I was just in the neighborhood and need someone to talk to."

I had met her about a year before. Del lived in Salem, still with her folks, even though she was in her early twenties. She wasn't a regular at our parties and her girlfriend had always been with her, but this day she was alone.

"Tell you what," Steve said. "Let's have a beer and talk about it. I'll turn some music on."

She pulled her long black hair to her back and followed Steve, with me behind. Her straight hair bounced at her butt.

"Thanks. Kym, how are you? I haven't seen you in a while," Del said.

"I was at Job Corps for a year. Just graduated and working a lot," I answered.

"That's good to hear. That's kind of what I wanted to talk to Steve about. I mean, Jo and I broke up and I was laid off from work, and I don't know what I'm doing with my life."

Steve thumbed through some records to make a choice while I sat down. Del sat down next to me. I didn't know Del well. She had been on the outer ring of our social circle, knowing Steve through her parents. The few times I had seen her, I saw her as Mona Lisa— Del was the spitting image of her. This time, though, she wasn't still in a framed picture. She was alive, with a sweet musky orange scent that warmed me. Her long black hair flowed to the middle of her back.

Following her visit, Del often came back, even when Steve wasn't home. I could relate to her feeling lost in this big world, and found it all too easy to be that shoulder for her to lean on. The more of myself I gave to her, the closer we became. Crossing the boundaries of my relationship with Steve, I'd embrace Del with my naked bashfulness, wanting to sensually please her as I brushed her long dark hair aside to melt lips with hers.

I never knew quite when she'd pop back in, but found myself

longing for her next visit. What strength Del had lacked in her life, she found in my arms. And once she was strong again, her visits tapered off as she set about making a life for herself, leaving me to remain with Steve where I respectfully belonged.

With Del gone, my craving to drink intensified, and I needed more than my limited dry vermouth or the allotted daily beer with Steve. I was frustrated when I was unable to get the next drink. I was too young to buy it. My heavy drinking wiped out any cohesive thinking I needed to make realistic goals, short or long term. I still looked for goals, but my common sense lagged when it came time to discern if those goals were a good thing or not.

Steve knew me well. It didn't come as any surprise to him when we sat down in the backyard and talked about how I wanted to move into my own apartment. I gave him a bunch of excuses and then tried to explain it better when I said, "I love you but can't be in love with you. I'm an adult now and have to go my own way."

He took his glasses off, pushed a tear from his face, and nodded.

CHAPTER 6

MRS. JONES

"How are you, since you parted ways with Steve?" Nana asked me.

"It's different without him but I'm good."

Nana took my hands and said, "You'll meet the right person if it's meant to be. Remember, you don't need anyone to make your life full. Life has a lot to offer if you go after it and make it yours. You're smart and intuitive, and you will always make me proud, as your Uncle Randy has. I knew he'd fix it to be here this year. It's good, Kym, to have you here this year, too."

It was Thanksgiving time and a return to the traditional family gathering in Nana's home. She hadn't skipped a year, but I had. And Randy, recently married, had to juggle family obligations. I was nineteen years old, feeling lost in my life, yet squarely rooted in Nana's world. Uncle Randy and I knew our place in the family, and with great respect for our family matriarch, we lived up to expectations she placed on us as the firstborn grandchild and great-grandchild.

"Doesn't your job with Social Security end soon?" my mother asked me.

"Yes, but I've lined up another job. It's a file clerk position with the IRS, downtown, to last until Tax Day in April."

It was an awkward conversation with my mother because it was a conversation. My mother and I had never practiced the fine art of talking. It would have been normal if I had answered her direct question with a direct yes. But I had to show that I was worthy of being credited as Nana's smart young woman, so I added the part about the IRS job.

Life had become drab. Parting ways with Steve, my outings in his circle of friends dwindled. Leif was the friend who stuck close by me. My apartment building was in a safe neighborhood with a fire station right across the street, but it proved useless. Shortly after I moved in, someone at the end of the hall had a kitchen fire, causing an overnight evacuation. Our fire department had been on another call, so we had to wait on another station to respond.

The only thing that took away my discord was drinking. I continued pot manicuring jobs for Steve to get my vermouth, and sometimes looked to Leif to get more to drink. I didn't want them to notice how much or how often I drank, so I tried to find other ways to get it since I was too young to buy it. I'd heard that lemon extract had a high volume of alcohol, but with that came excuses to the store clerk about how I had a lot of cakes to bake.

When I could drink, I drank without end. Alcohol made life

comfortable. It also put me in situations with precarious risks, but I usually didn't notice, or else stayed in denial. The few times I admitted my problems to myself, I shook them off over another drink. Drinking hid the shame of whatever it was I wished I hadn't done.

Drinking also gave me an escape from facing that, for the first time ever, Nana was sick. Shortly before our Thanksgiving gathering she'd had problems with her diabetes sugar level. Then it was obvious signs of Alzheimer's. Others filled me in, and I could hear it in her voice when on the phone with her.

Lastly, she got breast cancer, which canceled the Christmas tradition. Each new health problem only made the other health problems worse. And then, in early January 1987, her daughter committed her to a nursing home. Uncle Randy and I visited her. She lay still in her hospital bed, staring up into the ceiling, occasionally blinking. Randy took her hand and I took her other hand. She didn't squeeze back.

Two months earlier she could have passed as seventy years old, years shy of her eighty-third birthday in two weeks. Now, she seemed aged and tired. Her lips were pale without her lipstick. Her skin sagged with pale white rumples. She was not the woman I knew.

One day soon after, I woke up, inched myself up into a sitting position, and wondered what to do with my day, let alone my life. It was a Sunday, so I didn't have to get up early. Trying to get comfortable, I looked across my room to where the foot of my bed came close to the opposite wall. During the day, it folded into a couch. I shifted my weight on its coils.

I stopped fidgeting. Something caught my one good eye. In front of me, on the wall between my front door to the right and my kitchen entry to the left, I saw Nana. I knew it wasn't really Nana. That would be ridiculous. Besides, it wasn't a physically solid appearance. But it had to be Nana.

Her sea-blue jacket with wide shoulders and pristine pointed collar was solid against the white wall. Buttons at the top of her starched cream blouse were undone, which showed her neckline. The colors of her suit blurred then dropped into thin air from her waistline. Her youthful appearance made her look twenty-five years old. I recognized the younger Nana from the scrapbook pictures she had often shared with me.

Nana stared back at me with a smooth olive tone to her face, but neither frowned nor smiled. Our shared gaze was interrupted as she floated alongside the wall to the corner at her right, which bordered my kitchen. Her skin tone whitened, and her appearance became blurry again. As the colors cleared, she looked to be about forty years old.

Nana stopped. Her dark hair was pulled tight to the back side of her neck. A pearl necklace hugged her open neckline, and deep royal blue replaced her soft blue jacket. I watched intently. All too quickly, her appearance floated farther along, and into other droplets of color. No longer against a wall, but in my kitchen entryway, swirls of blues and purples morphed to an ebony blue suit, contrasting with her silvered hair. Her face had wrinkles and her look was solemn.

I called out, "Nana?"

Poof, with no transition and no warning, Nana disappeared. I looked down to the floor. All that was left to see was an open trash can. It overflowed with empty vermouth bottles. *Oh no!*

Nana was gone. My shame and remorse were not. The phone rang. I answered it.

"Kym, this is Uncle Randy."

We didn't have caller ID back then. I replied, "Yeah?"

"I have some bad news to tell you."

I pulled a blanket up on me for comfort. "I think I already know."

Uncle Randy continued, "Grandma—your Nana—passed away this morning."

"Oh."

"She couldn't take it anymore and refused to eat and refused all nutrition. She wasn't happy where Peg put her. She was happy in life, though. It was her time to go. I'll let you know when I have her memorial service arranged," Randy said.

I stared at the wall across from me. I wanted Nana back. "Okay."

"Do you need anything, Kym? Are you okay?"

I answered, "I'm fine. Just let me know when the service is."

"I need to make some other calls now," Randy said.

"Bye."

"Bye."

Uncle Randy didn't need to know Nana had visited me. It was my secret. Or a secret only Nana and I shared. That was the morning of February 1, 1987.

◆ ❖ ◆

Ashamed of that trash can of empties, I started going to AA meetings. But quitting drinking didn't come easily. When my government jobs ended, I turned back to the temporary agency but work assignments were too few. Steve suggested I help a home contractor he knew who needed an extra hand.

I helped the contractor hang wallpaper as his water boy, earning money to keep paying my rent. As one of Steve's drug connections, the guy had a soft spot and would get me wine coolers after work. Steve never thought highly of this guy. He stunk from poor hygiene, was old—much older than Steve—walked with a crick and was balding. The more I relied on him, the more degraded I felt, which, like a boomerang, made me want to drink more.

After work one day, the contractor came in my apartment with me and we started in on a bottle of vodka. Once intoxicated, my discomfort in our concocted conversation peaked. "I need cigarettes from the store across the street. I'll be right back," I said.

I had no need for the store. Instead, I boarded a city bus, getting off where I knew the Night Owls AA meeting was. It went on all night every night. I wasn't even trying to pay attention to the meeting's speaker when the woman next to me whispered in my ear, "Some of us are going to Pancake Alley. Come with us if you want."

I followed her out. At the restaurant, we settled in at a booth seat with several others. Soon, a young man showed up. I looked up at him while he chatted with someone. He was clean-shaven with a baby face but seemed a few years older than me. His sandy blond hair was cut conservatively, and his orange polo shirt hung at the belt line to his jeans. The woman who had invited me told him to sit.

He sat down across from me. Right away, he smiled and stretched out his arm to shake hands with me. "Hi, I'm Vance. And you are?"

I smiled back and said, "Kym."

I tuned out everyone except Vance, and twirled each French fry before putting it in my mouth. In our flirtatious small talk, he assured me a ride home. In the wee morning hours our group broke up to part ways. I walked beside Vance out to the parking lot, where he opened the passenger door of his orange '76 Bronco and then helped me climb up into it. We said little, smiling mostly as he drove out of the neighborhood.

Vance asked, "Where am I taking you, young lady?"

"I live near Lloyd Center," I answered back.

"I live on the east side too, but farther out south."

"Oh no," I said as I spoke my thoughts aloud.

"Oh no what?" Vance asked.

"I can't go home," I answered. "After work my boss came home with me and I didn't want to be with him, so I left and came to the meeting."

Vance asked, "You think he's still there?"

"I don't know, and I don't want to take the chance," I answered.

"Young lady, where do you want to go, then?"

I put my left hand on his right leg as he drove. With a strong grip, I answered, "Let's go cruising."

We went cruising and then some. The next morning, we woke up together in his bed. On the floor, a used condom lay on his AA Big Book, which eerily showed its face among the clothes strewn about. In AA there are the traditional Twelve Steps of Recovery, none of which I had done, and then there is the taboo Step Thirteen, which was precisely what we had committed.

On my twentieth birthday I navigated jagged edges among boulders, looking for a smooth spot to sit. Natural rock in sun-drenched oranges and reds formed an arch as if pointing upward to the gods in the sky. Del clasped my hand with both of hers and said, "Oh I can't believe you're really here, Leigh."

That was my new nickname according to Del, created from the last syllable of my full first name, but spelled differently. I was Leigh. I smiled and soaked in the beauty of the park, Garden of the Gods. My Portland life had stopped working. With Nana gone, I hadn't hesitated when Del had called me to reconnect. She was living and working in Colorado Springs, Colorado, and I grabbed the opportunity to make a new life by moving out there to be with her.

Here too, life soon became drab. I registered with a temporary employment agency and worked the few jobs they could give me. Mostly I was stuck at home. I should have been college-bound or married or doing something worthwhile as Nana had expected.

Each day when Del came home from work was much the same as the day before. The sink was full of dirty dishes, our bed was still unmade, and a mess of newspapers sat on the kitchen table with help wanted ads circled.

After coming home to the same thing again, Del plopped onto the love seat, looked around, and then said, "What do you do all day while I'm at work?"

I walked toward the kitchen. She got up and followed me. I got two beers out of the fridge and handed her one. She took it but then her arm relaxed. As I tapped the top of my can, Del answered her own question, "Sit around and drink all day?"

I popped open my beer, took a gulp, and said, "Your beer is going to get fizzy if you keep shaking it like that."

"This is not how it's supposed to be," Del said.

"Drink your beer and relax."

"No," she said, "I'll show you how it's supposed to be."

This time I followed her. Del marched into our bedroom, pulled out my luggage, and filled up suitcases with what items and clothing seemed to be mine. "Let's go," she demanded.

"Go where?" I asked.

Del yanked the beer out of my hand, letting it fall to the carpet, and pushed me out of our bedroom with my luggage in her other hand. She damn near pushed me all the way to her car. "Get in," she said. I pleaded with her, not knowing where we were going. She drove to the airport, parked, pulled my luggage out and again demanded, "Let's go."

I put my arm on her arm and said, "Del, I'm sorry. We can work this out."

Del pulled her arm away. "No, there's nothing to work out. All you ever do is drink. I'm buying you a ticket and sending you home to Steve. He'll help you figure your life out."

"Del, please."

"No, you'll be okay, Leigh. Just not here with me."

From the Portland airport, I hitched a ride to Steve's from the guy who sat next to me on the plane. I walked up the steps to the front door.

I'm home.

I opened the door and walked in. Steve wasn't expecting me, and he wasn't alone. He was with someone named Carrie and she was my replacement, or that's how I took it in my awkward arrival home. Steve got me settled on the couch, and the next day arranged for me to temporarily stay with Georgia. I knew Georgia. She was one of Steve's regular pot clients.

Georgia was a professional woman with a nice house in the suburbs. As she gave me a tour of her house, she said, "No smoking inside, and as soon as you get a job, you need to move out. I expect you to start looking for work right away."

My job came through Carrie. She worked in the radiology file room of a major medical center, Oregon Health Sciences University. She put in a good word for me to her boss, and I was hired. I moved in with Vance. It was early July of 1987, and my stay with Del had lasted only a few months.

I needed to be normal. That's what Nana had wanted. Vance was normal. He had a high-paying management job in a factory that made computer chips. He owned his own house, had friends, and on the weekends liked to take his nephews fishing. He was an all-American guy. If we got married, I'd be normal.

At the end of July, Vance and I took his nephews on a camping trip. The boys were asleep in their tent while we stood at the lakefront, looking up into the dark blue sky. Stars were out on this clear night and the moon glowed. I put my hand in Vance's hand and said, "I love you."

"I love you, too," he said.

I asked, "What do two people who are in love do?"

"Do you want to get married, Kym?"

"Yes."

Later that week, after work on Friday night, Vance took me out to dinner. I dressed in my finest dress with lace stockings. Vance always wore jeans, but instead of a polo shirt he paired his jeans with a button-down shirt, vest and tie. Pink linens and candles lined the glass tables and the waiter lit our cigarettes. Dessert was fried ice cream. And then Vance pulled a small box out of the inner pocket of his leather jacket. It was a wrapped gift, topped with a delicate pink bow. He handed it to me and said, "I love you."

Inside was a quarter-diamond engagement ring. Our engagement was official, and our dinner out was the first of many priced at over a hundred dollars.

This is normal. This is what Nana expected.

My focus became our one-year engagement. I had a wedding to plan, set for July 9, 1988. I needed a maid of honor and a bridesmaid or two to help me with wedding plans. I had only begun to make friendships in my newfound life, but I had AA and work where I could search out friends. Then I found Kandi. She went to AA and teetered between staying sober and not staying sober, just as I had done in the past. More than our AA connection, Kandi worked in the same department as me, although swing shift.

At four years older than me, tall and slender and muscular, Kandi had a creamy soft face that if only allowed to, I could have easily melted into. Vance knew Kandi was in AA, and therefore a good influence. He didn't know that she struggled with her drinking problem, or that she liked to dabble in cocaine, or that we often goofed off by going out to bars when we were supposed to be doing wedding planning stuff. At least I always drank plain iced tea when out with Kandi, whereas she ordered a Long Island Iced Tea, with complaints to the waitress that it was too weak.

Kandi did everything a bridesmaid could possibly do to make sure all the plans fell into place just right. An afternoon of picture taking to get my smile just right, considering my blind eye, which often appeared lazy, was her successful accomplishment to contribute to the engagement announcements in the local newspaper. A week before the wedding, my maid of honor and bridesmaids gave me a small bridal shower.

The evening before the wedding, Kandi and I got together for one last hurrah. We stepped into a trendy bar in the artsy area of northwest Portland. The waitress led us to a sitting area with white love seat chairs near a fireplace and a glowing fire. It reminded me of Nana's White Room. So much of our sitting area was white, except for the orange glow from the candle on the small table we shared. We were swallowed up by the ambiance of the place, without a care in the world.

After a few too many iced teas, we taxied it back to her place, a basement apartment. Inside, I sat back and sunk into her leather couch. Only then did it hit me hard that my white picket fence dream was to come true the next day. It was not an illusion, but my truth to be had.

I ignored my truth by not resisting one bit when Kandi sat her gorgeous body down next to me. Her perfume was sweet but daring, like how a black rose would smell if it had any scent to its artificial coloring. Before, the fire at the bar had overpowered her scent. Now I smelled her and it was good. Her gaze pulled me in as she leaned her body into mine. Her lips parted, and with an undertone of softness in her voice, said, "I feel good being with you and I want to get closer."

"Me too," I quietly said without any reservation.

Kandi asked, "Can I get closer?"

"Stop asking and go for it."

She leaned in closer and whispered, "I want to kiss you. Can I kiss you?"

Kandi didn't wait on my verbal answer. My green light was enough and she melted into me.

When I got home later, Vance asked me, "How was your evening with Kandi?"

I had no idea where my answers came from. "Oh, it was good. You know, we talked and stuff. She has things going on with her boyfriend she wanted to bounce off me. And we talked about the wedding tomorrow, and her mom has been getting on her nerves lately, so I let her get that out."

Fifty friends and family members filled the pews of a small A-frame wedding chapel in a wooded area in outlying Portland. Tulle bows of soft pink lace lined the aisle. Uncle Randy stood beside me with his arm in my arm as we faced the aisle he would escort me down. Randy was dressed in a plain dark gray formal suit. A translucent pink veil covered my face, which perfectly accentuated my traditional gown. I gripped my delicate bouquet of lavender, lilacs, and pink baby roses, which busied my hands and eased my nervousness.

If Nana's presence had been possible on that day, she would have been there with a prideful glow. To live up to her expectations was a daily ritual. If only Nana were still alive. She'd have been pleased with my choice of groom. Vance was the perfect package.

Ahead, I saw my matron of honor and my two bridesmaids, one of whom was the woman I had slept with the night before. All three were adorned in long formal gowns in light lavender hues. Kandi smiled at me, and without the need for words, I knew her smile meant that everything was all right and that I looked flawless.

The minister was front and center, cloaked in her religious attire. I knew her from my formative years. Nana had rarely gone to church, but when she had, she'd made her commitment to God known with her presence in the congregation of this minister.

Sunshine filtered through tall stained-glass windows. Next to the minister stood the man I claimed to love. He waited to receive my hand in marriage.

By the end of the day, I was Mrs. Jones.

Our two-week honeymoon in Canada began the next morning, following a night at the hotel where we had our wedding reception. Vance and I stayed a week in downtown Vancouver, British Columbia and took in every touristy sight we could. From there, we drove to Banff National Park, where we stayed at Fairmont Château Hotel, overlooking Lake Louise.

Rich, warm colors adorned the hotel. There were exquisite chandeliers and plush carpeting, yet the hotel was modern in its amenities. Our room was tiny, not even ten-by-ten feet. We didn't mind. The view from the window in our room displayed the majesty all around us. As if a true emerald gem, Lake Louise, which I had picked for its namesake to my middle name, was peaceful with pearl-like waves. Surrounding Lake Louise were arêtes, crisp white from crescent snow peaks.

Our favorite place to while away the hours was the outdoor pavilion, sipping flavored coffee. From this vantage point our view was wider than imaginable. Fellow guests told us actor and comedian John Candy was also a guest, although we never saw him.

When we returned from our honeymoon, I not only used Vance's last name, Jones, but I also petitioned the Bureau of Vital Statistics in Little Rock, Arkansas, to make the preferred spelling of my first name legal. I became Kymberley, with a "Ky" instead of "Ki," and ending in "ey" instead of only "y."

Our two spare bedrooms got filled with German exchange students who interned at the company Vance worked with. Then my half-brother, Scott, needed a place to live. He was having problems living with our mother again. I let bygones be bygones as Vance moved him upstairs into the loft. Scott turned his space into a sort of band studio with a set of drums Vance bought him. He did well when living with us. He didn't set any fires that we knew of.

Hiking and trout fishing soon became favorite weekend retreats for Vance and me. We'd plan weeks in advance for an overnight trip to Monon Lake in Jefferson County. With Vance's young nephews in tow, it was our favorite place to fish by moonlight. Another fishing spot was on the Washougal and Columbia Rivers, near Vancouver, Washington. His family owned a cabin there, tucked away on some hidden land. He taught me the fine art of trout fishing. It was more his love than mine. Fishing was too quiet of a pastime and I itched for something more thrilling.

In our drive to the family cabin, we often pulled off the road and into some private land owned by family friends. There, I found excitement. Later, it would be the monotony of fishing. If all we ever did was fish, I think I'd have been bored out of my mind. In that open land I learned to target shoot with his handgun.

I had finally found something I was good at. You can only use one eye to look through a gun scope. My eyesight and depth perception had always hindered me, but I only needed one good eye to shoot. Like a sharp marksman, I knocked over and shot up his empty Mountain Dew cans. I was in awe of the power in my hands. I felt in control, and acutely aware of the destruction I could cause, even if it only impacted pop cans.

In one of our trips to practice shooting en route to the family cabin, we stopped at a pawn store in Vancouver where I fell in love with a nickel-plated .22-caliber Jennings handgun. "Please, can I have it?" I asked, eying Vance with a puppy dog look.

"Yes, you deserve it. You know how to use a gun now." Vance always spoke clearly and formally without slipping into cuddly words. He was like Nana in his bold, direct, and straightforward dialect. With his yes, I knew I had proven myself in knowing how to use a gun. Finding seventy-five dollars in cash in his wallet to drop on an impromptu purchase was not at all difficult. Vance's financial decisions didn't hinge on if we could afford it, but rather discerning if the purchase was justified.

As we were Oregon residents, I couldn't take it home with me that day. First, I had to complete an application to buy a gun and then wait for a background check. Two weeks later, in our return trip, the store manager handed me my pretty gun and said, "Mrs. Jones, you are now the proud owner of a Jennings twenty-two."

I don't think Nana ever owned a gun. She had been powerful in her own way. As he announced my ownership, I was oblivious of where that gun would later lead me.

PART TWO

CHAPTER 7

SUSIE, I

It was a warm evening in early August 1989, and I didn't yet know I'd soon earn a near half-million dollars—or closer to a million dollars, depending on which reliable source you believed. The month before, at one year married, I had traded in the name Mrs. Jones for Ms. Jones.

Returning home to my one-room apartment, I said hello to the neighbor across the hall. Jim was tall, lanky, and in my humble opinion, the spitting image of Chuck Norris, sandy red hair included. Not that I liked Chuck Norris. I didn't. On nights I got home before him, I'd see him in his blue uniform shirt, stained with grease. He was a gas station attendant who pumped gas all day. Nana wouldn't have approved, so I quieted her voice that lived in my thoughts.

Jim's name was short for Arthur James. While I could do without the Chuck Norris look, Grandpa was named Arthur. Best yet, Jim rhymed with Kym, so I took that as a good omen.

The door to his cramped space was ajar as he watched TV from his bed. Often I'd join him for a TV show, sitting in his one chair, a wooden chair with a square seat pillow. Sharing our insecurities, aptitudes, and dreams, I was drawn to his self-confidence, which complemented his reserved disposition. He had been an Army medic in the Vietnam War, on the hill next to Hamburger Hill, when he was barely old enough. He was from Alaska, having moved to Portland recently with his best friend, Dan, and Dan's wife and little boy.

A detective show with a predictable storyline was on TV. As I watched the scene play out, I told Jim, "I can shoot better than that."

Jim asked, "Yeah?"

"Yeah," I said. "My ex-husband took me target shooting a lot. I still have my gun. It's a pretty nickel-plated Jennings twenty-two."

Later, I asked Jim, "Why'd you leave Alaska?"

"Something went wrong. My friend Dan and I got caught up in some burglaries, but then something happened and we had to leave."

"As much as you talk about Fairbanks, you must miss it. Alaska, I mean," I said.

"Yeah, but not as much as Dan and Tammy miss their daughter. She was with Tammy's mom and we didn't have time to get her. Couldn't even pack with the cops on our trail. Only their son was with us when we left. If you meet Tammy, you'll see how sad she is. There's nothing Dan and I can do about it. She misses her baby girl."

I looked at him and asked, "What went wrong?"

Jim answered, "That's something you don't need to know. The less you know, the better off you are."

He looked back at me but said nothing more. He wasn't budging on giving me an answer. I took a sip of my soda and then put the can on the floor next to my chair. We went back to watching TV. I never found out exactly what went wrong to provoke their split-second flee.

Day in and day out, I spent my days at work and my evenings with Jim. Life had become dull. Goals and achievements in Job Corps and Job's Daughters were behind me.

"I want to learn how to do a burglary," I told Jim.

"No, you don't," he said back without any hesitation.

"Yes, I do."

Our argument lasted for several evenings when he finally conceded and said, "All right. First you need to learn the basics and get a feel for it."

The next evening when I saw Jim come home from work, he said, "If you're sure about this, then get dressed in dark clothes. Black, if you have it. Dress warm. Get your car keys and bring your gun, bullets too, if you have any. I'm going to change out of my uniform. Knock on my door when you're ready."

It was September. The weather wasn't that cool, but I layered a black sweatshirt with my T-shirt and jeans, pocketed my gun and got my keys, and then joined him.

"You okay if I drive?" Jim asked me as we headed out to my car.

I answered, "Sure, I can't see all that good in the dark. I've got vision in only one eye, you know?"

Jim reached out his hand and said, "Let me have your keys then."

I handed him the keys. "Besides, I have no idea where we're going."

"We're going on a mail run," Jim answered.

As he drove, he told me he didn't have a license. "I've got an Oregon ID," he said. "Since fleeing Anchorage, I can't take the risk of trying for a license."

He parked in a visitor spot of a large apartment complex. I followed his lead. We got out and started walking. He took my hand and smiled at a couple who passed us going the other way. Holding my hand was not a sign of affection. We had never even kissed. It was his way of making us look like a young couple in love out for an evening walk.

We walked up to a row of square metal mailboxes and stopped. Jim looked around, then opened the boxes and pulled out mail, dropping it into a knapsack he carried from his shoulder.

When we got back to Jim's place, we emptied our bag on his neatly made twin bed. He didn't have a table, other than the small clothes dresser his TV sat on. That, his twin bed, and my wooden chair were all that fit in his place. About 200 pieces of mail, from utility bills to birthday cards, lay in a mess in front of us.

It was the first of several nights in a row spent on mail runs. Each night when we dug into our haul, I squealed when we got a music CD or cash. Even five bucks got me excited. Jim, though, liked to get touchy-feely with mail. He'd tell me, "Open this one. I can feel a credit card in it."

About a week into this routine, one such piece of mail he handed me had a bank card inside. It was for a woman, who as we learned from her other mail, was in the hospital. According to the letter from her bank, her pin number for the card would come in the mail soon. Each night we returned to her mailbox. Then it came.

Jim drove and then parked at a mall with an outdoor ATM. I think it was an unspoken agreement that I was the one to do it, since it was a woman's card. I got out and started walking to the ATM, looking back to see if Jim was watching me. He had warned me where the cameras were probably located. I kind of knew that already though, from working at the U.S. Bank when I was younger. Some places also had cameras on their buildings.

I pulled my hat down around my cheekbones. I leaned back from the ATM, stuck the card in, and opted for a balance inquiry. Good thing the camera couldn't see my leg. It was shaking. I was nervous. Balance was $8,000. Her daily withdrawal limit was $1,000. I took the max out. That left $7,000 and she was still in the hospital. I quickly turned my back to the ATM, stuffing ten $100 bills in my right pocket. "Damn I'm good," I said under my breath. Then I added, "Ha, that teaches people not to steal my Halloween candy."

It had been ten years since the dark stranger had attacked me, but I remembered it like it was yesterday. I learned in AA meetings that one of the Twelve Steps involves getting rid of resentment, but I hadn't done any of the AA steps and was two years sober. In eight days' time, we maxed out her card. My Halloween resentment was gone. I was hooked. I was ready for the big-time burglaries.

No more petty-ante pilfering in mailboxes for me. I want the real thing.

◆ ❖ ◆

The first week of burglaries came with a learning curve, inter-mixed with bravery and nervousness. First, we'd stop in for dinner and a visit with Jim's friend Dan, with whom he had left Alaska. Dan had turned away from crime to protect his family. His wife, Tammy, was quiet, never saying much, but she was always pleased to make a full dinner for all of us.

After dinner, she'd settle in the living room, reading the Bible to their little boy. Jim and I stayed at the table, talking more with Dan. It was my time to smoke as many cigarettes as I could. Jim didn't smoke, but he didn't mind that Dan and I did. Once we left Dan's place, it might be several hours before I could smoke freely again. I couldn't smoke when doing burglaries. The spark from the cigarette or a lighter could be seen in the dark from far away.

It was a fair trade-off though, as Jim, who liked to have a beer occasionally, never drank on a night of burglaries. Sobriety kept us sharply aware of everything.

Saying goodbye to them one evening, I picked up my black gloves from Dan's table. He saw I hadn't removed the ring from my finger. The stern look in his eyes brought back Nana's voice, which I tried to keep stuffed away. It was the same look that Nana would give me when disappointed. Dan's look should have been enough of a hint for me. But Dan was not about hints. Rather, he lectured me. "Take that ring off and put it in the glove box. Don't ever wear jewelry on the job."

I figured my glove would keep my ring on my finger, but Jim and Dan were not ones to take chances. If I were to lose my ring, it could be used as evidence. The fingerprint-matching system police used was evolving. My fingerprints were on file from when I worked with the IRS and the Social Security Administration. That made it doubly risky for me to lose anything that might contain my fingerprints. Jim, too, had been fingerprinted. Both of us had to safeguard our prints. Gloves were only one layer of protection from this risk.

Even our IDs, my driver's license for one, stayed behind, stashed in our car. If one of us didn't make it out alive, we didn't need anything to lead back to the other person. It was a dark thought but an imperative rule. Other rules also added to our protection.

I took my ring off and put it in my pocket. "I'll put it in the glove box."

Dan said, "I already lost my daughter and I don't need to lose anyone else. Jim means a lot to me. I don't know whose idea it was, yours or Jim's, for him to get back into these doings. What's important is that you two keep your wits about you. That's why I tell you how it is."

"I know, Dan. And I appreciate it. I care about Jim, too."

At first, I carried my Jennings, but soon I had my new gun. It was a .44-caliber handgun, dark in color, and not silver plated like my Jennings. It was a little fatter, its barrel a little longer. I liked its touch. With its safety on, I showed Dan my new gun. He responded, "Your gun is your lifeline. Is it loaded?"

"Yes—"

"At all times, you are to protect yourself and Jim."

I gave Dan my full attention.

"Do not be afraid to use your gun. Remember, homeowners are strangers to us. They'll be too pissed off to care if you and Jim live or die. Your gun is your power to stay alive."

"I understand, Dan."

"Good. Now get out there, Susie, and have a good night."

Susie was my alias when in burglary mode. Another rule. Jim became Frank, named for my father's middle name. When a little girl, I had been told my father went to prison, so it seemed apropos to me. Our aliases were an extra layer of precaution.

Years later I came to understand the vulnerability and emotional turmoil my victims must have felt when they came home to face the aftermath of our visits. However, at that time I saw my actions as nothing more than crimes against property and things, not against people. This excuse fueled my chase, always looking for the next burglary to overcome. Each new challenge brought me rewards, incomparable to my earlier achievements in Job's Daughters and Job Corps.

Like an alcoholic with a drink, one burglary was too many and two were not enough. In my stone-cold sobriety, I had to have more and thrived in my bold undertakings. Dressed to the nines in my black gear with no jewelry and no ID, gun in hand, known as Susie, and with a partner in crime, I had found my purpose and calling.

At times, my adrenaline rush was amped. I walked beside Jim, leaving our parked car at the curb behind us. Not a hint of bad weather was in the night sky, but a light breeze was in the air, which cooled me. My knit ski mask was awfully tight and a bit too warm. We walked down the sidewalk. Large well-manicured lawns separated the houses on this residential block. Dogs barked far off in the distance. We passed a few houses, then stopped. Jim pointed to the next house. Neither of us said a word. Hand signals were enough.

There weren't any cars parked in the long driveway and a hedge of bushes bordered the lawn. He crouched and walked with his back hunched over. I followed close behind. We kept our bodies lower than the bushes. The hedge led us to the back of the house, where it ended at a wooden fence. No lights were on anywhere that we could see. Not even a porch light.

Standing at the window at the back side of the house, Jim got out his flashlight and shined it inside. Venetian blinds were pulled up. I followed him while he walked to the next window and did the same thing. We circled the whole house, looking in each window we could. Two windows had curtains shut. Others gave us a good view inside. We returned to the window where we had started. He handed me the flashlight. It was my job to shine it on his work while he used a crowbar to pry open an old wooden door.

Ten minutes later, we were in. He put the crowbar in his tool bag, which hung tight over his shoulder, across his chest, and down past his belt. I handed his flashlight back to him and pulled out my own from my back waistband. And I pulled out my gun. Jim pulled his gun out, too. He walked in first. I walked right behind him. He pointed his finger at himself and then to the right. Then he pointed his finger at me and to the left.

He went to the right. I went to the left. Our outdoor perimeter check had given me a general idea of the layout of this single-level house. I used my left hand to point my flashlight forward to help me see where I was walking. While looking to make sure the house was empty of people, as we believed it was, I took a mental note of a boom box stereo I saw next to a sewing machine. *We'll want that stereo.*

I hoped no one was home, but I had no reason to be afraid. My right arm was outstretched, and my gun was in my right hand. It was ready to fire. It was my lifeline. I checked every room. The bathroom smelled overpoweringly woodsy. Once clear, I walked back to the doorway we had come in. I relaxed my arm but kept my trigger finger ready. Jim arrived back at the same time as me.

"All clear," we said in unison.

He added, "This house doesn't have much, but I got some cash off the kitchen counter."

"How much?" I asked.

"I don't know. We'll count it later."

It was in his pocket. After a few mishaps in prior burglaries where we needed to get out fast, we came up with a new rule. Any time we found cash, no matter who found it, it went right in our pocket. That way, if any stuff got left behind, at least we had the money.

He looked at me and said, "Susie, keep the back door open. That's the way we'll leave. I left the front door locked, but if we need to leave that way for any reason, you only need to turn the lock on the door handle. Anything you find, pile up by the door here. I'm going to start in the bedroom. Watch closely, Susie, in case anyone comes home."

When we were inside houses, my priority was watching for returning homeowners. Grabbing goods came second for me. Jim's priorities were reversed; his foremost job was gathering stuff. If a car pulled into the driveway, we had only three minutes to organize and get out. It nearly always took people a few minutes to get out of their car, to the front door, and unlock it before walking in. My job was to make sure we got out before they got in.

Jim walked toward the bedroom. I got the stereo and put it to one side of the doorway. Rifling through a cabinet, I saw some VHS movies. I stopped, walked to the front window, and looked out. All was still clear. Jim came back in the room and handed me three pillowcases, then turned to go back to the bedroom. I loaded the movies into a pillowcase and threw in some old-looking coins and other crap from the cabinet. I stopped and went back to the front window. All was clear. Jim walked back in, carrying something big, and set it in our growing pile. "You watching, Susie?" he asked.

I answered in a whisper, "I'm watching."

He returned to the bedroom. I unplugged the VHS player and the TV and added them to our pile. I looked toward the front window while filling another pillowcase. Headlights appeared. I ran to the window and looked out. Firmly, in a voice meant to carry to the nearby bedroom, I said, "Frank, a car just pulled in. We gotta go."

It must have taken us longer than the usual minute to get out, and less than the usual few minutes for the resident to walk in. The homeowner came through the front door as I was swinging my arm down to grab randomly at one of the stuffed pillowcases in my run through the back door. He was on our tail. We ran through his backyard. I followed Jim's lead as he climbed the fence. I started to climb, threw the pillowcase over, then finished climbing. The guy chasing us stopped at his fence and we disappeared into the surrounding landscape.

By Christmas 1989, burglaries had become our full-time avocation. I still worked at OHSU, but had switched to swing shift. No longer living in the shoebox rooms as we had when we met, we now lived together in a rented house. We were more than friends. Jim was now my boyfriend and I loved him.

We showered Dan and his family with Christmas gifts. Dan even got a baggie of pot that we had scored from a teenage boy's room. Like me, Jim had no want for pot or drugs. Like Nana had spoiled me with name-brand toys, we made sure Dan and Tammy's son had the best, even a brand-new bicycle. Tammy's look of appreciation couldn't hide her disappointment in knowing where their gifts came from.

TVs, computers, VHS players, movies and CDs, jewelry, cash, coins, collectible trinkets, food, new hygiene items, clothes, tools, knives, rifles, and handguns were commonplace items we took. If something was of value to sell to a friend, or valuable and unidentifiable to sell to a pawn store, we took it. If it was useful and easy to grab, we took it. Like department store shopping on a gift card, anything I saw and liked, I took.

If we could haul it, we hauled it. Or if we couldn't haul it, we found a way. In an upper-class home, with houses few and far between around it, we had an especially large stockpile to carry out one night. Jim suggested, "We could go get the car and park in the driveway to load up. There's no houses around here with neighbors to see what we're doing."

"Frank, there's no way all this is going to fit in our little car."

"We could take some of it now and come back later for more," he suggested.

"No, Frank, that's too risky. When we leave, we leave for good. We don't need the houses down the street seeing us coming and going, and what if they come home while we are gone? I mean, we'd have to do another perimeter check, and I've got to get to work tomorrow afternoon and I want to sleep sometime before then."

As I voiced my counter argument, I looked around and paced in circles. Not wanting time to be wasted, I chatted as I grabbed little stuff without much thought, tossing items into the pillowcase I held. That's when I saw it. Hung on the pegboard in the kitchen in eyesight of us—keys on a key ring. "Frank, what do these keys go to?"

"What keys?" he asked while I walked to the pegboard and pulled them off.

"These keys," I said as I dangled them in front of him.

He took the keys out of my hand and said, "There's a Ford SUV in the garage. These must be the keys to it."

Going on three in the morning, he drove their SUV loaded down to the gills, while I followed behind in our car, also loaded. As if I weren't already shaking in my boots, er, my black Converse high-tops stolen from a prior burglary, I saw a cop car one lane over from us. My adrenaline immediately kicked into overdrive to conquer my fear. It was no time to panic. *And schwew*, that cop car paid no attention to an overloaded SUV with a taillight out in an ungodly hour of the morning on the interstate.

Once we had both vehicles unloaded, we closed our garage door on the SUV. We hadn't planned what to do with it. It was a first for us. "I have to get some sleep. We'll figure it out later," I said.

When Jim picked me up at work the next night, our task was to get rid of the SUV. Again, I drove the car, following him. He left the SUV parked in a legal spot in front of the Hillsboro City Police Station. In our third week of drive-bys, it was finally gone.

Come spring of 1990, with six months of experience behind me, I was ready to tackle our next barrier. We were in a neighborhood where the only house that appeared lifeless was this square-framed two-story house. From the front side, we could see they had a heavy security door and bars on their front-facing windows.

Jim whispered, "Let's get a better look."

We walked around back. He shined his flashlight in the first window we came to. It also had bars on it. "Yeah, I don't think anyone's home here," he said.

Instead of proceeding to the next window, he stepped back a few feet and used his flashlight to see the whole back of the house as best as possible. He scratched his head with an empty expression on his face. I thought he wanted to pass on it, but it was hard for me to judge his face as he stared at the whole house.

With impatience, I asked him, "What?"

"What, Frank?" I asked again.

"I don't think this one is any good to do," he said.

"Why?" I asked.

"Why, Frank?" I asked again. Still not getting a response, I rephrased my question, "You gonna let some bars stop you?" I pointed to a second-floor window, likely a bathroom window from its size. "Look, Frank. Look at that window. I mean, I think they're the same bars, but look at how they're kinda sticking out like they're just hanging there, not fastened in like on the other windows."

As he looked intently at the house with his strange stare, I scanned the yard. "Look, Frank, a ladder!" I exclaimed as quietly as I possibly could.

Not the wimpy kind, but a sixteen-foot ladder and other items leaned against a small shed, chained together. I ran to the ladder, then turned to look at that bathroom window again. Without further discussion, other than my self-rambling, he cut the lock on the ladder and placed it against the house. I started my climb up for a closer look as he securely held the ladder in place. I reached the window to find bars, but with flimsy brackets, probably the $1.99 specials. The bars weren't welded to the house as they were on the windows to both sides of the lower level. I whispered to myself, "Ha, teach them! They think they can keep us out. I don't think so."

I climbed back down and told him what I had discovered. It was time to reverse our roles. Whereas Jim had always been the tool handler and I had always been the watchdog, ironically with a blind eye, this time it was his turn to keep watch. With a screwdriver in my back pocket and a small crowbar in hand, I climbed back up. A few minutes later, I had the frame of bars in my hands and waved it so he could see I had accomplished my task. He stepped aside, and I tossed it down to the ground.

Next was the window, and I had no proven experience busting open a window—that was usually Jim's job—but it wasn't even locked. The owners probably didn't think to lock it. The window was small, and on the second floor. I slid the window pane to one side and then pushed on the screen, using the screwdriver to push under it and prying with the crowbar as needed, until it flew forward and fell.

I put the safety lock on my gun and secured it in my waistband. The screwdriver went back in my back waistband and I tossed the crowbar down to Jim. I sat my butt on the top rung and swung my legs in, and then used my hands to work my way through. With a four-foot drop, I landed on the tile floor, feet first and knees bent. I made a quick jump into an erect stand, pulled out my gun, and released its lock.

I held my gun in my right hand, trigger ready and pointed forward. I used my left hand to hold my flashlight to see by. With each step I took, I checked to make sure no one was home. I walked down the stairs, out the back, and approached my partner in crime, who was still staring at the house. At least he wasn't scratching his head in bewilderment anymore.

I said, "We're in."

"What took you so long, Susie?"

I answered, "What do you mean? First, I had to find the stairs, then the front door, then the back door. The front door needs a key. Come on, Frank. I have the back door open for us."

"How much of a sweep did you do, Susie?"

"I didn't check the whole house, only the parts I had to walk through. We still need to check the bedrooms," I answered.

In each house we did, I was always ready to shoot if I had to. Thankfully it never came to that, although we did have our close calls. We walked into one house only to find a heavyset man snoring sound asleep on his living room couch, out of sight when we had looked in the windows. We immediately backed out quietly. He never woke up.

At another house, with people on vacation as far as we knew, all seemed fine in the early morning daylight. We got in through a back door. I never heard a car pull up, but when I looked out the window during one of my frequent checks, I saw a young girl, about twelve years old, walking up toward the house. She was only a few feet shy of the front door. "Frank, hide, now," I whispered.

He ran to me, grabbed my arm, and pulled me with him into a bedroom. We hid behind the bedroom door, leaving it ajar, with no time to shut it. She came in the house. I heard her head toward the kitchen. We peeked through the opening where the door hinges and the door frame met. She fed the cats, petted them, then started to leave the kitchen. We leaned back against the wall, not letting our eyes peer through our peek hole. She left.

There was a time I fired my gun. After doing two neighboring houses in a rural stretch of a state highway, we started our five-minute walk to our car. It was parked on the highway shoulder. We stayed close to the grass line, off the road, and walked silently in the dark without our flashlights on. Even the night stars didn't light up that desolate area.

Far from city noise, we heard voices at the halfway point to our car. As we got closer, we saw five young men stripping our getaway car. Two were bent over at its wheels with flashlights, which lit up the whole scene. We dropped our bags and reached for our guns.

"Freeze!" Jim yelled.

Pow. Jim had fired a warning shot into the sky.

In a split second, they ran to their car. The driver started the ignition while the back doors were still ajar. My reaction took three seconds to their one second. I spent that first second trusting Jim's warning shot. In the next second I reacted to the scene unfolding in front of me. *Forget a warning shot!* I thought.

My third second happened as their driver accelerated with three of them crammed into the back seat of their tiny car. My bullet shot through their back window, dead center. Glass flew with their bellowed screams, all while they kept going.

I stood on the rural highway and stared toward our beat-up car but couldn't see anything in the dark. We were in the middle of three crime scenes; the burglaries we had done, our getaway car vandalized, and my shooting. Jim ran to inspect the damage by flashlight. He looked back at me and said, "Quick, stash all our bags off the road. Hide them good. Every one of 'em."

I grabbed what I could, and he ran back to me, grabbing up the last bag. We couldn't load them in our car in case a sheriff car drove by. One look at our car would warrant suspicion. We hoofed it back to the last house we had hit. That was before the days of cell phones as we know them today, and we needed a phone to call Dan for help.

After another sweep of the house, Jim called home. No longer renting a suburban house, we had since moved into a large farmhouse, sharing it with Dan and his family. Another friend we called Big-Dan also lived with us. When we called home for help, it was Big-Dan who answered the phone. Jim said, "Our car broke down."

We walked back to the car and waited. With exact directions to find us, Big-Dan pulled up, got out of his car, and said, "What the hell are you guys doing out here?"

We didn't respond as Big-Dan tied a rope to the bumper of our car. Our roommate's exertion caused heavy beads of sweat to pour from his forehead. By the light of his car's headlights, I saw him push his neatly combed hair up off his round face and out of his eyes. Big-Dan was a heavyset guy with an overhanging belly, which likely added fifty pounds to his 300-pound physique. Earning his nickname, he was known for having a heart for everyone—a heart as big as his belly.

Big-Dan changed the pitch of his question as he asked, "What is going on here?"

My partner in crime answered for us. "You don't want to know."

Big-Dan clamored, "You know I don't mind helping you out, but I don't want any part of any shit."

Tightening the knots in the rope, there was exasperation in Jim's voice as he told Big-Dan, "Yeah, yeah, sorry. We had no one else to call."

Big-Dan said, "I mean it, Jim. I don't want anything to do with whatever it is you two are up to. I don't need trouble."

Opening the car door, Jim said, "You won't get in trouble. Get us out of here. Get us home." Our car dangled taut on a rope as Big-Dan drove us home.

Homebound for several days, Jim and Dan put our car back together. After that, it was business as usual.

One night our choice was a spacious five-bedroom, two-story house in the middle-income suburbs of Portland. We understood from our research that the family was on vacation out of state. That night our set of rules would be weakened until we had no choice but to execute damage control. It would be the catalyst to pissing detectives off—detectives we didn't know about yet.

Loading our car with the goods we got out of the house, Jim stopped to check his tool bag and several other bags. "I lost my flashlight. The big one," he said.

We went back inside and looked in every room. It was lost somewhere in that big house. Sure, he had worn gloves, but inside the flashlight were six C batteries, and he hadn't worn gloves to load those batteries. In 1990 the forensic process of fingerprint matching was tedious, but the job would be made easier because Jim and I already had prints on file.

What are we going to do? I thought.

We sat in our car for a good twenty minutes in near silence. I don't know who was more scared. "Come on, can't you remember where you left it?" I asked.

Jim turned his head to look at the house, then looked back at me to answer. "No, I was everywhere in that house. It's a big house."

"Where do you remember having it last?"

He turned his head and looked back at the house. "I don't know. I just don't know."

"We can't leave it behind, and we don't know where it is, but we have to do something," I said. He lowered his gaze, not meeting my eyes. "I refuse to go to jail. Look at me," I said. He looked at me. "You've been caught before when you were in Alaska, and I refuse to let us do anything to get caught this time. I'm not leaving here with that flashlight still in there!"

He lowered his gaze again and said, "I don't know what to do."

I flung my hands in frustration and said, "Well burn the house down for all I care."

He looked up from his lap and turned his whole body to directly face me. "You mean you'd really burn the house down?" he asked.

"I don't want to get caught. I refuse to get caught. I don't want to burn it down," I said.

He agreed. "I don't either."

I put my hand on his leg, softened my voice and asked, "Sweetie?" I didn't know what else to say. I didn't have any real answers. His look kept darting between the house and me and his lap, and back again to the house, each time resting for a few minutes.

I unzipped my sweatshirt then unrolled the window a little. Wearing several layers made me stuffy hot. What I really needed was a cigarette. It wasn't safe to smoke here, though. We couldn't let anyone see us just sitting here. We had to sit in the dark until we figured this out.

He fiddled with the radio dial even though the radio wasn't on. Everything was quiet.

A few more minutes passed. It was going on one in the morning. I put my hand back on his leg and broke the silence. "We've never done that sort of thing before."

He looked down at my hand on his leg. "I know."

With more sarcasm than seriousness, I raised my voice and said, "Shit, where's Scott right now? He's the pyro in the family."

Jim looked back at the house. I stared at Jim. Jim looked back at the radio and again played with the knobs. He then clutched the steering wheel. A few more minutes passed. Finally, he asked, "How would we do it? I mean, if we did do it?"

I answered, "There's a jug of matches by the stairs and we'd find some lighter fluid. As big as that house is, there's got to be lighter fluid or something somewhere." In the jug at the foot of the stairs leading to the upstairs bedrooms was a wide assortment of matchbooks. Apparently something they collected from restaurants and hotels.

Throwing his hands up, he said, "It's your call. You decide."

"Yeah, but—"

"I'll go with whatever you decide," he assured me.

I answered, "Burn it. Burn it!"

Come summertime that year, 1990, my half-brother, Scott, needed a place to live again. The three of us went in on a suburban home in Clatskanie, with only Scott's name on the lease. No landlord liked that Jim and I had a history of frequent moves.

Scott was bored living in Clatskanie, far removed from Portland, and he started joining us a few nights a week. He liked what he got out of it, and we appreciated his short stature. Smaller than me, he helped us gain entry through smaller windows.

Full throttle into our intensified burglary spree, we were busy all across the northwest corner of Oregon. When we exhausted an area, we moved on to another area. When we needed a break, we mixed it up with mail runs, which provided clues to who was away on vacation or dead.

A year into this routine, I was exhausted. While I worked my real job, Jim handled getting rid of stuff and scoping out new places to hit. At work I did my minimum, my hour lunch break spent with an alarm clock and blanket in a locked exam room. Our hits kept us busy from before midnight until past sunup.

At the end of each full night, I'd sleep while Jim drove us home. Clatskanie was over an hour drive from any Portland suburb. With only four or five hours to eat, shower, and sleep before returning to my real job, I squeezed sleep in whenever I could.

One night, after a full evening of burglaries, we were on our return drive home along a rural highway. I woke up from my nap to our car jerking wildly. Jim had fallen asleep at the wheel.

Our car bounced in the dirt gutter and bobbed back up onto the road, which jarred Jim awake. It was too late. He had lost control. The car careened through its next bounce into a triple roll.

Our predicament scared me and I feared Jim could be hurt. "Are you okay?" I asked.

"I'm okay. You?" he answered.

I touched my seat belt where it crossed my chest, keeping me strapped in. A tree limb protruded through a shattered window a few inches in front of me. Had I not been seat-belted in—and sometimes I didn't wear my seat belt—I would have fallen chest-first in that upside-down car onto that tree limb. "I think so, but I'm afraid to move."

We talked through the process of getting free as Jim kept me balanced to pull me away from the branch. With grounded footing on the car's ceiling, we crawled to the back, opened the hatch door, and jumped out, holding on to each other. As we tried to tidy the inside of our upside-down car, stuffing full pillowcases of stolen stuff out of sight as best we could, sirens headed our way. Jim started scooping up spilt mail, but before he finished, a fire truck pulled up.

Who the heck saw us out here in the middle of nowhere? I wondered.

I hoped our car appeared trashy and that they wouldn't have any idea of the real scoop. Whatever they may have seen, those firemen were only concerned for our well-being, nothing more. A cop also showed up and I hoped he wouldn't notice that the driver's seat was pulled back too far for my short legs. If he noticed, he didn't say so. He wrote a report that said I had fallen asleep while driving.

Before long, we were back to our normal daily routine. I was too preoccupied to allow Nana's voice to judge me. Jim, however, missed his mom dearly. There hadn't been time for a proper goodbye when he had fled Alaska. As Christmas 1990 neared, so did my need for a short break. On Thanksgiving Day, I gave him a present. It had cost me $1,000, but at the rate we raked in money with no accounting method, money spent went unnoticed. As he unwrapped his gift, two round-trip airline tickets to Fairbanks for a one-week stay at Christmastime, he shed tears.

I wanted him to reunite with his mom, and I secretly day-dreamed of starting life anew. We didn't have to return on those tickets. More than ready for a break, I was ready for a new journey in my life.

Will I be able to persuade him to stay once we get there?

CHAPTER 8

SUSIE, II

Radio boom boxes were in my way. I had to step over an open box of them to reach the washing machine. A plastic laundry basket was nearby, but it was being used for an overflow of VHS and cassette tapes, not dirty clothes. I think there were a few music CDs in it too. Straddling the basket of tapes was the only way to reach the washer in our garage that day.

The car sat parked on the right side of the garage. There was nowhere for it on the left half. It wasn't the washer and dryer that took up all the room. I reached up on a shelf for the laundry soap and a pile of clothes that I'd forgotten about fell.

Oh yeah, Jim liked the leather jacket and I can always use more black leggings under my pants, especially with summer gone.

Not all our goods were pawned off. We spent more time doing burglaries than pawning off what we got from those burglaries. Nana had taught me well to go after anything I wanted. She had been an aristocratic woman, using resources to better herself, whether through another marriage, business intuition, or as a changemaker in her community. In an era when women weren't meant to be entrepreneurs, she had ignored society's stigma. I was rich, but unlike Nana—there was a sharp difference between us. My accomplishments were illegal. Hers had not been.

I dropped clothes in the washer and added laundry soap. It was quality detergent, with a label claiming "stain fighting." No need to go to any supercenter for anything. We had everything, even this detergent. I set the laundry soap on the table next to me. A clustered mess of jewelry boxes sat on the table.

I turned the knob on the washer as Jim walked past me with some sort of tool in hand, likely headed to his Craftsman tool box, which stood high at the back wall. To get to it, he tripped over a short stack of beat-up metal boxes but caught himself before falling. Some were twisted beyond recognition, and some had white powder residue. "Dang it. Don't worry, I'll get rid of the safes today while you're at work," he said.

"Look at all this stuff, Jim. We've got tons of money. Let's quit while we're ahead and just enjoy it all."

"I'll think about it, Kym, honey, but not yet," Jim replied.

That day in our garage, me at the washer, and Jim doing what he did best, was the day I made the decision to get those airplane tickets. I looked forward to Christmas with his mom but kept quiet about thoughts that we could stay in Fairbanks. I didn't want to upset him. He had enough stress as it was, and so, in my secret hopes, I had to get him used to the idea through any hints I could throw at him.

Jim's remedy for my burnout was far from anything I could have fathomed on that October morning. After a visit Jim had with our friend Dan, it was decided our next big hit would be the Salem Armory. It would take all four of us—Jim, Dan, Scott, and me—to pull it off.

"Sweetie, I thought Dan was done with doing stuff like this," I said.

"This is different. It's not a house. It's the armory," Jim said. He beamed a big smile at me and added, "The armory!"

Jim explained that he and Dan would work out the plans, and then go over them with Scott and me. I saw no harm in planning. I could always say no later.

The armory job never got fully planned, and our trip home to Alaska never happened. But back in October 1990, we had no way of knowing what was coming next.

My nightly enthusiasm dwindled, replaced by mere obligation to my compulsion, as I pushed on in our life as I knew it. One dark night, Jim pulled off onto the side of a rural state highway in Columbia County and parked. We took a short walk to understand the physical layout of the ranch houses that sat off the road, deciding if it would be a good area to hit. When we returned to our car, we realized the keys were locked inside. Our tools were inside the car.

Nearby was an open shed. The nearest house it could have possibly belonged to was ten acres away. With flashlights in hand, we took what we needed from that shed to break into our car. With a flat, hook-like tool, Jim worked to pry open our driver's side door, while I stood ready to help pull it out from its frame.

A brown sheriff's car pulled up to us, headlights to headlights, but his were on and bright. Ours were off. Jim glanced up without moving his head, then looked back at his task and said, "Tell 'im we went for a walk to talk. That we weren't getting along and needed to talk."

Jim stared at his task while I raised my eyes to watch the sheriff, or perhaps he was a deputy. When he opened his door to get out, his interior light showed that he was alone. He walked up to us, flashlight in hand, not that he needed it with his headlights still on, and asked us, "What's going on here?"

Jim stopped and turned to look at him. I didn't say a word. That was another rule to go along with the rules of no jewelry, no smoking, and no drinking. Dan had lectured me many times not to say anything to cops. Not ever. I respected Dan for his experience.

I didn't answer the cop. I kept quiet. We weren't under arrest, but there stood a cop who questioned our strange presence at such a time and place on that deserted neck of the road. Jim answered him, "We locked ourselves out of our car and are just trying to get back in it so we can leave."

The brown-uniformed officer asked, "Why are you parked here?"

Jim answered him, "We went for a walk."

"I don't know many people who would choose to go walking out here this time of night. You're the first I know of."

Another brown county cop car pulled up, and again, a single officer got out of his car and joined us. "Hello. What's happening?"

The first cop answered him, "We have here, two people who got locked out of their car."

The second cop asked us, "Where did you get the screwdriver?"

It wasn't even a screwdriver. "Um—"

Before Jim could finish his answer, the cop pointed to the open shed and said, "We got a call from the owner of that shed over there that a couple of people were rifling through it."

"Sorry, we were just trying to get back into our car. I was only borrowing it. I was going to return it once we got the car open," Jim said.

"We need to see ID for both of you. And, ma'am, follow me please," the second cop said.

The first cop stayed to talk with Jim as the other cop escorted me a short distance away. There, he stood and faced me. "Your ID, please."

"It's in the car with the keys," I answered. It was a still night, sparse traffic, but we were too far away for me to hear what Jim and his cop were talking about.

"How did this happen?" my cop asked me.

"We went for a walk to talk. We had to discuss something and I was too upset to talk and drive at the same time, so we pulled over and went for a walk. I guess I was too upset when we got out of the car because I forgot the keys inside."

The cop started idle chat. "Nights are getting colder this time of year. My son had a ball game earlier and it was sure chilly out. If you got kids, best to not let 'em play outside on these cold nights."

I didn't reply. I turned my head and looked back at Jim.

My cop kept chatting, but I didn't respond. A few minutes later, he walked me back to Jim. The first cop was on his hand-held radio as he told the dispatcher the information from Jim's ID, old Morrison Street address included. We didn't correct him. While he waited for a dispatcher's response, he said directly to Jim, "Here's what we're going to do. I need you to take that tool, and any other tools you borrowed, back to the shed. Then we will get my crowbar out of my trunk and pop your door open so you two can be on your way."

Jim headed for the shed, turned his head, and over his shoulder said, "Thank you."

My cop added, "And ma'am, I'll need to see your license before you leave."

They got our door open and then I showed them my license. My cop wrote my name and birthdate on his pad of paper. I didn't think he took the time to write down my address, but it was still listed as the Boise Street address where I had lived when married to Vance.

"All right, I don't want you two to ever borrow tools again without asking. The homeowner could have pressed charges. So that's it. You're free to go," he told us.

"Thank you again for your help," Jim said.

We got in our car. I was in the driver's seat, and I picked up the keys from the console. I had to move the seat forward. There was no way I could reach the pedals where Jim had earlier stretched his long legs. I didn't want to make that obvious, so I fidgeted and moved the seat back farther, then forward again but far enough up for me.

I also feared one of the two of them would follow us, and sure enough, at the nearby fork in the road, the second cop went our way while the first cop took the other road toward town. We didn't want the cop to know where we really lived, nor what our itinerary was for the night. As soon as I rounded a bend, I gunned the accelerator and sped like a bat out of hell to lose him. I knew those back roads well enough to navigate the curves without worry over my poor night vision. For several miles, my speedometer passed fifty around the corners and ninety on the straight stretches. I got us the fuck out of Dodge.

With the cop ditched in the dust behind us, I took a road that led to an outlying area of Multnomah County. It would take an hour drive to get there. "That was close, real close," I said.

Jim said, "I know. I don't know why he didn't arrest us for taking the tools from the shed. I don't know if I buy that story of the home-owner not wanting to press charges."

I adjusted my rearview mirror. "I told you, we need to retire."

"Nah, we'll be fine. We just got to be careful from now on and make sure we have the keys before we get out of the car," Jim said.

I slowed down a little. It was hard to see the road in the dark. "But wouldn't it be nice to just relax and retire?"

Jim didn't notice my slower driving and kept yakking. "Just wait until after we do the armory. Dan and I almost have those plans worked out, and you wouldn't believe all the guns they have in there. The armory job is what you need to get you excited again."

Our routine picked up where it had left off, with more of the usual business. Or, almost usual. Two weeks later, we had another run-in with the cops. It was mid-evening in a commercialized sprawl of Hillsboro in Washington County. The sun had about another hour before it set. I was driving to give Jim a break. In my rearview mirror I saw a blue-and-white cop car tailing us.

I had no idea where we were headed next, so I made a left turn in hopes of shaking him off. He followed me, and then his siren lights signaled me to pull over. I parked, turned the car off, and left the keys in the ignition. I then rolled down my window just a little bit and waited for the cop to approach me.

"Your driver's license, registration, and insurance, please," he said. I handed them to him.

"And I need you two to step out of the car."

Oh shit, my hot gun is under my seat, I thought to myself. Hot, meaning it was stolen. And loaded. And bigger than the wimpy .22 Jennings I used to carry.

I pulled the keys out of the ignition and pocketed them, rolled up my window, and as I reached for my door handle, I looked at Jim and said, "Lock your door when you get out."

I pushed open my door and slyly pushed the lock button down. I stood up and shut the door behind me. Some loot was in our car's trunk, with only one pillowcase of stuff on the back floorboard. Since crashing the hatchback car, we had traded it in for one with a trunk. We had just finished our first burglary of the night. It was dusk and I didn't think the cop could see well back there. If he discovered my hot gun, all hell would break loose. That alone would be enough for disaster.

As the cop radioed in my license information, two more cop cars pulled up. Two cops got out of each car. Five cops stared us down. They detained us far too long, as the sun started setting. They weren't so much interested in my driving record as in doing a search of our car.

The first cop said, "I pulled you over because you seemed to have a hard time driving. You were weaving. Have you been drinking?"

I hadn't been drinking. I had more than three years of sobriety, never mind it had been a long time since I'd gone to an AA meeting. I recognized his ploy. I gave my one-word answer with no need to say more. "No."

Jim, though, got wordy. "She has vision in only one eye so that might be why her driving is not as good as it could be."

The sun had set to darkness since they had first arrived on the scene. One cop was handling our business while the other cops shined their flashlights through our car windows. "Are you sure you haven't been drinking?" the first cop asked me again.

"Yes."

"I think you've been drinking."

He instructed me through a field sobriety test, which I had never done before. That took time, which gave the other cops more time to keep searching by flashlight. Then, another cop car pulled up. Before long, six cops in all walked circles around our locked car with flashlights.

I passed the sobriety test with flying colors. At default and without discussion with the other cops, the first cop said, "We want to search your car for alcohol to see if you've been drinking."

"No, you can't search my car. I haven't been drinking," I said.

"We still want to search your car," the cop said.

I repeated myself. "No, you can't search my car."

As a professional burglar, it was my job to know the law. Just as Nana had instilled in me right from wrong, Dan had instilled how to handle myself in life-threatening situations. Considering the hot gun under my seat, this was life-threatening to me. I knew all too well the discovery of the gun would mean immediate arrest. In Oregon in 1990, the law was such that a cop couldn't randomly search a car.

"Why won't you let us search your car?" the cop pressed. He was the only one talking. The other cops were busy walking circles around our car with their flashlights.

"You can't search my car," I said assertively.

"Do you have something to hide?"

"No."

"Then let us search your car."

"No."

"Why not?"

As if to compromise, I answered, "You can shine your flashlights on my car all you want. But no, you cannot search my car."

At that point, one of the flashlight cops said, "Let them go. There's nothing more we can do here."

The cop handed my license, registration, and insurance card back to me. "Drive safe."

Leaving the scene, I drove us to a fast food place to regroup. Jim said, "You were driving fine. There was no reason for them to pull you over."

"I know."

Jim added, "Look, I didn't want to scare you, but I think something's up. A couple times this past week while you were at work, I could have sworn someone was following me."

I asked, "No?"

Jim said, "Yeah. Let's lay low awhile here in the Portland area. Hillsboro and Beaverton, too. Let things cool off. We haven't tried Veronia yet, or Warrenton."

I blew on my hot coffee to try to cool it down. "Those towns are a long drive from work when you pick me up at night."

"They're closer to home though. Let's just keep watching for any more funny business," he said.

After coffee, I handed Jim the car keys and we headed off for a two-hour drive to the inlying coastal towns. Our usual routine had resumed. We added to the stockpile in the garage and Scott added cash to his pockets.

◆ ❖ ◆

A couple months later, on an early December morning, the sun had barely risen when Jim, Scott, and I returned home with a large haul. I was due into work later that day, so sleep was the only thing on my mind. First, I checked on our cats. We had thirteen in all. Nimba, a Halloween-calico cat, had recently had a litter of nine. Tiger came to us as a stray, and then after him came Nimba. We'd also taken in two more.

I put on a Peter Gabriel CD to unwind. It was on its third song when I walked out of the bathroom and across our living room. Headed to the kitchen, I needed a light snack. I stopped in my tracks. Something had caught my eye. I was in the habit of looking out front windows for signs of life, and when I looked this time I noticed something peculiar.

Directly across from our house was a street that led around a corner and back to our house from the opposite direction, leading out of our cul-de-sac. I saw a car go by, go around the loop, but instead of driving out of our neighborhood, it rounded the loop again, not exiting our cul-de-sac. I called Jim's attention to it.

Jim looked and said, "You're just seeing things. Nah, everything's all right."

I thought Scott was noticeably concerned as well, but instead of freaking out like me, he looked to Jim as if expecting him to tell us what to do. "She's right. What do we do?"

Jim calmly answered Scott, "Don't worry about it, you two. Everything's okay."

My stomach fluttered. "No, this isn't okay."

The car rounded the cul-de-sac again. Scott said, "Whoa, we gotta do something, Jim."

With a high pitch to my voice, I said, "Look. There it goes again." Driving slowly, that same car turned the same corner again. It was circling our street again.

Jim gave a quick glance around our living room and then pointed at a pile of unorganized crap in one corner. "Get that stuff and get it into the car now. Hurry. Susie, keep your gun on you!"

"My gun's in the bedroom," I said. *We're not in burglary mode. Why am I Susie now?*

"Scott— Susie, help Scott with that TV. He's got the cord wrapped around some stuff."

We swooped up another armful of stuff and ran it out to our car in the driveway. Peter Gabriel was still playing in the background. The song "That Voice Again" started playing on the CD. The getaway plan Jim was orchestrating was stupid. The thought crossed my mind that I could escape through the backyard. That was also a stupid idea. I couldn't leave Jim behind.

Jim was in charge while Scott and I loaded our car to the gills. With an undistributed weight, or more likely because of the donut tire, the car leaned to the right. We had punctured a tire when on a gravel road recently and hadn't fixed it yet.

Scott and I were stuffing crap in the car when Jim ran into the house. In under a minute Jim came running back outside, my gun in one hand and the envelope with the Fairbanks plane tickets in the other hand. He handed me my gun. Just my gun and not my wallet. "Here, Susie, take it. Take your gun."

Jim motioned for us to get in the car, while he jumped into the driver's seat and slammed the plane tickets into the glove box. There was no time to question Jim taking the driver's seat. We also didn't bother with seat belts.

Jim didn't get us far. Not even as far as the nearest main road, the highway. Nope. I think it might have been the donut tire that slowed us down. Either that, or the heavy weight in the car on top of the donut tire. Either way, we couldn't get the car to pick up any real speed. We were barely out of our cul-de-sac when Jim pulled into the parking lot of the Safeway grocery store that cornered the state highway.

Where does he think we're going?

Jim drove around to the back of the store. We screeched to a stop, and instinctively jumped out of the idling car as Jim yelled, "Run!"

In flight mode, we embarked on the steep climb up a back-lot embankment. We didn't make it far on foot either. With our backs to the parking lot, I heard a loud scuffle behind us.

If we keep climbing, we might escape.

Behind us, the sound of cocking rifles echoed.

"FREEZE!"

It was the loud male voice of only one cop, so I exhausted fifteen more seconds and a few more inches in my attempted upward escape. Fifteen seconds may not seem like long, but on a stopwatch it is an eternity. No shots were fired. I accepted that I had taken my last step, and then I surrendered.

"DROP YOUR WEAPONS!"

I did.

"DROP TO THE GROUND!"

I did. I was already near to the ground with that hill demanding more of a crawl than a hike. I lowered my body and let my belly touch the earth. I was down. I felt my heart throb against my dirt landing. I heard more scuffling from a crowd in the parking lot. I turned my head to face Jim, who was next to me. I sensed that more rifles, in the far-off distance, were being cocked. Jim was already looking my way, but he didn't say anything.

Suddenly, the butt of a rifle was at the small of my back. "Don't move!"

As the pressure of the rifle was lifted from my back, so was my left arm. My arms were pulled behind me and my hands were hand-cuffed. A cop manhandled me up onto my feet. My head was still turned to Jim. Another cop was handcuffing him. I watched Jim, not turning my head toward Scott, who was farther away on the other side of me.

It was only as this cop escorted me across the lot that I saw for the first time what I had only heard up until then. Cop cars were everywhere—cop cars with red and blue sirens that silently twirled, unmarked cars, unmarked pickup trucks, and plain SUVs, all with no logical order to where they'd come to a stop, skid marks and all. Male cops were everywhere on foot, some behind the door to their vehicle, some not. Some were running, and some were walking with mad intent. Some cops were dressed in their blue-and-white uniformed attire. Some were not. And there were a lot of cops who would have passed as plain old fat businessmen if they hadn't been waving their guns.

I didn't feel dangerous enough to warrant that kind of attention. And Scott, who was as short as me, certainly didn't have a threatening hair on his tow-blond head.

So why are rifles still pointed at me? At me?

With his hand ahold of my arm, this cop walked me to a plain white cop car. As we stood by the car, he gave me a light pat down. "Do you have anything on you?" he asked me.

With my gut instinct telling me to stay quiet, I kept my answer short. "No."

He opened the car's back door and pushed on my arms as his way of instructing me to get in. A different cop got in the driver's seat and drove me out of the lot while the scene behind us continued to unfold. Jim and Scott were still back at the scene.

I was taken to the local Clatskanie police station. It was small, same as the town it served was small. As we walked inside, I noticed its parking lot made it look bigger than it really was. If not for my sunken reality, I would have thought I was at the Mayberry Jail. Instead of Don Knotts who ran the Mayberry Jail in the '60s TV sitcom, I was greeted by angry cops. They seemed royally pissed off at me, and yet at the same time, they smirked and gloated.

A cop took me out of my handcuffs and I spent the next several hours, or so it seemed, in an interrogation room. I stuck to our rule and didn't talk. That was the agreement Jim and I had from the get-go and I intended to stick to it like glue. A male detective finally gave up on me. He left our interrogation room, leaving the door ajar. In that Mayberry place, I overheard him as he said, "You go talk to her. She won't talk to me. She needs a woman to get her to talk."

That only heightened my attitude of defiance. A woman officer came in, sat down in the wooden schoolhouse chair across from me, and then proceeded with several different tactics. "Your husband, is he Arthur? He's in the other room right at this moment telling us everything we need to know. What is your side of the story?"

It wasn't surprising she referred to Jim by his first name. Only those who knew him called him Jim, short for James, his middle name. This was serious. I didn't answer her.

"Is Arthur your husband or your boyfriend?" she asked.

"I'm not talking to you," I said.

She tilted her head down and looked up into my eyes. "I would like to hear your side of the story."

I kept her gaze. "I'm not answering your questions." Our gazes hardened into stares. Our stare was a stalemate, seemingly unending. The door to our room was shut tight. I couldn't make out any of the conversations outside of our room. The minute hand on a wall clock kept ticking, also seemingly unending.

"Are you sure about that?" she asked. "It would really help you if you tell me what you can. You're only hurting yourself. Your brother is talking too, and I think he's putting all the blame on you. Don't you want to clear the air so we know what really happened, so you don't get the rap for something you didn't do?"

"I'm not talking to you." I looked up at the clock I kept hearing but didn't pay attention to the time. It was just something to look at other than her. I wondered where they had Jim. I wondered if Jim and Scott were together.

"Did you grow up around here?" she asked.

"I'm not talking to you."

She said, "I went to high school in St. Helens and was just wondering if you did too."

"I'm not talking to you."

"Is there anything you want to ask me then?"

Silence swept over us as I drifted into thoughts about Nimba and her kittens.

"My cats. I need to make sure my cats are taken care of. I have a cat who just had a litter of nine kittens a couple weeks ago, and we have other cats too. Thirteen in all. I'm worried about them. What's going to happen to my cats?"

"I can find out for you. See what I can do about your cats," she answered.

"I'm concerned for the little kittens. I don't want them killed or taken to the animal shelter. I need them taken care of," I said.

"Let me see what I can do," she said as she got up from her seat.

She left the room and I sat alone for a long time. I didn't mind the quiet. Quietness was a welcome relief from the tense silence of earlier.

When she came back in our room, she said, "All of your cats

are with a neighbor now. She's happy to take them in and they'll be taken care of."

"Thank you."

She took her seat again. "We have detectives going through your house now. I'd hate for you to get into more trouble than you already are. Tell me about the items in your house."

"I'm not talking to you."

She asked, "Your brother said he didn't do any of the burglaries. Is that true?"

My defiant attitude reared its ugly face. "I already told you I'm not talking to you about this. And trying to get to know me by asking where I grew up isn't going to work for you. I'm not answering your questions."

She looked down at the watch on her wrist. It was a delicate-looking thing, not rugged like you would expect in her line of work. She looked back at me and looked back at her watch. I studied her watch. Diamond studs decorated it, only they probably weren't real diamonds. Still, it would be worth some money. Not this day, though, not for me. I looked back up at her.

She sighed. I looked back at the wall clock, then back at her.

She got up and left the room. I overheard her just on the other side of the open door. "May as well process her. She won't say anything to me either."

Soon, a male cop led me to the one and only jail cell that I could see. It was a barred cage strategically placed where all could see it, as if Deputy Barney Fife oversaw that layout. I came to believe that

Scott and Jim were in interrogation rooms. I never saw them, and I could see everything from that cage, except anyone or anything behind the closed doors of the rooms that were alongside one wall. I hoped Jim and Scott weren't talking. That would piss me off. Well, not so much Scott, but Jim. Jim knew better. We had an agreement.

I'm sticking to my end of the agreement, but is he?

Eventually I was let out, handcuffed again, and driven to the Columbia County Jailhouse in St. Helens. Later I found out that part of the waiting game for my transfer from the city cage to the county jail was their need for a woman guard. Before her, the jail was solely staffed with male guards. Other than an occasional female drunk driver, brought in to sober up overnight, they rarely got women inmates.

This guard introduced herself. "I'm Rose and I will get you booked in. Follow me."

In a coat closet type of room, Rose watched me undress, which took a while. I was wearing black long johns, black leggings, and over that, black jeans. I also had on a black bra, a black undershirt, a black turtleneck shirt, and over that a black long-sleeved jersey sweatshirt. On my feet were thick black socks and black Converse high-top tennies.

Once undressed, she handed me my three articles of clothing to dress in, orange pants and tunic top of a cotton material, along with thin white underwear. She turned my bra inside out, then right side out again, and handed it back to me. "Keep your bra."

Lastly, Rose gave me plastic open sandals. My clothing was bagged and tagged and put in a locker in my presence. "What about my shoes, Rose?" I asked.

Rose answered, "Those are being held as evidence against muddy footprints."

No argument there. Besides, they were stolen. Fully dressed as best as I could be, Rose led me into another room, where a short, fat, balding male guard stood at a computer behind a four-foot-high counter. He helped Rose with her duties. He also informed me of my charges. "Twenty class A felonies of burglary and one class C felony of burglary, as charged by the County of Columbia."

The class C was for the open shed. Rose measured me to determine my height and then weighed me. She wrote her findings in a ledger on the counter. Next, Baldy fingerprinted me and my mug shot was taken.

With logistics out of the way, Rose walked me to an old-fashioned desk phone and told me I could make one phone call. I hadn't even thought to ask for a phone call. I had no one to call. My lifeline was Jim, and he was obviously a no-go. I had no friends left, other than Dan, and I certainly wasn't going to involve him. I wasn't close to any relatives other than Uncle Randy, Nana's other favorite, and even that relationship felt estranged. I called Uncle Randy. Our call was brief and to the point. I let him know the basic facts.

At long last, Rose handed me a box of indigent items, which included basic hygiene products and enough rolling papers and tobacco to make thirty-two cigarettes. I was informed it was my commissary and I'd receive the same twice a week, on Mondays and Thursdays. She further informed me, "Everything but the tobacco products are free of charge. Your limited allotment of tobacco will appear on a bill upon your release at one dollar and thirty cents per commissary."

With commissary and a bedroll and towel in hand, fully dressed in my orange attire, I was led into the female unit. I had been arrested that morning and booked in the early evening of Tuesday, December 4, 1990.

CHAPTER 9

JONES-NELSON

"I don't want to go this alone. I want us to get married," I told Jim as he stood beside me during our shared elevator ride up from the basement, destined for the courtroom. Two male guards stood with us, Jim and I sandwiched in between them. It was a small utility type of elevator, plain and rudimentary. The last time I'd seen Jim was when we were lying on the ground next to each other being handcuffed.

I had been booked in only twelve hours earlier, but that was too long for me to go without him. Well rested, and with three showers since then, I reasserted my plea. "The only way to get through this is together. As it is now, we have no rights that allow us to be with each other since we're not married. We need to get married."

"Okay, Kym, I'll talk to my attorney about it. How are you? Are you all right?"

"I'm fine. It's nice and quiet in my cell, but how are you?" I asked.

"I'll be okay."

In that first courtroom appearance, we stood side by side as the judge arraigned us. Jim was charged with twenty class A felonies of burglary, and I was charged as previously informed when booked. I had one more charge than Jim—the class C felony of burglary. The judge asked, "How do you plead?"

"Not guilty," I said.

"Not guilty," Jim said.

I had to fight my incarceration. The judge told me bail was $100,000, and that I'd receive a court-appointed attorney. However rich we were at the time of our arrest, it was stolen money and couldn't be used to bail us out or retain an attorney. We had a little money stashed in a bank account in his mom's name, up in Fairbanks, but saw no point in revealing that. I had what I needed in hygiene items and for smoking, and furthermore, any legal defense could cost more than that few thousand.

That elevator ride was the first of several to come in subsequent weeks, and all were too short. I wanted to be held by Jim and to feel his strong arms wrapped around me with love. Instead, we held hands or exchanged a quick peck of a kiss, if the guard who escorted us to court seemed cool enough to allow it. There was much more I wanted to say and ask in those brief moments, and so little time to express myself. I wanted to know what was going to happen to us, and I wanted to know what happened to Scott.

Jim's most common response to my unanswered questions was, "Keep the faith."

I was ignorant of religion but understood enough to know that when he said that, he meant something that had to do with God. I respected his belief that God would guide us and bless us and keep us safe, but did not share his views. God was not tangible. Life in jail was real.

Before the end of our first week in jail, my court-appointed attorney visited me in my pod. There was no reason to go to a conference room. I was still the only woman inmate. He explained that the court process involved several appearances. He further assured me he'd consult Jim's attorney to move forward with our petition for marriage.

Soon after his visit, another woman was booked in. She was also in deep trouble. Renae Rider was booked on felony attempted manslaughter. She had beat up a guy with a teakettle of hot water to protect her girlfriend. I was fine by myself, but if I had to have a cellmate, Renae was fine to fill that role.

Buff and heavyset with short hair that fell to her shoulders, Renae was all dyke, and my type at that, but in personality, we were too much alike. At times we butted heads, if only out of a mutual demand for respect between us, as if we were old friends. Her girlfriend, Tia, eventually came out of hiding as her co-assailant.

Our shared cell had an open floor plan with solid walls at the front and back. Another wall of the same sea-green plaster divided our two sleeping areas. Each sleeping quarter had a metal toilet and sink, a bunk bed, and a third bed. Our cell was enclosed by yellowed steel bars.

We shared the shower stall, which stood as an eyesore in our dayroom, next to our cement picnic table and bench. At our table, we often played cards or wrote letters. Our TV was anchored right outside of our cell. We used the open end of an empty plastic shampoo bottle to reach between the bars and change the channel to our compromised liking. In the opposite corner was a locked entryway with two sliding gates to our pod, also made of metal bars. Whenever that gate was opened, the bars clanked when slid shut.

There was no need for windows deep in the middle of an underground basement. No sunlight could be had. Jim told me the guys got outdoor rec time in a fenced area once a week. As the only three women, we weren't given that privilege. Our pleas for yard time went unheard for more than a month. Then, we got our one and only venture into sunshine.

That trip involved handcuffs. Two guards watched over Renae, Tia, and me while we stood behind the jail on the banks of the Columbia River. The day was crisp, and without coats, the sun warmed my arms. It was still winter. I breathed in a sweet smell of musty river and factory smoke.

Long before our outdoor adventure, my attorney let me know our request to get married had been approved. The jail staff scheduled our wedding for Friday, January 4, 1991, when they would have enough staff on duty to oversee it. We couldn't invite anyone to our ceremony for security reasons. Not even Uncle

Randy, and I was glad Nana couldn't see me marry someone she'd have disapproved of. Then again, Nana had always encouraged me to bravely do anything necessary for success. As Jim's wife, rather than merely his partner in crime, I'd have a better chance of controlling my situation.

As much as I wanted Uncle Randy to be present for our ceremony, I couldn't complain given our granted privileges. Randy had visited me only once since my arrest. His visit was more of an obligation than a want. He had to check on my well-being and lecture me. "With felony convictions, you'll never be able to vote again."

Not voting was the least of my concerns. Randy added, "I didn't tell your mother, but she found out anyway. The morning after your arrest, it was in the Salem newspaper. Your mother had no idea what you two kids were up to, and then she saw in the paper that her only two kids had been arrested and were responsible for this awful thing. I liked Jim, but now, to find out about this hidden side of him..."

Our story was covered not only in the *Salem Statesman Journal*, two hours away, but during the first week, it reached papers in Portland and from Seattle to California. Uncle Randy informed me there was no reasonable way to raise my bond money.

I assured him there was no need to bail me out. "The only way for me to see Jim is by staying here, in jail."

I'd have given anything to be free but was okay where I was. I still had Jim, if in a different way. In jail I slept well, and showered often, unlike when back in my dogged run. And twice weekly I was handed a clean set of orange scrubs to change into. All scrubs were orange, with small, medium, and large as the only difference. In exchange, I handed in my dirties to be added to the recycling rhythm. Even though cooties had been washed away in my clean set, a male inmate likely wore them before me.

Best yet, out of all my needs being met, the food was good. Our dinner cook was a retired chef from a cruise ship. In all my life, before, during, or since, I've never enjoyed a meal so much as those from that chef. Thursday nights were my favorite with a full course of Mexican fare. Lunches and weekends were different. We were at the hands of randomly assigned guards and male inmates instructed to feed us. Peanut butter sandwiches and lime Jell-O with green peppers for dessert were common when our chef wasn't on duty.

Renae and Tia helped me with my wedding arrangements. We used colored pencils to make wedding announcement cards. It was the next best way to include family in our celebration, however awkward the time and place. Valuing Jim's belief in God, I thumbed through our jailhouse Bible and found a scripture that I added to our announcement cards from Philippians 4:7, "And the peace of God which surpasses all understanding will guard your hearts and minds through Christ Jesus."

We could choose which fellow inmates would sign our marriage certificate as witnesses. Jim chose Scott as his best man and one of the witnesses. Renae was my maid of honor and filled her role well, making me a blue paper flower ornament to adorn my hair.

On Friday morning, January 4, a female guard escorted Renae and me from our cell to an anteroom that was also in the basement. The baby blue fake flower in my hair offset my bright orange scrubs. The first person I saw when we entered was Jim, who stood tall and smiled at me with a freshly shaven face. Jim stretched his arm out and took my hand as I stepped beside him. He smelled like fresh deodorant.

Renae stayed by my side, and Scott stood on the other side of Jim. At the edge of our small room, two male guards stood with arms relaxed, but guns in their holsters at their hips. A court clerk held legal documents and faced us.

The court clerk led us through our vows, then softened her voice and said to Jim, "You may now kiss the bride."

Jim took me in his arms and said, "I love you."

"I love you," I said.

We embraced with a long passionate kiss, unlike the quick elevator pecks. We could have stayed in our embrace forever if allowed, but after a few minutes, a guard cleared his throat and instructed us to, "Break it up."

We signed our documents, thanked the guards and court clerk, and then received our order that it was time to go back to our cells. As soon as Renae and I were safely locked back in our cell, the woman guard removed my name plate at our entry foyer and walked away with it. A few minutes later she returned to hang it back up, but with a name change. I was now Jones-Nelson, K.

At first, I was puzzled by my name change. However, since I'd kept Vance's last name when we divorced, and then was booked under it, Jones had to stay. My assigned hyphened name was the best I could get. So, Jones-Nelson I was.

With our marriage came visiting privileges two or three times a week, if the guards weren't too busy. Our visiting area was a divided room with two doors, one for each of us to enter. Inside, we each had a long steel bench for sitting, and an accompanying steel table on which to rest our elbows. A clear pane of security glass stretched the length of our table and bench. We talked through a phone, usually for thirty minutes.

I used discernment when talking with Jim. Guards could use anything we said as incriminating evidence. In our time together I looked to Jim for answers. He had experience in this sort of thing. I had never been arrested before. He had. I had no idea what to expect or how anything would unfold.

Incessantly, I implored, "Jim, you can't tell them anything."

"I want to protect you," he said.

"No, you can't say anything. The more you tell them, the more they'll know. We agreed in the beginning, more than a year ago, back on day one, we'd never say anything to anyone. I'm keeping my end up. You have to do the same."

He wouldn't say if he or Scott had talked when at the Clatskanie jail, but I sensed that he wasn't staying true to our agreement. Worse yet, Scott likely talked. He was released the day after Jim and I married.

Aside from the countless burglaries, the prosecution wanted a greater understanding of the arson. I refused to divulge information. My attorney suggested I take a polygraph test to appear cooperative and likely avoid the charge.

Although apprehensive in the days leading up to my appointment for the polygraph, I was determined to stick to my story, or that is, the story that I didn't have a story to tell. My appointment was in a dimly lit room, also in the basement.

Only the polygraph examiner and I were in the room. The first part of our time together was reserved for open discussion. The polygraph examiner and I sat corner to corner at a table, and I answered as reservedly as I could. He explained, "To get accurate results, I need some background information. Not thinking about these burglaries, have you ever stolen anything?"

I didn't want to appear unbelievable, so after much thought, I told him about the time I was a little girl and stole the lipstick from Hazel, which Nana had scolded me for. Once satisfied with background information, he wired my fingers up to his electronic gadget, which sat on the desk. Then he instructed me, "Just answer yes or no to each of these questions."

"Okay," I said.

The polygraph examiner asked, "Have you ever stolen anything?"

"Yes."

A green light lit up and the needle on the machine moved a little.

He asked, "When you were a little girl, did you steal lipstick from someone's purse?"

"Yes."

Again, a green light blinked, and the needle moved again, but not as far.

The questioning continued as he moved deeper into questions about theft, and then the arson. Sometimes a red light blinked, instead of the usual green. Sometimes the needle jumped far, and sometimes it barely moved.

In the end, the polygraph yielded "inconclusive" results. I had lied regarding the full scope, and came out of it in the middle of the spectrum. There was no indication I had lied, nor any indication I had told the truth. Once the prosecution reviewed the results, they determined they didn't want to spend more taxpayer monies on yet another polygraph test in hopes of something different. They accepted the results and placed the paperwork in my ever-thickening file. I was never charged with the arson. Jim was.

My attorney maintained his professional attention to my case but also let me know it was difficult. "My friends are upset I took on your case. I can't even get my hair cut without my hairdresser talking about it. You burglarized her house and it scared her."

He was right. I hadn't given it much thought until then. Stolen TVs could be replaced with new ones. Insurance would cover stolen jewelry, and my muddy footprints on white carpet could be washed away. These were only property crimes. As my attorney talked with me, I came to understand that people were affected. Before, I had been calloused. Now, I was shame-faced.

I was also ignorant of how my incarceration would either proceed or end. I imagined a crime spree of our magnitude would result in years of prison. I was relieved and eager to comply when my attorney suggested a plea-bargaining option.

"Here's the deal," he said. "We could go to court, but there is overwhelming evidence against you and confessions by your brother and your husband. To proceed through court would be expensive and time-consuming for taxpayers. Of the twenty-one counts you were booked on, the prosecuting attorney is offering a plea bargain—if you plead no contest to five counts of class A felonies for the burglaries you'll be given a six-month jail sentence with time already served counting toward it. That leaves you with three more months to serve."

"Wow, that's it? Just six months?"

"Yes," my attorney answered.

"I'll take it."

Jim pleaded guilty to several burglaries and the arson, refusing to let them charge me for arson. He took full responsibility. Jim refused to tell me how many burglaries he was convicted of, and more importantly, how long his sentence was. I asked my attorney for more information. He replied, "Sorry, your husband doesn't want you to know that."

◆ ❖ ◆

Jim was soon transferred to Salem to the Oregon State Penitentiary (OSP) for men. Renae and Tia were also soon transferred to the women's prison, also in Salem. Scott never saw another day in jail after his release in early January. With one month to go on my sentence, a male guard came to my cell and said, "Jones-Nelson, roll 'em up."

A decision had been made, without notice to me, that I was scheduled for transfer to another jail. Apparently it was a waste of taxpayer money to have a female guard on staff for only me, and it was more cost effective to sell me to another jail that could add me to their pool of women inmates.

I gathered my letters from Jim, my soap, shampoo, comb, and my tobacco. The guard walked me to the same closet-sized dressing room where Rose had given me my first set of scrubs. He unlocked one of many cubicle-sized lockers and pulled my clothes out of it. They were the same clothes I had worn into the jail, back on December 2 when booked in. He said, "Here, get dressed and leave your scrubs on the washer."

One look at them and I reacted. "These are musty."

"They're your clothes. Get dressed."

He walked out and shut the door behind him. Five minutes later, he returned and knocked on my door. "Jones-Nelson, are you dressed?"

"Yes."

He opened the door.

"These clothes stink and what about shoes?" I asked him.

My Converse sneakers were long gone, in the hands of the detectives.

"Keep your sandals on."

I slipped my feet back into my jail-issued plastic shoes.

"Turn around. I need to handcuff you," he said.

He bagged my personal effects and the extra clothes I hadn't bothered with. We took an elevator up and walked out a back door to his brown-and-white patrol car. The sun was near blinding but felt good with an indescribable warmth. A breeze caught my hair when he opened the back door for me to get in.

The ninety-minute drive made me near dizzy without any letup, but I didn't mind. It had been a long time since I was last in a car, or even let up from the basement to feel or see sunshine. Likened to sea-sickness when on a boat for the first time, I felt a whirling discombobulation from the motion of his moving car.

Inside my new jail home, I didn't have to wait long to get out of my itchy clothes that were desperate for a washing. They were bagged, put in a locker, and exchanged for jail clothes. Again, I was dressed in orange scrubs, but with a big stamp on the right knee that said: "Clatsop County Inmate."

My pod had the same basic layout as before, but smaller in scale. At any given time during my stay, there were anywhere between three and six of us housed together. Commissary issuance, laundry exchange, and smoking privileges were the same. And like before, time was passed in card games, letter writing, reading, and TV watching, so it was much like my old place, but without the chef's great meals. I called Uncle Randy collect to let him know of my transfer and reminded him, "I'll be out soon."

The promise of a six-month jail sentence turned out to be a falsehood. Marion County wanted their chance to prosecute me. Soon I was incarcerated in a larger jail with about forty other women, sharing a dayroom. In Salem at the Marion County Courthouse, I was arraigned on burglary charges yet again. However, at my second court appearance, I was informed charges were dropped. When I left the courtroom, I was escorted back to my cell with the familiar instructions, "Jones-Nelson, roll 'em up."

But then the guard added, "You're being transferred to Multnomah County to face charges."

Same routine, different jail, different court. Later that same day I was in my own jail cell with a door I could shut. Countless jail cells, each with only a bed and toilet, lined the circular dayroom of one of many pods in that metropolitan-sized jail. I was arraigned. I again pleaded not guilty. And again, charges were dropped. And again, I was transferred to another jail.

That time, to Washington County Jail in Hillsboro. I was used to countless institutions, when one jail would have been enough. After all, high school saw me in four different schools. Like burglaries, high schools, thirteen cats, and alcoholic drinks, one county jail was too many, and according to the powers that be, two were not enough.

Washington County wasn't so swift to send me to the next place, whether it be another county, or out on the streets. At my second court appearance, I was informed that enough evidence had been submitted by the prosecution to hold me on fourteen counts of class A burglaries. For better or worse, I had to make that jail my new home for a while.

My pod wasn't gigantic like at Multnomah or Marion Counties, but was large enough to hold twenty-five women, dorm-style with bunk beds. And we had a window, which made me smile, even though bars stood between a pane of glass and the street view. We had round tables, and benches near the window where we ate meals that were brought to us three times a day.

Unlike Columbia, Clatsop, and Marion County Jails, that jail, like the Multnomah County Jail, was nonsmoking. *Yikes.* Unlike Multnomah County Jail, I was going to be at this jail a while. *Double yikes!*

Nonsmoking was also a falsehood. I was hanging out on my bunk, chatting with the gal in the bunk next to me, when the door to our pod opened. A guard let in another woman inmate and pointed her to a bunk, then turned around and left. The woman tossed her rolled bedding on the bunk, ran her hand through her long grey hair, flinging it back. "Girls, it's party time."

She headed toward the bathroom, a long skinny room with toilets, sinks, and open showers, none of which offered privacy. Two ladies followed her, and as they passed the tables on the way, two more gals stepped in line with them. The gal who was in the bunk above me jumped down. She pulled my arm and said, "Come on, Kym, you smoke too, don't you?"

My bunkmate and I ran to the bathroom to join the others. The grey-haired woman had her back to us with a leg propped up on a toilet. "Got it," she said. Then she turned to face us, pulled some toilet paper off its roll and wiped the cigarette. "Who's got a lighter?"

"I do," my bunkmate said. She handed over her lighter. We formed a circle. Our new friend lit her cigarette, and then passed it to the gal next to her. We went around the circle, all of us getting a toke off the keistered cigarette.

At prior jails, I had limited my smoking to eight cigarettes a day to stay within my indigent allotment. Tobacco crumbs smoked out of a pipe made from an empty toothpaste tube always got me a few extra tobacco hits. It was like switching to menthol when I was running out. I didn't know how much longer I could go with only an occasional one-off in that jail.

As Washington County prosecuted me, they looked at my prior convictions as a prior criminal record, even though everything stemmed from only one arrest. The prosecuting attorney claimed I was a repeat offender. The judge said, "Jones-Nelson, you are a career criminal."

My fourteen counts were dropped to nine, and with my no contest plea, I was sentenced to fourteen months to be served in state custody. In total, from the day of my arrest, along with facing charges in different counties, that added up to twenty-two months of incarceration. And no parole.

A year before, in 1989, Oregon had done away with the system of paroling early. Knowing my release date, rather than guessing, was tension relieving. I'd be free in September 1992. Equally comforting was that I'd no longer be Jones-Nelson. Court sanctioned at the state level with the Department of Corrections, my last name was filed as Nelson.

Once my sentencing papers were signed and approved by the judge, I heard my assigned name for the last time. "Roll 'em up, Jones-Nelson. Today's your lucky day. You're going to the Big House."

CHAPTER 10

#8545044

Towers resembling rooks in a chess game were manned with guards, armed and ready to shoot their rifles at any moving target. I counted ten towers as I looked out the van window and ahead to the end of our road. I had seen the place from afar when I was a little girl, living here in Salem. This was the first time I saw the towers.

Oregon Women's Correctional Center, or OWCC for short, and Oregon State Penitentiary, or OSP for short, stretched alongside a polluted creek. Jim was at OSP. Built in the 1800s, these mansions stood with antiquity. It was a fortress all on its own, hidden from Oregon's capital city.

The women's Big House, as OWCC was aptly nicknamed, was once part of OSP, but in 1965 construction began to facilitate housing women inmates. OWCC and its big brother, OSP, have housed infamous criminals—from Diane Downs to the I-5 Serial Killer. In 2010 it was closed to women to accommodate population growth on the men's side, and women inmates were then dispersed to other prisons statewide.

I sat still in my seat. There was no point in fidgeting. That would only irritate my skin where my chains rubbed against me. My hands were handcuffed together, center and front, which led to the chain wrapped several times around my middle. I was in a belly chain, handcuffs, and ankle-cuffs, all connected by that mid-waist chain. I was all locked up and locked to myself.

A woman I didn't know sat next to me. She didn't say anything. An electronic barbed wire fence opened, and our van driver drove through our final entrance. I turned my head to the side. Two women sat on the bench seat behind me. I looked past them and the other women. Out the back window, I watched the fence slide shut.

Our driver parked under an outdoor carport and got out. Another female guard greeted her, then opened our van door to greet us. "Get out, form a line, and follow me inside."

I studied the women who went before me. On my turn, I followed their lead, leaning forward into a slight hunchback position, allowing slack in the chain. I had a chain from my stomach to my ankles. There was no slack to be had where my hands were cuffed, so I couldn't hold the side of the van. The driver stood by but didn't offer any help. I hopped down and out of the van. More women followed me as we formed our line.

Just inside, we each took our turn at the paperwork handled by another female guard, who stood behind a high wooden counter. "Name?" she asked me.

"Kymberley Nelson," I answered.

She said, "Nelson, N-E-L-S-O-N, Kymberley, K-I-M-B—"

"No, it's K-Y. Kymberley is spelled with a K-Y," I corrected her.

"Your paperwork from Washington County has it spelled as K-I, so that's how we have to do it."

"But that's not the right spelling." I was proud of the legally changed spelling of my name, unique to other Kims.

She said, "Even so, here you will be known by your Sid."

When she said "Sid," she meant the acronym SID, short for State Identification Number. It seemed I often had to learn the abbreviation lingo in the corrections system. With Nana, Kris, and Steve, I had conversed in real words, not made-up jargon, so this was an ever-present learning curve for me. Cheeks meant butt and can meant the bathroom. The guard's last words as she leaned over her counter to reach me were, "You are Number 8-5-4-5-0-4-4. Here's your intake papers. Next."

With my chained awkwardness, I took the carbon copies from her and moved to the next line. One at a time, about five minutes each, our line inched along as we each took our turn going into a room where a woman guard waited for us. No one who went in came back out in this hall.

"Next." That was my cue when it was my turn. Inside, a woman guard, short, stocky, and with hair in a bun, shut the door behind us. Walking farther into our small room, I saw another door. The women who had gone before me must have left through this second door. The guard said, "Face me."

I did. She unlocked all my chains and helped me get out of them, then tossed them in a box with other chains. "Get undressed. Time for your strip search."

I did. I was used to these by now. "I'm on my period."

"Not a problem," she said.

Maybe not for her, but for me it was a problem. It was a private matter. That's what Nana had taught me.

After the search, she said, "All clear." Without turning her back to me, she opened a cabinet that was behind her and pulled out some items. A stainless steel sink was above the cabinet, beside the countertop.

"I need to wash my hands," I said.

She didn't reply. Opening the other door to the room, she handed me a single-use bar of white soap, a tiny plain bottle of yellow shampoo, a new tampon, and a white coarse terry bath towel. Pointing toward a row of open shower stalls, she shut the door as I walked out. I didn't think I needed a shower just to wash my hands, but the shower was protocol.

After my shower, I joined the next line, all of us naked save for our towels. As we got deeper into our booking process, we got deeper into the prison. Women inmates in blue jeans passed us in the hall. I saw Renae, who had been my maid of honor, and her girlfriend, Tia. I paid no attention to the fact that I had no clothes on, and instead beamed with a big smile.

Renae saw me too. "Hi Kym."

I answered back, "Hi, it's good to see you."

My words were an understatement, not adequate to describe my relief at finding a slice of friendly familiarity in that great big unknown world. I could only hope all the women were as kind as

Renae. I wasn't a fist fighter. Sure, I knew how to use a gun wisely and wasn't shy about it if I needed to protect myself, but I was in a whole new ballgame, and I knew I had little physical gumption to protect myself should a situation warrant it.

If it weren't for my prior experience in an institutional setting, Job Corps, I could have been swallowed up. I remembered the pale green and peach paint on the hallway walls there. *Is that color a standard for institutions?* I wondered. Putrid peach and seaweed-green hallways welcomed me into its abyss. Likened to Job Corps, as an older facility, the OWCC building was even older. And there I was, no longer in a tiny jail cell, but at the Big House.

"Hey Kym," Renae said. "When you're done, come see us."

"Okay, yeah. Where do I find you?"

Renae answered, "We'll be out in the yard."

I didn't have time to respond or ask which way to the yard before a woman guard sternly encouraged me to move on. "Move it, ladies."

Our fitting for clothes was handled more casually. I tried on several different sizes. In jail there were only three sizes, and jeans fit differently than scrubs. Issued clothing consisted of two pairs of blue jeans, two blue T-shirts with the prison logo, one button-down light blue dress shirt, a flannel-lined denim coat, five pairs of white socks, five pairs of used sheer panties, two used white bras, one pair of blue shorts, and a cotton nightgown. Unlike in jail, it was my responsibility to keep them washed in the community laundry room.

I was also handed two yellowed sheets, a pillowcase and plastic pillow, and two blankets. I was told blankets could be exchanged once every six months. Lastly, my clear bag of personal effects, less the tobacco left over from jail, was returned to me, along with a padlock to use on my chest of drawers. Any new hygiene items or tobacco had to wait until the next commissary date, a week away, and were at my own expense.

A woman guard escorted us down a long hallway, and around the corner to another hallway. We passed private rooms, which weren't private at double occupancy or more, but private in comparison to where we were to be housed—a big square room, larger than a high school gymnasium. As we stood in the doorway, our guard met another woman guard, and one by one, we were allowed in. At my turn, the first guard said to the second guard, "This is Number 8545044."

The second guard handed me a small piece of paper with my bed number typed on it, and said, "Number 8545044, you're on that side."

She pointed me to the right half of the dorm. My limited vision kept me from doing a full scan of the room layout, but I followed the guard's cues to find my bed.

Our dorm was split into two partitions, with only a half wall to divide the two sides. I walked, head up, down the narrow aisle, and found my bed toward the end. I was top bunk to someone I can't even picture or remember today.

Next to our bunk bed, same as all the others, was a three-foot-tall nightstand. Its bottom half was padlocked and numbered. The top half had my bed number on its front and was mine to use for my clothing and any personal effects acquired during my stay. My padlock would keep my valuables secured, and any contraband belonging to others out.

I held no animosity, nor did I receive any disgruntled comments or looks as I settled into my assigned bunk space. I sat cross-legged on my bed, careful not to dangle my legs over into my bunkmate's space. I didn't know her yet, and as such, didn't want to stir up trouble. I squinted and looked around. At the front end of our aisle, off to the side, was the shower area, likely a double shower, and the only showers for one hundred women. Not much farther was the open bathroom area, with steel toilets and single sinks that lined a mirrored wall.

In the front space on the other side of the partition sat one guard, the same guard as before, front and center behind a tall desk. In the far pocket corner, a TV was fastened to a wall. A few round tables with chairs were in between the TV and beds on that side of the room. Full of women, loud chatter echoed incoherently against competing conversations.

I soon found out from my bunkmate that to go to the yard—or anywhere—meant to go on "line movement." About once every seventy minutes, a bell rang to indicate line movement. That was the time to walk the halls, as long as we moved along and didn't loiter. Once I scoped out the dorm, which didn't take me long at all, I used the next line movement.

♦ ❖ ♦

When I met with Renae and Tia in the yard, I felt at ease to be with two friends, one of whom had been my maid of honor. I looked to them for answers, same as I had looked to Jim nine months earlier, when first in jail. They knew how everything worked in that place, while I had yet to get acclimated among several hundred women.

Tia shared her cigarette with me, and like the school kid I once was when I snuck out back of the apartment in Bothel to smoke, I again had to be sneaky. Sharing items was considered contraband, yet with the week's wait for my first commissary, there was no way I was going to last without smoking.

I made a deal with Tia. She kept me stocked in cigarettes through my first week, and in exchange, my mother-in-law deposited money on her books from the nest egg she held for us. I needed money anyway. Cigarettes were no longer an indigent commodity as they were in jail. Cash was not allowed, but anyone on the outside could send in money for deposit into an inmate's account, to be used as needed at the weekly commissary disbursement.

I adapted well in my dorm, but whenever I could get out of that crowd, I did. I made myself aware of events or activities to attend, and often took advantage of line movement for church services, the reading room, rec hall, the activity room for bingo, and out to the yard. However, in the yard, I was reminded of my loss of freedom all over again. As much as I wanted to walk out to the street, that was an impossibility.

If anything took practice in my dorm, it was tuning out constant noise. The only stillness and peace came at night, shortly after lights out at eleven until shortly before lights came back on at seven in the morning, in time for breakfast at eight. During those hours of the night, I was too tired to do anything but sleep. Funny, I'd once been a night owl only to have calmed down into a normative schedule.

Although we had a guard, I knew to trust no one, padlocking my half dresser before I nodded out for the night. As it was in jail, lights out didn't mean complete darkness. The bathroom with no door kept its bright lights on always, and the guard had a small low-wattage lamp at her desk. Ceiling lights down both aisles of the two partitions switched to a dark amber night light for sleeping hours.

With only one TV for one hundred women, it worked in my favor that I had no dependency on, nor any real interest in TV. I couldn't remember when I had last watched TV prior to my arrest. Between burglaries and the hospital filing job, TV hadn't fallen into that overloaded schedule. I wasn't hooked on any TV series or soap, and instead found comfort with a book high up on my bunk. I liked being on the top bunk. That gave me a view of most everything, and with that came a sense of security. I wasn't afraid for my safety, but vigilant in my independence.

Comradeship among the women was prevalent, and in contrast to horror stories I believed prior to my arrival. Respect and kindness for one another were actually normal despite the few brawls that broke out between more troublesome inmates. Still, with an ingrained survival mechanism, I never became complacent and was ever mindful of where I was.

When I showered, I kept my change of clothing draped inside my shower stall, and my locker key on me. I never left my bed area with my items out in the open and unlocked. Had I not locked my stuff up first, a minute or two to use the bathroom would have been letting my guard down for a minute or two too long. As a former career burglar, I knew timing was everything.

Any racial disparity rarely broke out into girl fights. In my back corner, I was among a diverse racial mix. There was a black woman named Buffy, who invited me to a friendly, one-on-one domino competition in the yard. Like TV, it had been years since I got wrapped up in games. Before our burglaries became nonstop, we had sometimes played the board game Risk with Dan. And we had played darts at a bar when Jim and Dan wanted a beer.

Nana's past influence, rich with card games and puzzles, brought out an inner instinct that motivated me to learn dominos. My intuitive plays brought favor from my black domino-playing friend, and soon we were partners in full-fledged tournaments. I was the only white woman to play in those, for no other white woman could master the game as well as the black women knew it.

And then there were the letters. Jim and I wrote each other often, several times weekly. In our letters, we doted on each other with love and colored pictures on our envelopes. My truth at the time, which I poured out in my written words, was that I loved him and couldn't imagine my future without him. His letters to me always had a biblical scripture, but I was aloof in reciprocating with religion. Rather, I pressured him to reveal his sentence length, but he never gave in.

I filed for visitation privileges with Jim and was informed a decision and visiting schedule would take several weeks to be determined. In the meantime, I had his letters, however dismayed I was at not knowing his release date.

My freedom was gone, and I was powerless. When involved in the burglary spree, its surge of excitement overcame any awkward feelings I had about life. But the burglaries were over, and I felt worse than ever in my own skin. I had to have something to fill my itch.

Over a game of dominoes, a gal across the table said, "We're going to get drunk tonight. Join us, Kym, if you want."

After dinner hour, some women went on line movement to the game room, or the library, or other places. I stayed behind and joined my domino friends. Five of us huddled, sitting together. Buffy, whose bunk we were on, got on her belly and hung her head over her bunk. She reached underneath to the floor and pulled out a clear plastic Hi-C jug.

A thick murky brownish beverage with floating fruit shavings filled the jug where orange Hi-C had first filled it. The guard sat at her desk with magazine in hand, out of view from our lower bunk. We went unnoticed, polishing off the sixty-four ounces of tongue biting, foul-smelling pruno.

I knew I had to behave, but I was far from a novice at drinking alcohol. I had a good rap sheet from my days of drinking at Steve's house, enough to strongly believe I could handle my liquor. We played Uno and reminisced about the crimes that got us there.

One of the other gals asked, "Why are you doing so much time for burglary, Kym?"

With a cackle, Buffy answered for me, "She shot the sheriff but didn't shoot the deputy."

Her joke became a mainstay, even after our night of drunken fun. It felt good to let go and not give a shit about everything Jim hid from me. For once, I didn't care about that, nor anything else serious. I felt independent and alive, and not dependent on my maid of honor or her girlfriend or anyone else. Smart from my survival in jail and then prison, I felt like a real trooper, as Nana had been. I knew I wasn't special, but felt special anyway. And I knew I wanted more of that sweet putrid stuff they called pruno.

At commissary, I bought a jug of Hi-C and finished it off while I gathered other needed ingredients. We were patted down for contraband on our way into and out of the dining hall, and it was against the rules to take food. One item from one meal at a time, I acquired dinner rolls for yeast, plums and oranges for fruit, and sugar packets. I also managed to take several servings of fruit cocktail in heavy syrup by emptying my bowl into a small, well-washed-out shampoo bottle that I damn near keistered to pass the pat down. Fruit cocktail was for sugar and a taste boost.

Shown how to make it, we used an old thinning sock to cover the neck of the jug and a rubber band to tighten it. Every couple of days

I squeezed the sock, which encouraged fermentation. Six days later, the sock had blown up like a full-sized balloon, which meant the concoction had fully fermented. I wanted to invite Renae and Tia to our party, but inmates who didn't live in the dorm weren't allowed.

Days later, a guard said, "Number 8545044, roll 'em up. You're being transferred."

I rolled up my bedding, gathered my belongings, handed my latest brew in progress to my party friends, and bid my farewells. I was sent to the Women's Release Unit, or WRU for short. It was minimum security, unlike OWCC. And small, adjacent to the State Hospital, which housed incorrigible mental patients, many of whom were convicted of serious crimes but found mentally insane. The hospital was a large institution, also in Salem, and they leased an unused wing to the Department of Corrections.

There, my incarceration began with an assigned bed in a dorm, which was closer in size to the Washington County Jail dorm. Before long, I was out of the dorm and housed in one of sixteen rooms that lined one side of the only hallway, each with two inmates. Our dining area, shower room, and bathroom lined the other side. With the dorm at the rear end of the hallway, the common area was up front, with an open TV room on one side, and a dayroom on the other. A guard shack was strategically placed, front and near center.

In our dayroom, we played cards and wrote letters. But the room did double duty as the visitor room, closed to our free use during visitation hours, twice weekly. We had both male and female guards, but male guards stayed inside the office. Women guards roamed our small common areas, but usually didn't bother to go any deeper into our place, with the exception of the early morning hours. Alarm clocks were contraband, and unlike at the Big House, an overhead light didn't light up at seven sharp. Instead, we requested wake up times, then depended on guards to wake us up.

My cellmate was Anne. She was an older woman with a deformed face. I never asked her what happened to her, and she never told me. Her kids had run a drug business out of her house, which got her convicted alongside them. Next door to us was the ostracized inmate, convicted of rape.

Of everyone I befriended, Jacquie was my best friend at WRU, my Spades partner, and who sat beside me as we wrote letters. She had applied the same smarts, seriousness, and survivalist attitude to her career as a shoplifter that I had shown to my burglaries. She had kept her thefts under a certain dollar amount to avoid a felony, but then had racked up too many misdemeanor charges, putting her over the threshold, which sent her to prison.

Two others, Leslie and Shannon, were also in my clique. Leslie taught me to crochet. Quiet, with a peaceful aura, she was in her last year of a seven-year sentence for kidnapping seven dead bodies. She explained, "It was really six, not seven. My husband, Larry—he shot them all. In our house. I was just trying to get rid of the evidence. They were dead anyway, or I thought they were all dead when I loaded them in my car. I had to get them out of our house, so I took them somewhere they might not be found for a while. Turns out, one person—he was a young guy—wasn't dead. He lived and here I am now. Larry died last year at OSP."

Leslie's bosom friend, Shannon, was in her last months for arson. Without telling my secrets, I ardently listened to her confessional account.

I earned three dollars daily for a seven-hour shift in the kitchen at the State Hospital, while most inmates worked in another wing. The kitchen I worked in was the same one that brought meals to our place, WRU, three times daily. Holidays were an exception. State employees ran on a skeleton crew on Thanksgiving, Christmas, and Fourth of July, so we got only brunch and dinner. Everything was a privilege and not a right, including the number of daily meals we received.

Twice a week, Mondays and Thursdays, things were different. Those were my two days off work to visit Jim. I'd dress in my nicer pair of the two issued pairs of blue jeans, and while no makeup was my norm inside, visiting days were an exception. I used a bold cherry-red color of lipstick, more so to feel good about myself than to please Jim. Perfumes, colognes, and scented cosmetics were not among commissary items, but a dab of strawberry-scented shampoo on my neckline worked wonders.

Midmorning on Mondays and Thursdays was a waiting game for me. I never knew when in this three-hour stretch I'd be called to the outtake room. Following my outgoing strip search, with an incoming strip search expected on my return, I was handcuffed to be made ready for transport to visit Jim. With each strip search, I was once again excelling at excess. At no less than four times weekly for over a year, without adding in the times before and after and in between, I may have broken the world record for most strip searches.

At OSP's open visiting room, I met Jim with a great big hug and kiss. His knobby pale white hands gripped me with safety, assurance, and love, as we sat across from each other. His touch was real and tangible, not something to only dream of, as it was back at Columbia County Jail with its glass partition. We talked idly. We had no more court appearances looming over us, or none that I was made aware of. The only serious mention came when I pleaded with him to tell me the length of his sentence, but as always, he brushed me off. "You don't need to know. I'm just glad you're doing well. Has Randy visited you lately?"

Uncle Randy was the only person who visited me. Or sent me cards. Or acknowledged me. Two birthdays and two Christmases passed without word from family, with the exception of Uncle Randy. He even managed to get past his initial shock and hatred toward Jim and visited him often. He was Jim's only visitor. I was an outcast to the family, but certainly not the first to be shunned.

As a child, hushed tones ensued when I asked about Great Uncle Dick. As Nana's bad son, he had been banished from the family for something unthinkable, but what that something was, I never knew. I did know that if you royally messed up, then you were kicked out of the family. Nana had also expressed to me in confidence that she grew up among three mean brothers, and once married, she cut off those ties. And then there was my father, who was left behind in Arkansas.

Nana was long gone, but her role as family matriarch lived on. My mother and extended relatives followed her lead when it came to decisions about who to reject and why. My fall from favorite to outcast in the familial tribe had been forewarned by Nana and expected by everyone else. Only Randy kept his bond with me, but I think that was out of habit. Our bond centered around his place as Nana's first grandchild, and mine as her first great-grandchild.

My visits to Jim and from Uncle Randy remained constant until early August 1992, when I was again told, "Number 8545044, roll 'em up. You're being transferred."

In that same week, Jim was also transferred. He went to a prison in eastern Oregon. Our distance was a barrier to our privileged visits. I was patient. I had less than two months until my release.

CRCI, Columbia River Correctional Institute, was a modern prison near Portland. WRU and CRCI were both pilot programs designed to alleviate the problem of overcrowding—the result of an obsolete parole board system. But, unlike WRU, and unlike any other prison in the state, CRCI was non-smoking inside, with smoking limited to outside yard time. *Yikes.*

And it was coed. *Double yikes.*

Like WRU, both male and female guards patrolled the place. Unlike WRU, gender didn't define roles for guards. They saw my feet where the stall doors fell short in the bathroom and shower area. That invasion of privacy made me uncomfortable.

I had good reason to feel threatened by that change in atmosphere and surroundings, but couldn't foresee the life-altering change it would evolve into. It was there, at CRCI, that a chain of events was conceived that led me to my future. It began with Richard.

Not Rick—he liked to be called Richard. Standing at six feet tall, buff, and filled out by muscle weight, he had a robust stature at more than 200 pounds. He was naturally dark tan as part Native American. Resistant to any authority, his appearance reflected this defiance. He had long curly hair and tattoos, with the most prevalent tattoo on his right hand. It took all four of his finger knuckles to spell out a word, one letter at a time: f-u-c-k.

I met him in the yard during one of my countless line movements to go outside to smoke. I occasionally snuck a cigarette when inside the steam of a hot running shower, but I couldn't stay in the shower all day. And unlike the times I had smoked a keistered cigarette in the Washington County Jail, guards at CRCI were literally on guard, with no qualms about stopping a naked woman in a shower.

Gone were scenic fir trees that lined a prison yard. Instead, it was dry lawn with a circular rubber paved track to walk, and a big open weightlifting area where men sweated profusely. To me, it was hideous. I had nothing to do, and nothing good to see when in the yard, but it was the only place to freely smoke. Visits with Jim were gone. Visits from Randy were behind me. Crocheting with Leslie and letter writing with Jackie were no more. One day as I walked the track, Richard fell in line with me. "Hi, I'm Richard. Sure is ugly out here. And hot."

Bored, I said "hi" back, and let him walk with me. Over several yard visits, we discovered we had things in common. He too was in for a property crime, and had an upcoming release date. It wasn't so much that I liked him, but that he filled the void.

We talked about who we were as people on the outside. He expressed his tendency to wander and his love for travel. With no idea where I belonged, from Arkansas to Oregon to a family who rejected me, I related to his wanderlust.

He also strongly warned me that if we were to see each other on the outside, to never, ever let him drink whiskey. He said it turned him into a person he didn't like to be, paranoid and violent. I was oblivious that anything could be worse than the alcoholic problems I had exhibited back when Nana died.

Afraid I'd fall out of love with Jim, my friendship time with Richard was an intrusive thought in my head. I was afraid that if I strayed from my commitment to Jim, I'd hurt him. Having never been married before me and faithful to biblical virtues, he took marriage seriously. Frustration over not knowing Jim's release date superseded my warning signs. I didn't ignore these signs, but I didn't run from endangerment. I knew better, and yet, succumbed to my wayward ways. As our time for release neared, Richard and I made plans to see each other on the outside.

CHAPTER 11

SAMANTHA ANN MILLS

Released in September 1992, I had nowhere to go but to a women's shelter and halfway house in Salem. I registered with the parole office as required, and found work making $4.25 an hour at a Sizzler's restaurant in salad bar prep. My kitchen job at the mental hospital when at WRU had proven worthy of credit on that job application. I cleaned out the Alaskan bank account that Jim and I had in his mom's name and bought a cheap secondhand car.

My letters to Jim waned, replaced by letters to Richard. I hated that Jim refused to answer my questions. If only I knew his release date, then I could have a date to look forward to. Acting on what was real and right in front of me, I let go of my connection to Jim.

After an afternoon of apartment shopping, I returned to my place at the women's home. I'd need another paycheck before I could move out. One of the women told me, "You have a visitor. He's out back."

I wasn't expecting anyone. The other women at the house were the only people I ever spent time with. It housed ten women with a full suite of bedrooms and a spacious living area. Some women were down on their luck and would have been homeless had it not been for that home. Some had family who were not safe to live with. And me, fresh out of prison, with family in Salem who didn't want me.

I made my way past the long wooden dining table in the open galley to the sliding patio door. Like a plantation house out of a southern charm magazine, our home was picturesque among smaller houses in a tree-lined neighborhood. Bushes with pink flowers released a sweet aroma in my walk along the pebbled drive. We had a garden sitting area at the end of the path. There, I saw someone sitting on one of the garden benches.

He looked up at me, then stood up and walked toward me. I could tell by his attire, a suit with a clerical collar, that he was somehow involved with religion. "Mrs. Nelson, I'm Father Smith with the Oregon State Penitentiary. Can we talk?"

We sat down on the bench and turned our heads to each other. "Mrs. Nelson, Arthur hasn't had a letter from you in a long time."

Like other official people, he called Jim by his legal first name, but I was used to that. I turned my head. Roses were still blooming this time of year. I hadn't noticed that before.

Father Smith asked, "Mrs. Nelson?"

I turned my attention back to him.

He asked, "What are your plans?"

I pursed my lips. If only Jim were in front of me wanting answers, instead of a third party. I'd ask Jim, "When? When will you be released? When will we get to be together?" As it was, Jim kept me in the dark regarding his charges and sentencing. *When?*

Jim was far away and untouchable. I parted my lips, opened my mouth, and said, "I have to move on."

One month after my release, I drove to CRCI to meet Richard when they opened the prison gate to let him out. I had what few belongings I owned on the back seat of my car. That morning had been my last morning waking up in the women's home.

I stepped out of my car and opened my arms to Richard. He hugged back and said, "Hi babe. Gawd, it feels good to see you."

With a smile, I said, "Get in, let's go."

He flung his discharge papers behind the seat but didn't notice my few sacks. "They say I have to show up at my mom's place today. Fuck that shit. You got any ideas?"

I answered, "Let's find a place to be alone together, but first we need to get out of Portland."

Richard hung his head out the open passenger window. The autumn breeze blew his dark wavy hair into tangles. "Oh, it feels so good to be out."

I said, "I know. Two years inside was too long for me."

Richard asked, "So, where do you want to go?"

"It's a surprise."

He went with the flow and surmised we weren't on our way to the women's home, where he last knew I lived. We couldn't be alone there. He was as happy as a chirping bird, too ecstatic to care where I drove.

Nearly an hour later, we pulled into downtown Salem and I parked in front of an older brick apartment building. Without bothering to explain myself, I got out of my car, opened my back door, and picked up my sacks. He got out and followed my lead.

"Here, carry this one," I said.

As we walked, he peeked into the sack like a curious cat. "It's champagne?"

I opened the lobby door. "Yes, it's champagne, to celebrate."

I stepped across the hall to the first apartment, put my key in and opened the door. "Welcome home."

Richard had his parole transferred from Eugene to Salem, and as required, secured a job. Neither his parole officer nor I had room to complain over his career choice. His work as the day manager at an adult bookstore paid his parole supervision fee and half the rent.

The sixteen hours a week he worked earned little less in pay than the thirty hours I put in at minimum wage. I always held a job. After Sizzler's, I worked at a neighborhood thrift store, Value Village, in walking distance from home. My used car was not worth any more than the few hundred dollars I'd paid for it. As much as we needed a new car, we couldn't afford one.

My parole office appointments were required only once a month, and then in January the requirement dropped to unsupervised parole. Richard, though, had a twice monthly requirement to his parole officer. Random urinalysis was sporadic yet routine for his parole visits. Even though alcohol was against his parole rules, those UAs only tested for drugs.

The no-alcohol rule wasn't part of my parole. Unlike Richard, who had been drunk during his robbery, I had been sober during my crimes. Without fear for a drug check to test for alcohol, we drank freely and often. That is, until I saw what drinking did for him, which was violently erratic and not a pleasant diversion, as drinking was for me.

Each day after work, I liked to come home to a tall beer. I walked into our apartment one day to see Richard had started drinking without me. Depending on my shifts, sometimes Richard got home first. He cackled, "Hi-ya babe."

It took only a couple bounces of his wobbly steps for him to reach me from the other side of our tiny apartment. Swinging his arm out, pointing to our kitchen counter, he said, "Let me get you a drink."

Richard's glass of beer splashed. "Oh-oops, there's more where that came from." He pulled what was left of a forty-ounce Olde English Ale out of the fridge. The same brand that Steve, from my younger days, always drank. Richard pushed the bottle at me, then grabbed an open pint of whiskey off the counter. "This is mi-i-i-ne."

"I want a shot of that," I said.

"Oh-oh-if you be good. Here, fine, take a drink." He handed it to me.

I took a swig out of the bottle then handed it back. Drinking my glass of beer, I watched him dance nonsensically with the whiskey in one hand and his beer in the other. There was nothing else to watch but him. He set his glass of beer on our table. It was a card table, which doubled as our eating area. Our thirteen-inch TV and boom box radio also sat on it. Richard turned the dial up on the radio. Hard rock music overpowered our ability to talk.

He danced by himself for a minute until he plopped down onto our carpet, his back to me. Raising his voice above the loud music, he said, "Le-e-eave me alone. Go on, get goin'."

"Babe," I yelled, "what's going on here? We can't have the music up this loud. Neighbors will complain."

He turned the volume back down, and then said, "Oh-yurr ru-ining everything. Go on, get out." Turning the volume back up, he waved his arm behind him, directing me to go away.

I took a few more gulps of my beer, unsure of what to do. Richard sat cross-legged on the carpet. He put the lid back on his whiskey bottle and slammed it down on the floor next to him. He then went into a rocking motion. He stopped rocking only long enough to turn the music down a little, although not much. Back to his rocking motion, he chanted a wail of unintelligible words and put his arms up, even though there was nothing above his head to reach for.

In one tilt of my head, I downed the last of the beer in my glass, turned around and walked out. This wasn't fun. That was the first of many powwow dances for him, which came when he drank anything stronger than beer. I walked out each time with nowhere important to go. My go-to place became the neighborhood park, dawdling, waiting for enough time to pass that he would pass out from drunkenness.

After several of his powwow episodes, we agreed over morning coffee that alcohol was not a good choice. He then made a connection with a customer from the porn store where he worked. That customer turned him onto methamphetamine, or crank as we called it.

Richard managed to keep high on crank, plus go to work at the porn store, plus make his regular parole visits. My life had become a purposeless accumulation of events, spun with a cyclic lack of solutions or meaning in my life. I was embarrassed by the life we lived, if only to myself. I had no friends. Richard was my life.

My mother and half-brother, Scott, as well as some distant relatives, also lived in Salem. I tried to stay in contact, but any phone call or drop-in visit was awkward. I hadn't forgotten or overlooked that there had been absolutely no contact from any kin, with the exception of Uncle Randy, during my two years incarcerated. No birthday cards, no Christmas cards, nothing.

Scott could get along with our mother no matter what he had done wrong. However, the estranged relationship I had with her never evolved and seemed to have no chance at this time.

Uncle Randy lived in McMinnville, less than an hour's drive

from Salem. In one drop-in visit to my mother's place, where Scott was also living, Uncle Randy was already there. Randy was helping her fix a kitchen appliance. When done, he said, "That's the best I can get it, Kathi."

She stayed in the kitchen and Randy walked out to the living room where I was standing. Scott was gone. Randy told me, "Listen, your mom and I were talking. These visits aren't doing anyone any good. It upsets her. That was a real bad thing, what you did."

He was talking about what Scott and I had done with Jim, the burglaries that had sent me to prison. I looked away from him and picked up a framed picture on the mantel. It was a picture of Scott and our mother.

"Listen," he said. I put the picture back and looked at my uncle. We had once been the two special people in our family. He had been Nana's firstborn grandchild. I had been her firstborn great-grandchild. From the tone in his voice, I didn't feel special anymore. It had been a long time since I felt special.

Randy stood still in front of me. Much taller than me, he had to look down at me. I looked up into his eyes. He said, "We can't have you around. The family doesn't want you and your problems. You have to go your own way now."

He walked to her front door, opened it, and held it open for me. I didn't say anything. I walked out and returned home to Richard.

They excused Scott's criminal lifestyle as if he'd simply made a mistake. However, my wrongdoings were inexcusable. I failed to live up to my imposed expectations. Although Nana was gone, her value system still ran the family. Scott wasn't special, and as such, it didn't matter that he was an ex-con.

I was abandoned by my family and engulfed by a three-year parole commitment, irritated at monthly fees for my required parole. I didn't like Salem, which had grown up from a sleepy bedroom community to an ugly conglomeration of commercialization. My distaste was especially haunted by memories of Nana. I failed to live up to her expectations. If only I could have blinked my eyes and awoken to a whole new existence, one without baggage, to live in a different time, space, and place.

That was my mind frame when Richard returned from one of his many parole visits. He raced across our nine-foot room, turning the corner toward our bathroom. He flung his arms and opened our shared closet just outside the bathroom.

Richard explained, "He UA-ed me. Tomorrow he gets the results, and if it's dirty I go back to the joint. You know it's dirty. I've had too much crank in me for too long. It's going to show up dirty."

"Shit," I said. I hadn't peed for him that time. I was also dirty, and not from pot.

Richard grabbed his backpack out of our closet. It was the same backpack that went with him when he traveled. Before me, he had hitchhiked often from his mom's place in Eugene to his dad's place in Sacramento, California. He pulled out a stack of shirts and said, "I'm leaving. I'm packing my bags and hitchhiking out."

I didn't look away but watched and listened. He turned to me, and with a brief stare, said, "You can come with me if you want."

I stared back with nothing to say.

Richard added, "You can stay, but I don't see how you can get caught up on rent by yourself. Look, baby, there's a better world out there for you and me."

I didn't need him to ask—or to explain anything to me. I already knew everything he said. We kept our shared gaze as I replied, "Hell yeah. Fuck this shit we're living in." I walked toward the closet where he stood and said, "I'm ready. Let's go."

He turned to stuff more clothes in his pack, but then looked back at me. "Get packing."

"Where are we going?" I asked.

"Did I ask you where we were going when you picked me up at the joint?"

"No, I guess not."

He stepped to the side of the closet to make room for me. I pulled out some of my crap. "Should we pick a place?" I asked.

He answered, "I don't know. No. No plans. Just go. We have to go at least five states away for any police check to not pull up my parole violation—or yours. You'll be on the run too."

I was indecisive about what to take and what to leave behind. My indecision must have shown. As if to pacify me, he said, "I'll get out my map. We'll look."

He laid out our map on the floor. We looked at it but were stupefied at the forty-some states to choose from. I looked up from the map and looked at him. He looked back at me and said, "Hang on."

Richard pulled an empty V8 bottle out of our overflowing trash can. Sometimes juice was the only nutrition we got on top of beer and crank. He crouched over, put the plastic bottle on the map, and spun it. It twirled erratically on the four corners of Utah, Colorado, New Mexico, and Arizona. The bottle's open mouth rested on Wyoming.

Like magnets to the West Coast, leaving Oregon was new to both of us. Sure, I was born in Arkansas—but was brought west when still a baby. My venture to Colorado Springs a few years before didn't count. That was short-lived. Richard was experienced at hitchhiking I-5 between Eugene and Sacramento. But to leave the West Coast was something new. I yearned for a new adventure in my life, different from the life that hadn't worked out.

With his experience to guide us, we slowed down our frenzy to pack right. We had until morning before his parole officer would find reason to come knocking. First, we made a quick trip to a pawn shop and bought a backpack for me. It wasn't expensive, or anything all that good. Plastic and cheap was all we could afford.

Once back home, he pulled our Murphy bed down and laid our packs on it. His was a full-sized backpack with a frame to support his back. It had leaned against the closet's back wall for six months, ready to grab at a moment's notice. Any moment—like the moment we were in. He also brought out his bedroll, which was a sleeping bag bungee-corded into a tight roll.

With both packs in front of us, he showed me the art of packing. The secret is in rolling the clothes. That takes up less room and helps prevent wrinkling. To this day, I roll, not fold. Our packs got loaded with our must-have clothes and a few tiny personal trinkets like his pictures of his family. We filled both packs.

Flashlights, candles, matches, a deck of playing cards went in. A can opener, some food staples like peanut butter, some basic tools and bungee cords, a small first aid kit, a bar of soap, and a small sewing kit went in. All got packed in tight.

A lot goes into building a basic survival kit for highway living. My backpack was full, but Richard seemed loaded down to the gills. He didn't seem to mind. Again, he was experienced at highway travel by hitchhiking, and being a heavyset man, he could handle the weight.

The crank run was over, but rolling out of the last high cold turkey wasn't feasible, so Richard scored a small baggie of pot. After he smoked a little pot, he packed it away. With finality, he tied the bedroll, a duffel-bagged two-man tent, and a water jug to his backpack.

At dawn, we took one last look at what we were leaving behind. Not much of anything important. We didn't need the dishes, so those stayed put, in the sink, dirty. We couldn't hang a poster on our tent wall, so it stayed, pinned on the wall behind the Murphy bed, which we left down. The woman in the poster smiled uncannily. She was larger-than-life—an enormous 600-pound naked woman with roly-poly wrinkles, clad in a ball and chains, courtesy of Richard's job he was leaving behind.

We shut the door and started our walk with our packs on our backs. It was a few blocks to the downtown Greyhound bus station and a crisp morning that early April day in 1993. Convinced I was doing the right thing, I stayed beside him, content to follow his lead. My family had made it clear I was unwanted, and I wanted nothing more to do with Salem.

Where do I belong?

I was already a quarter-century old. Nana had always marked the passing of her life in quarter centuries. I heard her sharp voice in my memory-saturated fog, *When I was three-quarters of a century old, I... At a half-century old, I was... But, when I was a young woman at a quarter-century old, I was already aware that it was all up to me to make my life as I wanted it, and you will too.*

Will I?

I had to change my life. One month later I'd turn twenty-six years old. I had nearly run out of time to be where Nana had expected me to be at a quarter-century old.

The ticket attendant took Richard's cash for our tickets to Cheyenne, Wyoming, and didn't ask any information from us in return. We didn't show ID, reveal our names, or tell why we were going where. Unlike license plates or airlines, we left no paper trail for anyone to follow. It was our perfect clandestine departure, provided by Greyhound.

Wyoming was shy of the five states away we needed. It was,

though, a head start with three directions farther to choose from once we got there. It was not a direct eastward route. First the bus had to go north an hour, then a layover for two hours in Portland, and from there, eastward through the Baker Mountains by interstate, out of Oregon.

When we got to our Portland layover, we saw a bar and grill. Hungry, Richard promised me he'd be fine on one beer. His powwow chants came only with whiskey. Before we got to the restaurant, we stepped into an alleyway where he smoked two tokes off his pot pipe. He held his breath for a long minute, then as he released the skunky sweetness through his mouth, he coughed, and said to me, "Not to be rude, you want a hit?"

"Sure."

I overlooked that I didn't like pot. I had to leave the abyss of a black hole behind me. I had to shut my mind off from Salem. I had a new window to crawl through, figuratively. A hit of pot could only help, not hurt, I reasoned. I only took one hit, and as I did, he eyed me with surprise.

In the bar, we each had a beer and sandwich, but my pot high kept me from enjoying it. We put our wallets on our table and did a cash count. We had no income to take with us. What we had was all we had. I gulped my beer.

Returning to the Greyhound station, I felt paranoia from the pot hit me. Everywhere I turned my head, I saw derelicts and hoodlums. They seemed to stare at us, but why, I didn't know. I clasped Richard's hand and followed his lead to our bus seats.

I drifted in and out of sleep. After a good stretch of real rest, my pot stupor was over. A stretch of highway with cold, icy mountains in the distance could be seen from my window view. I tugged at my zip-up sweatshirt and shifted in my seat to see better out the window. Something wasn't right. My wallet wasn't in my back pocket.

Where is my wallet?

Richard noticed me squirm, ready to freak out. "What's wrong?" he asked.

"My wallet. Do you have my wallet?"

"No."

"It's not in my pocket," I said. I double-checked and then triple-checked the pockets of my jeans. Twisting and turning in the seat, I checked all my pockets, then stumbled over Richard to pull my pack down from above us. I opened its side pockets and fingered through the stuff. "I can't find it. I don't know where my wallet is. I can't find my wallet."

"Oh no. Don't tell me you left it at the bar," he said.

"Shit, yeah. 'Betcha I did."

"Well, there goes twenty dollars. Is that what you had in it? Twenty dollars?"

I answered, "Yeah, and my ID. My driver's license and my Social Security card. I have no ID now. Shit, now what?"

Richard tugged at my jeans and sweatshirt. He damn near felt me up and patted me down, same as prison guards had. "Think. Are you sure you don't have it?" he asked.

"I'm sure," I said.

"Good thing I have most of our money—"

"Which isn't much, huh?" I interrupted.

He answered, "No, it's not. But we'll be okay. You need some sort of ID to show who you are, though."

"Since I can no longer prove who I am, and I'm wanted now anyway, I guess it's time for me to be somebody else."

"Okay, who do you wanna be?" Richard asked.

We had plenty of idle time to name me. I wanted my middle name to be Ann. When I was a little girl, Nana's housekeeper was Ann. And I had a fondness for Raggedy Ann dolls. I liked the last name Mills, after Donna Mills, the actress. She was my idol. I loved how the look in Donna's eyes dramatized any TV shows or movies she played in.

We were indecisive about a first name. "Jennifer?" I asked.

"No. What about Summer or Kenzie?"

"Babe, it has to be a normal name. We can't have people asking me how I got my name. Erin and Elizabeth are normal run-of-the-mill names."

"Quinn?" Richard asked.

"A name like Amanda or Samantha or Lisa," I said.

Richard said, "That's why when I named my daughter I gave her two middle names. With four names and not just three, she can choose what name to go by if she ever has to."

I set his latest input aside. "And I may as well change my age too. I look young for my age anyway, and for someone to not have ID, they must be really young. Every woman's dream is to be younger. This way I can be. I'll be twenty again—that'll put me six years younger. What do ya think? Can I pass for twenty?"

"Yeah, definitely," he answered.

We turned our conversation to something different. I eventually drifted off, in and out of sleep. Traffic kept passing our bus. I paid more attention to the scenery around me than the traffic. I wondered if I'd miss the northwest. It was full of tall snowy peaks and evergreen trees and lush green grass.

Late afternoon, a day later, the Greyhound bus pulled into Cheyenne. I was stone-cold sober and had fully accepted my lot. I helped Richard into his backpack and adjusted the straps on mine. We walked off into the distance. The interstate was close. Richard's foremost thought, which he voiced, was for us to camp for the night and get an early start the next day.

We walked on. Then a city patrol car stopped. Oh, how cops could give me the heebie-jeebies. Only one officer was in the car. He got out and approached us. "Hi, can I talk to you two a minute?"

Richard answered the officer, "Yes sir."

The cop looked at Richard. "How are you two doin' tonight?"

Richard answered, "Aw, we're good. Thank you."

"And where are you two headed tonight?"

"We just got into town and are looking for a place to sleep for the night, then we'll be on our way in the morning. Are there any good places around here for us to crash?" Richard asked.

The officer said, "We used to let people camp out at the city park at the end of the street here, but we stopped that a while back. Seems there were some problems in keeping the park clean. I'd say be discreet, stay away from the park, and you should be fine." The officer then asked, "Do you have some ID I can see?"

"Yeah, yeah sure," Richard said, as he handed him his ID. The officer called it in on his radio. From my burglary days, I knew the difference between a local check and an NCIC. We weren't far enough away to pass any NCIC, but I heard the officer do a simple local check, so I felt confident we'd be cleared. Again, that was in the early nineties, when police checks weren't as thorough as today.

"And ma'am, can I see your ID?"

"I don't have any," I replied.

"That's okay. Give me your name and Social."

Put on the spot, I rattled off one of the many names we had come up with when back on the bus. "Samantha Ann Mills."

"And your Social?" the officer asked again.

"I don't have one. I've never worked. I've never needed to. He takes care of me," I said, as I gestured my shoulders toward Richard.

"What is your date of birth?" the officer asked next.

I had to think quick for a fast answer, and my ages-old sobriety date was the first fixed date I could come up with. For the year, I easily thought of 1973. It was a nice round year, next to the current year of 1993. And so I told the officer, "Eight—seventeen—nineteen seventy-three."

The officer radioed in, "Samantha Ann Mills, eight—seven-teen—nineteen seventy-three, Eugene Oregon."

As the officer waited for the dispatch reply, he said to Rich-ard, "Just be careful tonight. But I don't think you have anything to worry about. This is a pretty safe city. We don't see much action around here."

Dispatch came back with an "All clear."

"Okay, here's your ID back, Mr. Park. You and Ms. Mills have a good night. Be safe."

"Thank you. Goodnight," Richard said.

The cop got in his car and drove off. We walked on. Kymberley was a wanted woman for absconding from parole. She was ostra-cized by her family. But I was no longer Kymberley. In that moment, I became Samantha Ann Mills, nineteen years old, going on twenty. I was a young woman who was barely starting out in this world, and too young to buy alcohol. Good, I had a problem with alcohol anyway, so that was one way to curb my problem.

Richard took my hand. "Nice to meet you, Samantha."

PART THREE

CHAPTER 12

SAMANTHA, I

Who am I? Vibrations in the cement foundation shook me from my self-questioning. Another semitruck had passed over. My rest under that overpass was a welcome relief after a long day of hitchhiking. With almost an hour until it would be dark out, we talked idly and passed our bottle of rank wine back and forth. Unable to answer my own question, I turned my attention to Richard, lest I drift back into memories. He had asked me about my birthday. That question, I could take a stab at.

"My birthday is another month away. Besides, I'm Samantha now. I have to wait until August for a birthday."

"Our secret. No one has to know," Richard said, then wiped his lips with his hands. "We're free." He passed the bottle back to me. "We can go anywhere you want. Where do you want to go?"

I took another gulp of wine. "To the East Coast."

"Then to the East Coast it is," Richard said with his teddy-bear smile.

"No, really. I want to reach down and feel the ocean water on the Atlantic Coast." I tugged at our unrolled sleeping bag. Its creases where I sat made it lumpy. I reached in my pack for another sweater. The wine hadn't warmed me up yet.

Richard smiled and looked around at our surroundings. The eastern seaboard stretched several states, so it would be easy enough to get to, unlike if I had picked one exact place. Other than east, we saw no point in making plans. We were at the mercy of where highways led, and who drove those highways, and who among those drivers gave us a ride, and how far.

Gone was the counterculture era of hitchhiking. It had been a friendly means of transportation to help returning soldiers following both World Wars. Up until well into the 1970s, hitchhiking was popular. The 1980s wasn't yet ready to let go of hitchhiking, giving companionship for the driver on a long trip. As risks increased, so did local ordinances restricting hitchhiking. It took one full decade, the '90s, to reshape hitchhiking culture. In the early '90s, when Richard and I hitchhiked cross-country, it was still a viable mode of transportation.

I remembered Nana's stories of when she was a young woman and ran away from home. She too had sought a better life, away from her mean brothers. With her then boyfriend and another young couple, they went to Canada for several weeks before returning home to her parents. That must have been in the year 1921. With Nana in my heart and Richard as my protector and confidante, I looked forward to where I—not we—would end up.

"Here, take the bottle," Richard said, nudging me on my shoulder. I took the bottle out of his hands and took a big gulp to wash my memories away. Richard pulled our well-creased map out of the side pocket of his pack and unfolded it. Pointing at a city on the map, he said, "Since we're already in Nebraska, we need to stop in Lincoln for a few days."

"We had a week camping at Lake Ogallala," I said.

"Yeah, but that was so we could get our heads on straight," he said.

It had been only a few days since leaving Salem, Oregon when we stayed a week at the campground on Lake Ogallala, just inside Nebraska. From Cheyenne, the week before, we hadn't made it far on I-80 when the driver who gave us a ride into Nebraska suggested we visit their lake. "It's a beauty and no traveler should pass it by," our driver had said.

Camping that week had given us a chance to chill after our Salem life. Richard moved his finger along the map. "From here, and no matter who takes us how far, it's going to take us a few days to get to the East Coast. We need money."

Lincoln was an industrialized city, and as with any big city, the likelihood of a plasma bank increased. In Lincoln and from then on, whenever we landed in a big city and we were low on cash and willing to hang out, plasma banks were a place for Richard to earn money. It meant registering at their plasma bank with a fake local address so he could sit for an hour to donate plasma cells from his blood. For his plasma donation he got anywhere from ten to twenty-five dollars cash.

For safety and health reasons, all plasma banks had two common rules. Clients had to meet weight requirements, usually weighing in at 150 pounds or more. Donation frequency was also limited, usually to no more than twice weekly, with three days in between visits. With my hatred of needles, it was in my favor that I weighed fifty pounds underweight. Richard always weighed in at well over 200 pounds.

We were never on a fervent search to find a plasma center. We'd use them as needed, and if convenient. Otherwise, we made do with what we had. Routinely, Richard's first dollar and a half earned bought us a forty-ounce Olde English Ale. With his blood thinned from his donation, Richard got his beer buzz on much easier. It was his reward for earning us a few bucks.

In Lincoln, Nebraska, we stayed long enough for Richard to give plasma twice, and we spent our nights in woods on undeveloped land. With our campsite well off the beaten track, we left our heavy stuff inside our tent, traveling only with our valuables when we went on foot into town each day. Keeping our valuables on us was an ingrained rule from my days with Jim that I passed on to Richard.

Like many places we homesteaded overnight, we trusted our tent and belongings were well hidden. Even a short walk was cumbersome with our heavy packs. With our packs stashed behind in our tent, we could blend into the community.

On our last morning in Lincoln, we woke early, as soon as the sun started to come up. We were rejuvenated, had stocked up on tobacco and supplies, and had a little cash in our pockets. We were ready to head to the East Coast. A sundress was my choice in clothes that day, leaving my jeans rolled and packed away. I had yet to get used to spring weather, so unlike Oregon's mild temperature swings. We were in the middle of the United States. It was a stale blanket of hot air, unbroken by warm coastal streams.

Richard was packing away our flashlight, candles, and our deck of playing cards. He looked up at me and asked, "Are you done with your coffee?"

"Yeah," I said. One cup of lukewarm instant coffee was enough for me.

He said, "Wipe it out and I'll give you some water. I'm ready to shave."

I wiped out my coffee cup with a dry cloth, then shook some coffee granules off it and set it aside. Richard undid the bungee cord that held our plastic gallon of water, then poured water in my cup. He pulled a small plastic bowl from his pack and poured water in it. I dipped a wash cloth in his bowl of water and then wrung it out.

I handed the bowl back to Richard, and he went about washing and then shaving, except for his mustache. That stayed. I rubbed a bar of soap on my wet washcloth and wiped sweat and dirt off me as best as I could. I never wasted our water on shaving my legs.

Richard then brushed his hair to tame his coarse curls. That took a while, more time than it took me to brush my teeth from my cup of water. He pulled his long waves back into a ponytail and put his ball cap on to further hide his mess of long hair he chose to keep. We had our morning routines down.

In under an hour, we were at the interstate on-ramp, eastbound on I-80. Thumbs erect, we watched car after car go by, but no one was stopping. Several cars with windows already rolled down slowed in passing to extend an apology with hand signals. Cupping the finger toward the thumb with an open gap meant it was too short of a distance to bother. Pinching finger to thumb meant there wasn't room for us in their car. And a shrug of their shoulders was a polite excuse of "Can't help."

Bored in our second hour, I kept my right arm out and thumb up while Richard etched our initials into a nearby wooden utility pole. With a pocketknife he carved a heart, "RP and SM" inside, and below the heart, "AK to FL." Of course, we weren't truly from Alaska. And why Florida, I don't know. It was at the far opposite corner of the country from Oregon. More so, the initials for Florida wouldn't let us forget our goal, to reach the Atlantic Ocean. It became our trademark he'd scrawl into many more poles as we traveled cross-country.

In our ongoing travels, we were sometimes picked up right away, while other times it took anywhere from fifteen minutes to an hour or more. But gee, with our carved initials on the pole behind us, the sun was now high in the sky. Finally, our only taker was a driver who looked like Pee-wee Herman. And not in a friendly way, from what I could see when he rolled down his window. We longed for a ride, but I learned from Richard in that moment that safety comes before wants. It is always okay to say no.

Quiet-mannered, this driver stared at me through his oversized, round, black-rimmed glasses. Richard exchanged a few words with him, leaning in where his window was rolled down. The only part I heard was when Richard tapped the side of the car and leaned back to stand upright. He told the driver, "No thank you."

As Pee-wee drove on, Richard looked at me and said, "Something wasn't right about him. I don't know what it was, but he gave me the creeps."

"I know. I know." I put my thumb back out to face traffic. "Me too."

Before we had a chance to say any more, we saw Pee-wee's car about an eighth mile up, still on the on-ramp. Pee-wee's car slowed down and pulled over again. We watched. A few minutes passed before he proceeded onto the interstate. Not more than fifteen minutes later, Pee-wee was back, but this time he passed us by. He had to have taken the first off-ramp from the interstate—it was the only way anyone could have made it, backtracking through town, to check us out again on our on-ramp. Earlier, Richard couldn't tell me why that driver freaked him out, but Pee-wee's return was all the reassurance we needed. We had been right to say no.

Freaked out, not knowing if he'd return yet again, we needed a late morning break. Several hours had passed with Pee-wee as the only possibility. We discussed stashing our packs in a hidden area to go get coffee at a diner before resuming our stance.

Immediately beside our ramp was a downhill grassy mound with overgrown fields of weeds, sparse young trees, and thorny plants. We started our way down through the field.

Once downhill on level ground, and with the interstate above and behind us, I walked ahead of Richard. Without warning, the terrain I crunched through changed in front of my one good eye. I hollered back at Richard, "Honey, is this pot?"

Richard lifted his head from the tangled bushes he was stepping over. With a full gaze, he hollered back his answer. "It sure is. Start grabbing." In that same instant, he leaped forward with a half-run, half-jump, to find we were in the middle of a pot field.

It had been a few years since my marijuana manicuring job with Steve's harvest, but I remembered pot and its stages of growth. That pot field was intentionally planted in a squared-off designated area surrounded by overgrown brush. They weren't quite ready for picking, but at nearly mature, their buds had begun to flower. While I took a minute to observe the horticulture facts, Richard didn't hesitate. He pulled black trash bags out of his pack and handed me one with his command, "Pick. Start picking. Pull up everything you can."

Some stuff from Richard's pack got moved to my pack to make room. We picked and pulled pot plants and stuffed his backpack full. Without counting one by one, I easily estimated the rows yielded a harvest of fifty plants. When there was nothing more to grab, our break was over. We had to get out of Dodge. It was unknown territory for us, and the farmer could have watched us through binoculars from a far-off apartment window.

With overstuffed packs shut as tightly as possible, we resumed our post at the on-ramp. As quick as we put our thumbs out, a driver was quick to stop for us. Relaxing my thumb, sweet air wafted past my nose. My fingers were sticky sweet.

Our driver was on the conservative side, a polo shirt neatly tucked into his slacks. In mutual small talk, we explained ourselves with a fabricated story about being newly married and traveling. Our driver played along with our honeymoon story and informed us he would see to it we had a hotel room for the night.

We hadn't asked for any gift from him. A ride, in and of itself, was always greatly appreciated. We never asked for more. But this time we had a driver who offered more. Who were we to argue, considering we hadn't planned our next move with an overflowing backpack of pot?

We also didn't object when our driver explained he was taking I-29 North from Omaha. The farther away we got from our pot picking, the safer we were. In Sioux City, our driver's hometown, he pulled into a parking lot right off the interstate and left us in his SUV while he went inside an upscale hotel lobby. Minutes later, he returned and handed us room keys. "Enjoy your honeymoon night."

When we first walked into our room, I wanted so much to shower and cool off from the heat of the day, but Richard had other plans. "Clear off that desk. I'll get scissors out. We need small trash bags, too. Are there any in our trash cans?"

I checked beneath those that lined the cans. "Yeah, there are."

Richard got out his pot pipe and pinched off a bud for it. He lit his pipe, inhaled it, and then fought to let out a long smoky breath. After he choked on it, he asked, "You want some?"

"No. Not now," I said. I had no desire for a weird physical sensation or unintelligent mind frame. It was an unstated understanding that we had less than eighteen hours to manicure all fifty plants and clean up our mess, plus shower and watch TV. We got started right away. We worked side by side to clip and trim away twigs.

Ziploc bags from supplies in his pack helped divvy it up. Some pot went into single-use baggies for later. Some got packed tight and doubled wrapped in the small clear trash bags. Richard put a few of those in a black trash bag, then rolled the excess from the black bag over it. He did the same with the rest of it.

We got all the pot bagged up, piled high on the desk. Richard then started fussing in his pack. That was normal. He seemed to always be rearranging stuff in his pack. The pot that was in the black bags went on the bottom of his pack. Then he put his clothes and other stuff on top of that. The single-use bags of pot went in pockets and zippered compartments in his pack.

Early the next morning we cleaned up our room as best we could without a vacuum. Then, we carried several trash bags full of stems to the laundry room trash cans. Richard said, "Imagine, Samantha, the tip the maid will have in finding all these pot stems."

Eastward into Iowa, we discovered the remnants of a flood-ravished state. One night, our chosen spot to homestead was an abandoned campground. Thickened lumps of otherwise limp grass in long strands were all that kept picnic tables from sinking in deep ravines of water. In our rides through the state, our scenic views revealed outhouses, sheds, and tractors that floated by as if they were houseboats.

One ride at a time, we were making our way down a congested expressway. Signal lights were every few miles, making traffic stop and go. A driver in a Pinto station wagon pulled over for us. Richard sat up front with him and I sat in the back with our packs. At the next signal light, he moved over to the fast lane. He wasn't speeding past cars; he needed the retainer wall to keep his Pinto in his lane. It was a concrete median several feet high.

Our driver didn't have a care in the world as his car bounced with a big thud on and off that wall, guiding his way down the road. He was a happy, jovial guy, but stoned out of his gills, if not drunk. I felt safe enough in the back seat, cushioned between our two backpacks, but wondered how Richard was in his front passenger seat.

"Whoa, buddy," Richard said as our driver came a little too close to the car in front of us. He didn't hit it though, and at Richard's comment, slowed down, rubbing against the wall again. It was his car, not mine, so I didn't care how beat up it got.

Some fifty miles later, and still not hitting a car, our driver said, "I need a drink." At the next intersection, he swerved to the right lane, then turned into a liquor store parking lot.

Richard turned around in his seat and told me, "I'm going in with him. Going to get us something for later tonight."

While they went into the store, I stepped out of the car and smoked one of our rolled cigarettes. Returning to the car, Richard carried a small paper sack with the bottle he bought in it, then put it in his pack. Our driver carried a pint of whiskey. He started the car and pulled out of our parking spot, but before pulling out onto the highway, he opened the bottle and took a big swallow.

At least we're going eastbound, I thought to myself. But at the next light, he turned off our expressway.

Richard said, "Where are we going, buddy?"

Our driver said, "This-a-way."

"We should stay on the main drag," Richard said.

Our driver took another swig. His pint was almost gone. "No. What-you-u-u mean?"

"How about pulling over and letting us out?" Richard said.

Our driver didn't answer back. He had his pint tipped up at his mouth. After the last swallow, he pulled his Pinto to the side of the road, stopped, and turned his car off. He slumped his arms and head over his steering wheel. Through his muffled voice, he said, "This is it. This is as far as I'm going."

I reached for the door handle closest to me, the back seat driver's side. The door wouldn't open this time. I climbed over our packs and opened the other door. We stepped out onto a dirty graveled road. Corn fields were on both sides of the road. Richard pulled his pack off the back seat. "Get your pack. Let's go."

In our two-mile hike back to the expressway, Richard said, "Yeah, when we were in the liquor store he bought two pints. The cold ones were in a cooler in the back, and by the time we got to the counter he had already downed one. He paid for it, though.

Put it up on the counter, both the empty one and the one you saw him open."

Our next jaunt by thumb took us to Kansas City, and following an overnight stay, we embarked on to Springfield, Missouri from I-49 South. With a population of 100,000, we understood it was rich with resources for homeless people. After we set up camp in the backwoods of Battlefield Mall, we walked downtown to Commercial Street to check out The Missouri Hotel, as folks had suggested.

Its lobby was grand with high ceilings, murals, sculpted architecture, and curved staircases. There were chipped black-and-white hard tiled floors throughout. Pictures of Missouri hung on the walls, or at least I thought they were Missouri. If it wasn't for the fact that the hotel was a homeless shelter, it could easily have made its way into a fancy coffee-table book.

A brief session with an intake worker informed us if we stayed in their hotel we'd be placed in separate sleeping quarters. As Richard was my protector and provider, I refused to be separated from him. Perfectly content with our backwoods homestead, we declined the offer. However, we accepted clothing vouchers and our place in line for the soup kitchen.

Each day for a week, we trekked into downtown to hang out for another free meal. It was easy to befriend others. Richard had his pot to share. Unfortunately, our afternoons often brought drunkenness with others. With Richard drunk, I returned to my eggshell uneasiness. The more we hung out, the more time we wasted. Our shared goal to reach the East Coast felt more like my goal, and not our goal. In my morning pleas, I had to reel him back into our reality. "Honey, you promised we'd get to the East Coast for my birthday."

Through Nashville, Tennessee, and Atlanta, Georgia, we thumbed our way along I-16 into Savannah. From there, it was but a short jaunt to the coastal town of Tybee Island. Contrary to popular understanding, Savannah isn't oceanfront—not to anyone on foot—but is instead about twenty miles inland from ocean tides.

Savannah had resources, unlike Tybee Island. We needed to stock up on tobacco and food. The city also had a plasma center so Richard could earn cash. Savannah was a major city with lots of homeless people in its backwoods. We methodically chose our homestead in an undeveloped patch of land beyond railroad tracks. It was in easy hitchhiking reach to the coast. On our third morning, we felt confident enough to leave our campsite for our coastal day trip.

Approaching the north side of the beach, we stepped over a small rock border that edged the sand. I dropped my day bag, kicked off my shoes, and ran straight ahead, ignoring the seagulls and pelicans as they fluttered to get out of my way. With sand under my feet, into the water I ran, yelling, "We did it. Oh, isn't it beautiful?"

I splashed and kicked and picked up scoops of fresh ocean water to toss back at the waves, which kept rolling in at me. An enormous wonder was in front of me. I had touched the Pacific Ocean countless times, but had forgotten how vast the ocean was. To touch the Atlantic Ocean was breathtaking. I brimmed with pride at such an accomplishment—to have hitchhiked from a western state to here, feet in the salty water, on the far opposite side of our wide country.

I remembered Nana's stories of her vacation to see the Continental United States. It was back in the 1960s, I think. My great-aunt and Nana had made that trip by car, sightseeing, shopping, and staying in nice motels.

I bent down again, grabbed an armful of as much water as I could possibly hug, and splashed my face with it. Not one to like salt on my food, I didn't mind one bit that I got a mouthful of sweet, salty wetness. It came with a crisp invigorating sensation.

Seagulls, oh so many seagulls, frolicked with me. The air was fresh as the water purified and cleansed me, much needed after days without a shower. If only I could have soaked up the sweetness of that warm day in May 1993 to take with me forevermore.

After our Savannah stay, and then a brief stop in Memphis behind us, our thumbs next got us into the northeast corner of Arkansas. With one of our drivers, we shared a beer run through the Ozark hills to a wet county. He suggested we try a homeless camp he knew of.

Tent City, as the homeless camp was known, was out in the boonies. A dense forest enclave of twenty acres with yellow tents and marked-off cement slabs for tent sites were purposefully situated. Even though we had our own tent, the campground management assigned us one of the yellow ones, much bigger than ours.

It was there, around a communal campfire, that I tried crawdads for the first time ever. The men spent the morning hours bringing in traps they had laid in the river the day before. Next, the women put the crawdads into a big black iron pot on the fire to boil, along with a wide range of vegetables and peppers and spices.

Richard took part in the crawdad hunts, and I helped with the vegetables. Afternoons were spent over beer and wine and the peppered smells of our stewing pot. It was enough to feed the whole camp, about forty of us, and I quickly acquired a taste for it.

Off the beaten track of cops on interstates, we fell into a life with our newfound community that stretched several days. Moonshine was rampant, but I didn't need to over imbibe, sticking to beer and weak table wine. There was still a learning curve to maintain the facade of my alias identity. I sure didn't need anything to needlessly slip out. At times I was quiet, as if shy, but I was always on guard. I shared only as conversations demanded of me, and made up stories as I went along. To them, I was Samantha.

Richard, however, wasn't so careful when it came to what he drank or when. And of course, when he drank too much, or drank the wrong stuff, his pot was not strong enough to counteract his drunkenness. He was the risk taker. I was not, or not anymore, that is. I had to protect my identity. He got into a fist fight with someone. It was probably over something trivial, or a result of his zealous and unprovoked jealousy. Cops showed up to break it up, only to arrest Richard.

Overcome with grief over my separation from him, I could only hope his stay in jail would be but one night. The longer they kept him, the greater the chances of them doing a deep background criminal search. We'd be in deep shit if they found out about his parole violation.

I had no choice but to stay put. His stuff was with me, so that was reason enough for his return. I looked to a few fellow campers for solace and general information about what usually happened when someone in the group got arrested.

One man took me under his wing without concern for what caused the fight, and with no concern or favor for the other fighter who didn't get arrested. It was an awkward friendship. I stayed on guard while emphasizing my dilemma. I told him, "Richard is my protector. It doesn't matter how I feel about him or even if I love him. I can't lose him."

He'd reply, "It'll be all right."

I said, "You don't understand. There's so much you don't understand. I can't go anywhere without him. I have to have him."

"It'll be all right. No matter what happens, you'll be all right," he'd respond.

I believed my words and could only hope this man's words were also true. Without legal identification as Samantha, I had to have Richard for survival. He was my trusted confidante in my ascension to Samantha.

Richard was my soulmate. We had a shared history in our great big world. Cognizant of my future needs, I didn't lie to myself about the longevity of our relationship. Eventually we would go our separate ways, if only so I could get a life that would please Nana. But it was too soon. I couldn't survive by myself.

Overnight for two nights without Richard, I refused to drift into deep sleep. I fell asleep holding a hammer and kept a baseball-sized rock under my pillow. I was ready to pounce on anyone who would dare intrude on my space. But nobody did. I was left alone to sleep. Midmorning on day three, Richard strolled into camp on foot. I ran up to him and gave him a great big hug. We packed up our bags and walked out of Tent City without saying goodbye to anyone.

On a state highway, thumbs erect again, I saw Richard's hand and arm were badly swollen from the fight. "Shit, they didn't do anything about your hand when you were in jail?"

"No," Richard answered. "I didn't want to make a big deal out of it. I had to get out of jail before they started running background checks on me. They never fingerprinted me, just threw me in a rubber cell."

Our first ride out of the area was with a gray-haired hippie woman. She was a lot older than us, maybe in her sixties. I sat in the middle up front, between her and Richard.

While driving she fumbled in her purse, which was pressing on my left hip. Pulling out a handful of pill bottles, she handed them to me, all but one. I passed them to Richard. Popping the lid with only her thumb, she said, "I have some pills. Here, try this." She swallowed one and then handed me that bottle, too.

Richard let his handful of pill bottles fall in his lap while taking the last pill bottle from her. He took one pill out and tried to swallow it but started to gag.

"Coffee. Here, swallow." She handed Richard her cup from the mug holder. It was a porcelain coffee cup with daisies painted on it, stained with lipstick. The coffee looked cold and was light brown from too much creamer. Richard didn't hesitate. He finished downing his pill with her coffee.

He leaned back and smiled. "Thank you. I hurt my hand real bad from a fight I got into."

"Oh no, dear. Here, I know what you need." She called him dear, even though we had told her our names when getting in her car. With one hand on the steering wheel, she rustled through her purse again and brought out a different pill bottle. She popped the cap, took out a pill, and handed it to him. "Here, take one of these for that hand of yours."

Richard downed the pill with more of her cold coffee. Her hand went to the glove box, where she pulled out another pill bottle. That time she handed him the whole bottle and said, "Here, you and your wife enjoy these when you get alone together."

Richard said, "Samantha doesn't do pills."

"Oh, that's a shame." She let Richard take the bottle of pills from her and then put her hands back on the steering wheel. "Well, dear, you try it. Go ahead. I don't need it. I can always get more."

Richard popped the cap. Only two pills were inside. He took both.

Once that ride was over we soon found another ride, but not long after getting into the cab of a pickup truck, Richard nodded off. In and out, and back into drowsiness. The pills were doing a real number on him. He was the one who always did most of the talking with our drivers, and I had no choice but to explain the scoop. "He took some pain pills after hurting his hand something awful."

Our driver gave us a ride all the way to the front door entrance of the emergency department at University of Arkansas Medical Center. Richard was taken in for treatment right away. How surreal it felt as I waited out Richard's day-long stay. I was in the city in which I had been born. I had achieved a great feat to find myself back in the place I was from, far from Oregon where I'd been raised, even though it was without any planning.

The wait was boring, but I didn't mind. The air-conditioning was a welcome relief from the stinky hot Arkansas air. Nurses wrapped Richard's broken wrist in a cast and said it was to come off in four weeks.

Late in the day when we left the hospital, we got a bottle of Olde English Ale and then laid out our sleeping bag on a hillside well-populated with homeless folks. It was too hot to get in our bag, and it was not a safe place to set up camp. We were exhausted, burnt out, and wanted nothing more than to somehow survive the over-night temperatures that reached above one hundred degrees.

Fat bushes were everywhere on that hillside, some as high as nearly four feet tall. The bushes had tangled hardwood branches and overhanging leaves. We drank our beer, sitting on our claimed spot. We said little and mostly watched as some folks scurried into the bushes, pushing the branches aside to claim their own spots. The next night, we returned to sit out the night on the hillside.

On our third day of recovery in Little Rock, with little enthusiasm for standing on a boiling hot interstate on-ramp, we meandered on the south side of the Arkansas River. Soon others, also homeless or otherwise transient, joined us. It was a river likely not meant for public swimming, but nonetheless, we took advantage of the endless supply of cool water that streamed by.

Richard dangled his bare legs in the river. Clad in cut-off shorts and a tank top, I flopped around carefree in the river as others jumped in. It was our only escape from the scorching humidity and skyrocketing heat. Days of perspiration rolled off me.

Among the wayward stragglers who joined us were a couple of scruffy men, one seriously older than his counterpart. He introduced himself as Smitty. As we talked, they shared that they were homeless and living out of their van. With a beer run in mind, Richard and I walked to the nearby Piggly Wiggly shopping center to meet up with them as they pulled their bluish-brown van into a center handicapped spot.

When we got to them, Smitty had the side door of his van slid open, which revealed open boxes of canned food. We hung with them for an hour while Smitty played the salesman, approaching shoppers both coming and going from the grocery store. He had an offer for them, a much better deal on food, or so he claimed. "Cheerios too. Everyone likes Cheerios. You can have this big box for just one dollar," Smitty told them.

Peanut butter, and Folgers coffee, and boxes of Hamburger Helper, and lots of canned vegetables were among his stash that he offered up to reel in cash. When his work for the day was done, we got our beer, and with packs back on our backs, hiked the return to our river spot to meet up with Smitty and his sidekick.

As the day closed in on us and the sun neared its time to set, Smitty posited an idea. He had an air conditioner in his van, but it was one of those apartment window box types that needed to be plugged in. We threw out ideas of where we could park for the night that would have the needed outlet.

"The cemetery?" asked Smitty's partner.

"Nooo," answered Smitty.

"The golf course?" Richard suggested. Without further ado, we piled into Smitty's van and drove to the golf course. With his back seat folded down to make way for the boxed food, Richard and I resigned to riding as best we could, sitting wherever we could find a free place for this leg or that leg.

Smitty hooked up the AC by plugging it into an outlet from a pole beside the paved path through the golf course, meant for the caddy drivers. We settled in for the night with Smitty in the driver's seat and his companion next to him in the front passenger seat. They were soon fast asleep. Richard and I were in the tailgate section with our sleeping bag laid out, partly for privacy. We drifted off to sleep in the cold, cool air of the humming air conditioner.

I couldn't see Richard's watch to know what time it was. It was likely well into the wee hours of morning when I was startled by a tap, tap, tap. Richard and I opened our eyes and looked at each other, but neither of us moved a muscle, not even to blink. Smitty rolled down his window. I heard a man's direct voice from outside the van. "You two can't be using this golf course's electricity."

"Yes, officer. Sorry, officer. We were just trying to cool off for the night," Smitty said.

"I need to see your ID," he told Smitty.

I tilted my head up over Richard's shoulder and saw the back of Smitty's head and a cop outside. I dared not move anymore. Neither did Richard as we let the moments pass.

"And your friend? I need to see his ID too," the cop asked, bobbing his head to point at Smitty's partner.

Another minute of quiet stillness passed.

"Thank you. Is it just the two of you tonight?" the cop asked.

"Uh, no sir. We picked up a couple of hitchhikers earlier," Smitty answered.

"And where are they?"

"In the back," Smitty answered, "sleeping."

Damn, there goes our cover.

The cop walked to the back half of the van, knocked on a window, and said, "Come on out. Let me see your faces."

Richard pulled our sleeping bag cover off our backs. In a sleepy voice, and with great force that might have fooled others, but not me, he whined at the cop, "Yeah, I was sleeping."

"Anyone else back there?" the cop asked Richard.

"No, just us."

"Just us who?"

"My wife and me. That's it."

"IDs please."

We crawled forward, climbing over who knows what in the dark. Even that cop's flashlight didn't shine well enough for us to see our way through Smitty's maze of stuff. Richard handed him his ID and told the cop, "She doesn't have any ID."

The cop glanced at Richard's ID with the other two IDs still in hand, then passed them back to each person. "You all have to leave. You can't be using the golf course's electricity."

At least our last night in Little Rock was relatively cool, but I could have done without the wake-up call. We parted ways with Smitty and got a ride out of Arkansas that morning.

Over a campfire dinner, somewhere along the interstate stretch, smack in the middle of our big country, we made plans for Richard's birthday. He expressed he had always wanted to see the Sturgis Bike Rally. That was happening soon. And so, as directly as we could while at the mercy of our drivers, we headed up to Sturgis, South Dakota.

When we arrived in Sturgis, local townsfolk told us we had a week to wait until the rally, scheduled for the last few days of July and first few days in August, but that bikers would start showing up soon. During lunch at the Road Kill Café, they also informed Richard there was a construction site that was always looking for day labor workers on some place being built.

A man explained to Richard, "It's a temporary job, lasting only as long as it takes them to finish work on that site. If you show up Monday morning, I bet the job is yours for the taking. You'll see the place. Just twelve miles east on Highway Thirty-Four."

Still several days away from the big motorcycle event, the town was quiet with just a few neighborly people lolling about their sparse downtown. In the backdrop was a tall hillside, so tall it seemed as if it had been naturally erected to reach the gods in the sky. Huffing and puffing from the weight on our backs, we hiked uphill, almost to its top. There we found a spot among the trees to camp. From our spot on the hilltop, we easily looked down on all the houses. It looked like city life was nonexistent, but a walk into town the next day reminded us that life there did go on.

During the week, I bided my time at camp with crossword puzzle books and a radio while Richard went to work. Each morning he made his way downhill, then hitchhiked out. After he put in a good day of labor, he hitchhiked back home to me with forty dollars cash earned for the day. Surprisingly, he didn't bother to stop at any bars or liquor stores, but instead was a good boy. I think he liked the opportunity to work a few days, with his pot to come back to.

Thursday evening Richard returned to tell me his boss said there would be no work the next day. They needed to break for the rally.

Friday morning we decided to make a business day of it by going into town to stock up on supplies.

Before Richard crawled out of the tent, he smoked some pot. I stayed outside the tent when he did that. I didn't need a secondhand high from his pipe as he lollygagged to get dressed in between hits. We still had a lot of pot left, no matter how much he smoked. Fifty plants was a lot to go through. The last thing I needed was more of his chanting to the gods when drunk on whiskey, so I was perfectly okay with his marijuana preference.

We left our homestead neat and tidy for our trip to town. Nothing was left strewn about on the tent's outside. Inside, the bed was made as usual, with clothes and supplies each in their respective places. We didn't have any concern for the safety of our items. Crime didn't seem to be a part of Sturgis. And we hadn't ever seen any other life on that hillside, save for the squirrels.

After a full day of spending Richard's money on tobacco, candles, batteries for the radio, and some hygiene stuff, we hoofed it back uphill to our tent, day bags over our shoulders.

We set our bags down. Richard unzipped our tent. But the tent wasn't exactly as we had left it. Glaring at us right inside the tent was a good-sized rock, about the size and shape of a football. Under the rock was a handwritten note.

You are not allowed to camp here. This is private property. Please pack up and leave.

It was signed by the sheriff.

Under his note was Richard's folded sweatshirt as he had left it. Under his folded sweatshirt was an eight-gallon black trash bag with pot neatly packed in tight, like a soft brick. Under the pot was the foot of our bed, where the sleeping bag stretched to our tent's edge. The note had been left for us, and nothing of ours had been disturbed.

Richard said, "Shit, he never did find the pot."

"Wow," I said. "Everything is right where we left it. He didn't even bother looking through our stuff."

"Nope," Richard said. After a calming breath he added, "He just left the note."

"That was a close call. What if he had found it?"

Richard answered, "Good thing he didn't."

I lit a rolled cigarette to calm my nerves. "Now what do we do?"

In that stern protective voice of his, Richard answered me. "Pack up and find another place in town to camp. We don't want to miss the bike rally."

No more words were needed as we worked together in our pre-determined roles to pack up and move out. Just as Jim and I had once had specific roles when hitting a house, Richard and I each had our own tasks to make rolling up camp as smooth as possible.

Later that day, we walked into Deadwood Campground and found ourselves a tent site in the back-row area. Over the following two days we saw bikers arrive to set up camp as we had done. Evenings during the rally were spent around group campfires, and Richard's share of his pot stash was greatly appreciated. Rumor had it that Bob Dylan was in town too, but we never saw him.

At the close of the week-long festivities, we said our goodbyes and well wishes to those we had befriended, and made our way to the highway, eastbound. Thumbing our way, we traveled through Minneapolis, Minnesota, then through the corners of Wisconsin, Illinois, and Indiana. We'd find our next ride somewhere on the Indiana-Ohio border of I-80. That ride would take us farther than we could have imagined, and move me closer to strengthening my life as Samantha. I didn't know that when hopping into his truck.

CHAPTER 13

DONNA BLANK

Since our Salem departure, we had traveled from coast to coast. We had thumbed our way through fifteen-some states and went where our rides took us. We often tried to manipulate our itinerary with our weathered map in hand, which I had learned to read like a well-read novel. Yet we were content even when we got off the beaten track.

We received several rides from lone drivers who either wanted some company for their time on the road, or who felt compassion for us. Many of the lone drivers were men, and some were women. Some had long-distance plans, and some were doing their daily commute.

One woman who picked us up drove a two-seater sports car with a tiny luggage area behind the seats. We piled our packs in the back and Richard sat in the passenger seat up front. I was scrunched between his heavyset physique and her apple-shaped body. Every time she shifted gears, her hand brushed against my leg. When her leg moved to switch pedals, her short black skirt would hike up. I believe she was wearing a garter belt with her sheer black stockings.

Her white button-down blouse couldn't hide her full bosom below the plunging neckline.

It was rare for a whole family to give us a ride, but one such offer came when we traveled through the Midwestern states. The driver and his family took up all the seats in their full-sized car. Their boat was hitched to the bumper, and that's where we rode on our afternoon lift. Open and airy on an especially warm day, powerful breezes slapped at my face. I laid back on the boat's floorboards for a nap, and later awoke with sunburnt cheeks.

Back in Iowa, we had several rides besides the drunken guy in the Pinto. One was a pig farmer in overalls with a pickup truck. The bed of his truck had a homemade wooden slatted fence built around it, about four feet high. The bed floor held hay shavings and ten pigs, who roamed freely in their cramped space.

Of all our drivers, only one person got overtly weird with us. When he pulled over to drop us off, he asked me for a ten-dollar favor. "No," I said, and Richard backed me up.

And there were the long-haul truckers, whose stories became familiar. Regulations and rules infringed on their long-established freedom. They now had to log their hours, accounting for their travels, with daily driving hours limited. Weigh stations popped up with great frequency to stop those who were overweight and to inspect for contraband. For commercial trucking companies, that meant hitchhikers were no longer allowed. Some truckers went along and some resisted. Of the rebellious truckers out there, it was in Ohio that one such trucker picked us up.

With Minnesota, Wisconsin, and Illinois behind us since leaving Sturgis, South Dakota, we traveled through Indiana. It was right past the border of Indiana to Ohio on I-80 when that trucker pulled over for us. He reached across his cab, opened his passenger door, and stretched his upper body out the doorway to shake Richard's hand. "Hi, I'm Mitch. Hop in."

"Thanks," Richard said, tossing our packs in. I climbed in, moving our packs to the back of the cab with me. Richard followed me up into the cab, taking the front passenger seat.

Our driver, Mitch, wore a heavy flannel shirt with his blue jeans, likely to ward off the crisp air of late September. Like Richard, he had long scraggly hair. Unlike Richard, he didn't hide his untamed curls, letting them fall around his face.

Richard shook hands with him and said, "I'm Richard and this is my ol' lady, Samantha."

I leaned forward and elbowed Richard.

Richard smirked and added, "I mean, my girlfriend, Samantha."

Mitch let out a small laugh. "No worries. My wife is the same way when I call her my old lady. I'm a Sagittarius. What sign are you?" he asked as he steered his truck into the trucking lane of the highway.

"I'm a Leo," Richard answered.

"And you?" directing his question to me with a dart of his head to see me from his rearview mirror.

"I'm a Leo, too." *Shit*, I thought to myself. *Why did I say that? I'm not a Leo. What sign am I? I have no idea.* I tried to sound convincing as I corrected myself. "I mean, I don't get into the whole horoscope thing."

Mitch said, "Oh. Uh-huh."

I tried to keep quiet and let Richard do all the talking. Making up stories on the spot was awkward. It wasn't easy with Mitch. Sometimes he directed his questions right at me, however casual he tried to make it sound. I knew when someone was probing, and I could hear his probe.

The burden of answering his questions was lifted as he fell into a natural conversation with Richard, caught up in a world of similarities. Mitch said, "I'm headed home to Scranton. Been on the road for a while and I'm ready to get home to my wife."

In all, he had 500 miles to go on I-80 from where we had first climbed in. At each weigh station, Richard and I hid in a cubbyhole behind Mitch's seat. It was a few hours into our drive when Mitch got excited as if a thunderbolt of lightning had hit him. "Hey, if you two want to come home with me, I can take you tomorrow to meet a friend of mine who runs a diner."

Mitch turned his head to Richard, telling him, "Maybe he can hook you up with a job. You ought to settle down. Take it easy for a while. Pennsylvania is a great place to live. It's the oldest state in the country."

Like a travel agent, Mitch implored us to take the viable opportunity to make change, in Scranton, of all places. We hadn't planned on Pennsylvania. If anything, before Mitch had picked us up, we wondered aloud why in the heck we were headed north. We should have been southbound to flee the impending winter weather. A snowfall was on the horizon.

Maybe—just maybe—we could settle down. We were well past Oregon, on the opposite side of the country.

Where are we going? If we don't know where, then why not Pennsylvania?

Arriving at Mitch's house, we followed him in. Mitch kissed his wife, hugged his son, and then introduced us. His wife said, "Sit, dinner's ready." Her forehead furrowed, and a line appeared between her brows.

She hadn't bothered to say hi or anything else while Mitch and Richard talked through dinner. As soon as she finished eating, she stood up, and started her way to the kitchen with her plate in her hand. Their son, who was ten years old, asked, "Mom, can I go play?"

She turned around and answered, "Yes, honey, go play in your room." She returned to the table and set her plate back down and eyed Mitch.

Richard said, "Let me help you clear the table."

"No," she said, "get your packs. I'll show you to your room." She seemed to study us as we gathered our belongings.

The next day, Mitch stayed true to his word and drove us out to a diner in Moosic, a small outlying town. There he introduced Richard to his friend Terry, owner of Terry's Diner and Motel. With a handshake on the deal, Terry offered Richard a job starting right

away as a daytime housekeeper. We left Richard to work and returned for him later.

Each morning, Mitch gave Richard a ride to work and back
home again. Mitch's wife also worked during the day, and their son
had school. Sometimes Mitch was at home and sometimes he went
out for a while. Not wanting to corner myself into another situation
like the one when we talked horoscopes, I often got out of the house
and took a walk.

In neighborhood walks, I fell in love with the beauty of the city.
Brick Victorian houses with lush, well-laid-out yards were new to
me and much different from the neighborhood I had grown up in.
Its cityscape was not jutting modern skyscrapers, but buildings of
antiquity with carefully crafted architecture.

In its fall foliage, trees were near bare and leaves were everywhere—on streets, on sidewalks, and on parked cars. I was blanketed in a warm collage of reds and yellows. The more I appreciated
the beauty and friendliness of people, the more I believed I could
live in Scranton.

Aside from simple pleasures, I had to make good use of my time.
I needed to solidify my identity. Excuses made when we were transient had to be set aside. I had shelter, a little money, and easy access
to resources in town. My secret couldn't float forever on Richard. I
dared not live in such falsehoods. I had no concrete plan, but had to
do something, anything.

When Mitch went out, I turned my attention to my plan, however undeveloped it was. As a retired burglar, my skills proved their

worth as I snooped through his files and kept an ear out and an eye open for his return. I looked for any documentation that might help me, without knowing what I was looking for.

That's when I found it. Paperwork that showed his son's Social Security number. In the mid-1990s, unlike today, a child usually didn't need a Social Security number. It wasn't required for tax purposes or health care needs or anything else it's mandatory for today. It'd be several years before he'd need his number, so I wrote it down and saved the note.

I also found their marriage certificate. In my diligent strategy, I worked one logical step at a time. First, I borrowed the document and went for a neighborhood walk to a photocopy place, where I copied it. I stashed the copy in my stuff and returned the original to where I had found it not more than an hour earlier. The rest of my plan would unfold later.

In the evenings and weekends when Richard was off work, our idle hours were filled with irresponsible beer drinking and troublemaking when we were under the influence. Mitch's wife made matters worse with her attitude of condemnation.

Not long after we had moved in, I was sick and tired of her unfriendliness. One too many beers in me caused me to explode. Richard and I were in our room, rolling our clothes for packing. I had used their washing machine and dryer earlier that day.

Our door was open. We hadn't shut it when we brought the clothes in. Downstairs, at the foot of the stairs, Mitch's wife exclaimed, "How dare you bring strangers into our house."

Throwing a T-shirt at Richard's backpack, I said, "I can't stand how awful Mitch's wife is."

Richard said, "I know." He picked up the shirt I had thrown and said, "Help me here."

I raised my voice and paced our floor. "Why does she have to be so fuckin' mean? Did you see how she took over the TV when Mitch was watching it?"

Richard pulled me to him, tried to bury my head into his hug, and said, "Quiet."

I quieted myself into his hug.

Richard whispered, "I know. It's none of our business though. Don't let her get to you."

I whispered back, "It's not right." Pulling Richard's arms off me, I stepped backward, breaking our hug, and screamed, "How can I not let his wife get to me?"

Our open door slammed against the inside wall. Mitch stood at our doorway. "I'll have no disrespect for my wife. You're out of here. Get your stuff."

Neither Richard nor I bothered to apologize. We started stuffing our laundry in our packs.

Mitch said, "Hurry up. Now."

We stuffed as best as we could, and when Richard pulled the zipper shut on his pack, Mitch spoke up again. "Out, now."

We walked out to the sidewalk across the street. I took my pack off and set it down to put my coat on, which I had carried in our frenzied exit. It was cold out, thirty-five degrees Fahrenheit.

"Shit, now what?" I asked Richard.

He answered, "Don't worry about it. I didn't like living there any more than you did. Let's get to a pay phone. I'll call Terry."

Richard's boss, Terry, put us up in one of his motel rooms. It was a small room of less than eighty square feet with an overpowering queen-size bed. It felt more like a mansion to me. It had head room, unlike our two-man tent. We hunkered down in our motel room, sheltered from the falling snow.

With less stress on us in the motel than when living at Mitch's place, our problem drinking eased. Work tired Richard out and I kept busy at building my identity as Samantha. This was before the days when one could buy anything off the internet. This job needed my patience and creativity.

Our motel room worked in our favor as a stable mailing address. It's not that homeless people can't get mail. They can. Mail can be sent "General Delivery" to any US Post Office, and then it's up to the recipient to ask for their mail. Richard had received letters from his mom twice when passing through towns. He'd call her collect from a pay phone, telling her which post office to send it to. "We should be in downtown Birmingham by Tuesday. Send it there."

I bought blank ID cards and lamination sleeves from a mail order company. Richard was going to get an ID, too. These blank cards needed our information typed on them. We needed a type-writer so I could do the typing. Our motel sat on Birney Avenue, a state highway with residential homes, and we didn't have much in walking distance. A mile away, Kmart sold typewriters. We walked there and bought typing paper and a typewriter, then carried the thirty-pound thing home to our room.

Typewriters came with a ribbon that made the print appear on the paper. I was careful when using this ribbon to keep it from looking used. Once done typing our names, birthdates, and other details, I was ready to return the typewriter. We carried the thirty-pound typewriter back to Kmart, taking turns holding it as we walked the mile. Inside Kmart at the customer service counter, I said, "I need to return this. My dad bought it for me, but I already have one."

Passport photos came from a travel agency in Scranton. We rode the bus to get there. Our pictures got glued on the cards, and then those cards got sealed in their lamination sleeves. Considering it wasn't an official state ID, it wouldn't pass in a food stamp office or other government agency. It would, though, support my word. I no longer had to tell a cop I had no ID.

Richard held his new ID in his hand. He didn't have to be Richard anymore. He could be Joshua Axl Mott, DOB 07/04/1969, and with a Social Security number like mine but with the last four digits differing. Research in books from the public library taught me how Social Security numbers were issued. Our numbers, his made-up, and mine from Mitch's son, showed we were both from Pennsylvania.

Richard said, "Looks like me."

"Of course it does. It's you. Different name so cops don't pull up your robbery," I said.

"So far, nothing's come of my police checks to cause us problems. Maybe I'll use it." He tossed the ID on our bedside table.

"I'm putting mine in my wallet. My wallet has been empty for too long. I'm not taking any risks. I'm Samantha now," I said.

I also altered Mitch's marriage certificate I had photocopied, making it look like a photocopy of an original document. It showed Josh and I were married. With a marriage certificate, ID card, and memorized Social Security number as seen on that ID card, it sure seemed official to me. With confidence, I was Samantha Ann Mott, neé Mills.

While motel living was our safe harbor from the unrelenting snow, it was also expensive. A room wasn't part of the deal when Terry hired Richard, and most of his paycheck went to pay for our room. In one of our walks, perhaps to Kmart again, we found someone's ID on a snowbank at the edge of a parking lot. It was a woman, nearly thirty years old, named Donna Blank, and ironically, an Oregon State ID.

A factory a little farther from our motel, also on Birney Avenue, was hiring for full-time production workers. As Donna Blank, I got hired at six dollars an hour. The ID card I made to use as Samantha couldn't compare to the state seal on Donna's official ID card. When asked for my Social Security card, I said I'd lost it and would bring it in as soon as I could. Every few days I was asked for it again, and each time I said I'd get it to them as soon as I could.

My excuse could last only so long, but for the time being it was getting me a paycheck.

I counted down the hours each day as I counted tator tots or fish sticks, placing them in the correct compartment of cardboard TV dinner trays to later be distributed to schools. Non-stop chatter from coworkers talked over the clanking hum of the assembly line belt. "Donna, we need only one cookie per tray," or "Donna, I need you to help over here," or "Donna, are you from Scranton?" Sometimes it was, "Donna, do you have kids?" or "Donna, where did you work before here?" *Donna, Donna, Donna.*

At the end of my second week, I went into the bank from which my paycheck was drawn, a U.S. Bank. My first job, back when I was sixteen years old, was at a U.S. Bank. Nervous, I was glad Richard was beside me to cash my first paycheck. I resembled the true Donna, but if someone took the time to study her picture on the ID, it would be obvious I wasn't her.

"Next please," the teller behind the counter said with a smile.

I approached her and put my paycheck on the counter. Richard stood next to me. I said, "Hi, I need to cash my paycheck, please."

She asked, "ID please."

I laid Donna's ID card down. Richard smiled and told her, "That's a pretty blouse you are wearing."

The teller blushed. She picked up my ID card.

Richard asked her, "What do you call that shade of blue?"

I could answer Richard. It was cornflower blue. He didn't need my answer, though.

This time, as she blushed, her eyes blinked shut and she set my ID back down. I pocketed my ID. She picked up my paycheck. Not once had she looked back at me when holding my ID.

Richard's flirtatious rapport lasted while she pulled the cash from her drawer and counted out my money. As I picked my money up off her counter, she said, "Have a good weekend, Donna. See you next Friday."

She saw both of us the next Friday and the Friday after. Routinely, each visit went much the same as the time before.

How many more Fridays do I have to be Donna? I'm supposed to be Samantha.

Being Donna was too fake. We had been at the motel a month when I called a few different landlords who advertised apartments for rent.

"Honey," I said to Richard one evening over another boring cable TV show. "How happy are you here?"

He didn't take his gaze off the TV. "It's okay."

I rolled over, turning to him. "It's great you're working. It's keeping us in a room, but we need more."

"You called about some apartments," he said.

"It will take us a long time to save up enough for deposits to move in," I said. I soft punched my pillow, squishing it to get it just right, then propped it behind my head. Everything we did in that room was from the bed. Nothing else fit in the room. "Sweetie, are you happy here in Pennsylvania?"

"What about your job?" he asked.

I patted his big belly. "I'm not Donna. I need something different."

He touched my hand. "What are you thinking?"

"I'm thinking about all those telephone poles. Whenever we wait for a ride, you get your pocketknife out and carve our initials in. You always add 'from Alaska to Florida.' We may not be from Alaska, but we could go to Florida."

He turned his head away from the woman getting strangled in the TV show. His brown eyes looked at me and he asked, "Is that what you want? Florida?"

I answered, "Christmas is soon. Let's go to Florida."

CHAPTER 14

SAMANTHA, II

Florida-bound, we unfolded our map again, trying to make sense of the state highways out of Pennsylvania. Red leaves were still on the trees, frozen in time by icicles. The divided highway gave us little standing room, dropping off into a shoulder with soft snow. I double-checked my coat to make sure it was all buttoned up. Richard, now Josh, but still claiming to be Richard, said, "You've got us lost somewhere on Highway Six."

Soon a ride took us to Port Jervis. Although no longer lost on Highway 6, we still weren't sure where we were. Port Jervis crossed three state lines. We spent a night in our tent, hillside, still in Pennsylvania. Across the street was a small grocery store with a New Jersey address. Next door was a liquor store in New York state.

The next morning we moved along I-95 Southeast, out of Port Jervis, into New York City, and then southbound. Soon our beaten map seemed pointless. The greater Washington, DC area was a conglomeration of interstates in an unending circle. On foot and by thumb, we navigated tollbooths, junctions, and a sea of exit signs.

Sometimes a police car was in the string of bumper-to-bumper traffic. Those cops would get on their bullhorn. "No hitchhiking."

I'd relax my arm, let the cop car pass by, then stick my thumb out again. We had to hitchhike. No single ride took us far, whether in Delaware, Maryland, the DC area, or Virginia. Any driver on any expressway that pushed us farther south got us that much closer to Florida.

Into North Carolina, our late afternoon ride dropped us off in the downtown part of a city. We walked a few blocks then stopped at a newspaper stand. Richard hunched over and leaned his arms on it. My pack was much lighter. Across the street, teenagers loitered in clusters. Decayed buildings overshadowed small stores and businesses. Sea salt in the air bit my tongue, and a warm sticky breeze hid any hint of late November.

A guy in dirty clothes sauntered down our side of the sidewalk. He stopped when he got to us, and with a smugness in his smile, said, "Hi."

Our faces must have shown we were indecisive about where to turn in for the night. Quick to conversation, the newcomer pointed across the street and down about a half block. "That's where I stay. Over there. 'Used to be a Section Eight place."

Richard asked him, "Is it safe?"

"Sure," he answered. He explained, "Every night a cop runs through to get as many people out as he can, but if you lock yourselves up in a room, you'll be cool. He won't mess with you."

Richard looked at me and said, "It's an idea."

"Come on, I'll show you," he said. "You two party, don't you?"

"Yeah, I party," Richard answered, as he adjusted his pack's frame where its straps hugged his chest, and then took my hand. We followed the guy to the building he had pointed out. His room was on the ground floor, with one streak of evening sun where drapes parted in the middle. He waved his hand to direct us to take a seat on a trunk, while he sat in his rocking chair and scooted in closer to an upside-down barrel in front of us. He pushed some white stuff in the bowl of his bong, lit it, and drew a long breath. He handed the bong to Richard.

After a hit, Richard shrugged his shoulders. He seemed to be getting nothing out of this. The guy with the bong seemed oblivious. Richard thanked him, and we parted ways.

Flakes of paint and wallpaper hung from plastered walls through dank hallways. Dirt was caked in wall crevices. Food wrappers, used toilet paper, and empty tin cans lay about. Stained burgundy carpet had long ago lost its thread bearing. We took two flights of stairs to a long hallway and checked several rooms until we came across the perfect one.

Inside, we angled a heavy beat-up clothes dresser against the door. Kitchen and bathroom fixtures had black spots of rust where water had once dripped freely on its porcelain. Cobwebs lined corners of the one-room apartment. The bed still had blankets tucked in. Our room had a sliding glass door, which looked out onto a parking lot. I pulled the drapes back to let the late evening sunlight filter in. We had to save our flashlight batteries.

We laid our sleeping bag out on top of the bedding on the bed and slithered in for the night. When at Terry's motel, I had gotten used to sleeping in a real bed. It took only a few nights out on the open road to remind me how to sleep on grass, or a rocky bluff, or up under an interstate overpass. That dilapidated building was a welcome respite, both in comfort and in safety from anyone walking up on us.

Later, in the still quiet of the night, a thunderous bang from downstairs woke us up. It was the beat cop our acquaintance-friend had warned us about. Heavy footsteps ran the hallway below. Every door got banged on, and every so often we heard a door open to slam against the inside wall, and then a southern drawl commanded, "Get out. Get out. No trespassing."

From the floor below, he ran up the stairs to our floor. A big stick hit our door, but our barricade kept him at a running pace, as if he too were in a hurry to get out. I fell back to sleep in Richard's arms and woke the next morning to a clear sunny day, ready for us to hit the interstate again.

Had we stayed on I-95, it would have been a direct route into Florida. But we went where our rides took us, and where those drivers dropped us off. In the deep southern bowels of Georgia, we stood with thumbs erect on an unknown stretch of state highway. Leaves on magnolia trees grabbed any crisp breezes on this warm day in early December.

An older pickup truck pulled over for us. We tossed our packs in the bed of his truck and climbed onto the bench seat with him. He was a heavyset, middle-aged white man with a belly that hung out of his button-down shirt and open light jacket. When he said hello to us, it was in that southern drawl still new to us.

Richard returned his friendly greeting. "Hi, I'm Josh and this is Samantha."

I wasn't taken aback that he switched identities on me again. Casual times, not scrutinized by authority figures like cops, meant he could freely use his alias, Josh. In our friendly talk with our driver, we learned his name was Pastor Schick.

His pickup truck took us east and south along sparse state routes, giving us a new outlook on our diverse country. Whenever we saw a car pass by in the opposite direction, it was as if we had stepped back in time, each passing driver demanding a friendly wave. Peach and pecan and oak trees with overflowing moss, along with the magnolias, served as a canopy on that stretch of backroads. Any signs of metropolis life couldn't intrude on this route. Richard told our driver, "We're hoping to find a place on the beach to camp for Christmas."

Pastor Schick said, "You should try Fernandina Beach, where I live. It might not be the Florida Keys, but it's peaceful this time of year." As he drove out of another curved bend, into an unusually straight stretch of the road, I saw a tall skinny black man hitchhiking. Our minister friend stopped and picked him up. That put all four of us on one seat, but it was roomy enough.

The black man was much older than any of us, and sat quiet and reserved, yet polite. Our minister friend took him all the way to his house, not leaving him on the main road. He got out of the pickup, looked at Pastor Schick, and said, "Thank you, sir. That was mighty kind of you."

He then proceeded down his long driveway. Normally, skin color was not my first thought, but in that neck of the woods, as Pastor Schick explained to us after he let the man out, skin color came with a deep unchanging history in power balances between folks. Georgia's backwoods had hidden hollers of black folks who had never been outside of the area. They assumed the ingrained role as instilled in them by the generations who came before.

When Pastor Schick made me aware of the racial disparity in their social construct, it broadened my narrow understanding. Years earlier, under Steve's guiding values, my appreciation for multicultural differences hadn't influenced me in any adverse way. However, then and there, I became acutely aware of existing prejudices, which varied across our great big country. I believe Pastor Schick's values for human worth prevailed. Shortly after his time with us he built up a homeless shelter, which has grown exponentially in his community.

After seeing the black gentleman home, Pastor Schick's driving led us into the top northeastern corner of Florida. Leaving the hollers of Georgia behind, it was like we drove through a time warp. Bypassing Jacksonville, we arrived in his hamlet.

Like a well-photographed scene out of a coffee-table book, Fernandina Beach was a place all its own with quaint streets and picturesque houses. Elongated front lawns dotted its main drag. Our minister-friend pointed out his church, and then pointed straight ahead to the ocean which was in sight, just a half-mile farther.

Pastor Schick pulled into the parking lot where our road dead ended at a beachfront city park. "It was real nice ridin' with y'all. I hope to see you at church this Sunday morning if you decide to stay on 'til Christmas as you say."

Richard shook his hand. "Thank you so much for the ride and we might do that."

Pastor Schick pointed northward. "I think you two will find a good camping spot if you walk up thataway."

As we waved goodbye to him, we took his suggestion and with packs on our backs, began our hike. I walked beside Richard as he led. While we were farther south than our Tybee Island beach day, it was also later in the year. It was much colder on this oceanfront, too cold to kick off our shoes and layers of socks. I gripped Richard's hand. We stopped for a moment to breathe it in. I gazed at the vast, hazy blue-grey waves. Ships could be seen far off, and a walking pier, perhaps for fishing, was not far north of us.

We kept walking the sandy line to the north. Wherever we camped, it had to be off the beaten track for our stretch into Christmas week. While houses on the main street had full grassy lawns, houses along the beach had rocky sand at their backsides. The farther we walked, the less beachfront homes showed their faces. Two miles later, houses became nonexistent, leaving a greater expanse of sand dunes with overgrown sea oats.

Tumbleweed and sagebrush followed us, blowing in the light wind. It was an ideal place to stop. Had we kept walking, we would have hit the Georgia line before long. With a light dusting of snow all about us, we found an ideal spot to set up camp. Deep in the brush, natural weeds a foot or two tall did their job to keep us well hidden.

With three weeks until Christmas, we passed time with nature walks close to camp, and once weekly took a long walk to the local Winn-Dixie grocery store. Pastor Schick's church office was on our way when we walked to town, so we always stopped by for a visit. Sunday mornings, too, became a regular occurrence for us, and right away, I was baptized.

I had no real passion for finding Jesus or becoming religious. What I did have was a resource to strengthen my identity. Research had taught me that government offices often accepted baptismal certificates as supporting proof of one's identity. That minister and this church were a godsend. I told Richard, "You could get baptized, too. Pastor Schick knows you as Josh."

Richard shrugged me off. He wasn't as needy as me when it came to starting a new life. He wasn't going to let his relationship with his mom cease forever. The pictures he carried in his pack proved his loyalty to kin. Staying on the teetering edge, he was Josh in places it didn't matter and Richard where he had to have a legal identity to get something.

I was making a new life. As such, I was not an ex-con. I wasn't twice divorced, and I didn't have a history of four high schools or an accumulation of name changes. No photos, heirlooms, or keys tied me to that past. In my new identity, I accepted my limitations. The Salvation Army always turned me away from their soup kitchen. They required a Social Security card to get a meal. Reciting my number wasn't enough for them.

With a new name, however randomly selected, I had a birthdate to match my young appearance. I had a memorized Social Security number, which showed I was from Pennsylvania. I had a laminated ID card with a Pennsylvania address. My photocopied marriage certificate supported my name and birthdate. And, thanks to Pastor Schick, I had a certified baptismal certificate. Kym had evaporated. It was a start. I was Samantha Ann Mott, with Mills as my maiden name. My fresh start gave me hope to make something of myself, as Nana had hoped.

Unlike Richard's indecisiveness, once I became Samantha, there was no going back for me. The more I built up my identification, the stronger I became. This strength intensified in our next trip to the food stamp office. Back then, in the early '90s, the food stamp program hadn't yet become electronic for beneficiaries, so an in-person visit was needed each month wherever we were. Our benefits were always for one person—Richard.

In our walk to town that day, Richard started a discussion. He asked me, "Now that you got more ID, you think you could get food stamps, too?"

I answered, "I'm not afraid to try. We're as far away as we can be from Oregon."

We walked into their office. It was small, without any line. In other cities we had passed through it was common to have to take a number and wait. A bubbly round woman in a floral dress greeted us and offered us a seat across from her desk. Richard told her why he was there and then asked, "Can we add her to my benefits?"

Our caseworker asked for my ID. I handed her my ID card and baptism certificate. Being in a relaxed community absent of big-city problems likely swayed any hesitation a government worker might otherwise have had. She filled in lines on paperwork, writing down information from our IDs. All went well. I, Samantha, was declared Richard's dependent.

She pulled a binder down from a bookshelf next to her desk, turned to a page, ran her finger along a few lines, then looked up at us. "Considering your relationship to one another, here in Florida, under state guidelines, we consider you as married."

My eyes bugged. "Married?"

She answered, "Yes, married. You two have been cohabitating, sharing in expenses, and are now receiving government benefits together. As such, you are considered married, having equal rights and privileges to one another."

Richard looked straight ahead, over her shoulder, into thin air. "We're married."

I thought of Nana. She had been much older when she married for the third time.

♦ ❖ ♦

We held tight onto our December food stamps. Christmas was far off, and we were determined to have a good holiday dinner. The trip to the Winn-Dixie grocery store for frozen Cornish game hens had to be timed right. We relied on outdoor elements, with daytime highs in the upper thirties, as a slow thawing method, keeping the hens from going rancid.

Early Christmas morning, Richard stepped outside of our tent first. I sat at the open tent flap to put my shoes on, but dawdled as I looked out at the ocean. The sun had begun to show its face, first as a small ball of orange. Its rays stretched out like an octopus's arms to warm an icy blue expanse of endless rolling waves. We still had a dusting of snow on the ground, but no precipitation in the air, and not even a hint of gusty winds. It was a calm Saturday morning weather-wise at about thirty-three degrees.

I bundled up in a heavy, warm flannel shirt and put on my knit hat. Lastly, I gathered sticks, which had lain in our inside corner for a few days to dry out. With my armful of kindling, I stepped out and greeted Richard with a good morning peck. His skin was rough. He hadn't bothered with shaving.

Richard pointed to his large raincoat on the ground. "Put the kindling down there to keep it dry. Let me show you how we do this."

We patted the inside walls of the hole he had dug in the sand to firmly pack it, making it a secure pit. He arranged the kindling in our earth oven and lit it afire. Meanwhile, I prepared our potatoes, pricking holes in them, coating them with margarine and then wrapping each potato in tinfoil. The margarine would keep them from drying out while cooking.

Richard laid out two large sheets of tinfoil and laid one Cornish game hen on each. He used a stick of margarine, rubbing each hen well, inside and out. After adding seasoning that we had splurged on, he wrapped each hen in its tinfoil.

Once the fire sizzled down to a hot smolder, he laid our two hens on the bright orange coals in our oven and covered the pit with sea oat stems. An aromatic rosemary scent was released as our hens cooked. An hour into their cooking, he removed the sea oat stems, added our potatoes, then covered it back up. In our final dinner preparations, we heated up canned mixed vegetables in a small saucepan on our one-burner propane stove.

A driver had given us the stove. Before camping here, some nights on the open road were downright cold. When our brandy had worn off we'd wake up shivering, then turn the stove on for five minutes until we couldn't see our breath anymore. We rationed our use of the stove. Propane was a precious commodity. This day was different. It was Christmas.

Early afternoon, we loaded our plates and sat back against the outside wall of the tent. Ocean waves rolled with clapping echoes. Dolphins, whales, and big fish slapped about the deep water. Seagulls didn't bother traveling the beaten sagebrush tracks to check out what smelled so good. Those seagulls always stayed close to the tide.

My sweater and flannel shirt made me especially warm on this sunny day. But it didn't melt the sprinkled snow, which glistened. I couldn't ever remember having Cornish game hens that tasted so darn good. I was at peace, away from daily risks of the open highways. Even though we were homeless, Christmas 1993 gave me tranquility.

Early in the new year of 1994, our travels moved us slowly west and then north from Jacksonville. We were let out in Albany, Georgia, where our latest driver ended his trip. Hunkering down, we set up camp in a hidden holler under the interstate. The next day, a rainstorm rolled in. We stayed put, passing time over cards and cribbage marathons.

That night it rained more, and again the next day it rained. In yet another night of rain, we were awoken to the feeling of being in a busted waterbed. We scrambled to our feet as rain fell with intense fervor. Ankle-deep in rainwater, Richard grabbed my backpack, swung it onto his shoulder, and then grabbed his jeans from the foot of our bed and threw them on top of my pack. He next grabbed my shoes and shoved them into my hand. All in one motion, his right hand swooped up his own shoes and his left hand grabbed my free hand as we abandoned ship.

We waded at a brisk pace to come up out of the holler, and then crossed the street to the dark backside of a nearby motel. In their darkest corner to avoid being noticed, never mind that everyone should have been asleep at that ungodly hour, we changed into dry clothes. We added any warm overshirts we could find in my pack, which didn't have much to offer Richard.

At the convenience store next door, we bought a bottle of Night Train and then huddled under the overpass to wait out our dark rain. Our blood needed alcohol to get through the rest of the night. A few quick gulps of it took my shivering away.

Come late morning we walked to our camp's embankment. I stared down at the aftermath. Our tent and all it held was in knee-deep water. Richard said, "It's gonna take a few days for the water to recede."

"Shit, now what?" I asked.

Richard answered, "Let's head downtown. Find us something to eat and a place to help us with clothes and stuff. I don't want to do another night under that overpass without something to keep us warm."

On that walk, we stopped at a church and knocked on the door. Surely someone in their congregation had a spare blanket in their hall closet for us. Rather than the kindness that the Bible talks about, we were met with hostility. The woman who opened the door slammed it on us when she heard what we needed.

A social service agency gave us two sleeping bags. One was a Holly Hobby kid's bag. We ate at a soup kitchen and then returned to check on our camp. It was still swallowed whole in standing rainwater. We crossed the street and then followed railroad tracks into an industrial wasteland. "We got to bed down somewhere," Richard said.

I looked around, same as he was doing. Nothing looked promising. To the side of the tracks was a large graveled area. One work truck was parked nearby. Richard walked up to it and tried the doors. It was locked. We had slept in a parked truck once before, somewhere back in the Midwest. We had also slept in an unlocked camper trailer once. Richard opened the bottle of Night Train that we had spent our last three bucks on during our walk from downtown. "Here, ladies first."

I took the bottle and took a big swig of the bitter grape stuff, then handed it back to him. He took a sip, then put it back in my pack, which he was carrying. His pack was back in the flooded tent. "Over here," he said.

I followed him to the back end of the truck. He stepped up into the truck bed, then held his hand out to help me up. "Watch it, there's a huge blade in here."

"I see it. What kind of truck is this?" I asked. An arched blade about four feet long ran down the middle of the six-foot open bed of the truck. It was only about six inches thick and a foot or so high.

He answered, "I don't know. Something they use for construction work or gravel moving or something." He sat down on one side of the truck bed and opened his arms out. "We each got a sleeping bag and there's enough room if we each take a side."

We set our packs down and took our shoes off. Richard bedded down in his Holly Hobby sleeping bag and I crawled into the other. We passed the bottle of Night Train between us, once again warming our blood so we could sleep the night through. Safe and sound with Richard as my protector close by, I fell asleep next to a big huge blade.

The next day was much like the prior day, with soup kitchens and bedding down with Night Train and a truck blade. By day three, while the water had not fully receded, our camp was on relatively solid ground. However, it would be wet getting down to our campsite. Much of the land was still waterlogged. Richard put my backpack on, letting it rest high up on his back. He had our rolled bedding tied on top of the pack. "Let's go. Let's try this."

Pushing tree limbs aside, we started downhill. The water got thicker. I let myself sink, partly swimming, partly wading to make it to the gully where our campsite was. A black hairy thing swam past me. "Eww."

Richard, who was farther ahead, looked back at me. "What is it?"

I hollered, "An otter or a beaver or something."

At the bottom of the embankment, only a few puddles were left to conquer.

Together, we pulled everything out of our tent, took stock of what condition our stuff was in, and changed into jeans that weren't soaked. The jeans we wore to get down to the gully needed to be wrung out. We hung rope from one tree to another and then hung up our clothes and gear to dry out as best as they could.

We couldn't take stuff to a laundromat. That cost money, and besides, it would be a cumbersome feat. We would have had deep water to cross before even attempting to find a laundry place. Later that week, our stuff was in much better condition than when we had found it. Deep water leading back to the road was gone, having sunk into the earth below. We would likely pack up and head out in a day or two. For now, we decided to come up out of our gully for a trip to the convenience store.

Stepping up onto the road, we stopped and looked across the way. A woman was standing at the interstate off-ramp by herself. She held a cardboard sign. Resting from our hike up, we kept watching. Some cars stopped and passed cash through their windows to her.

In the early 1990s, working the homeless sign was not completely unheard of in smaller cities, but neither was it a common practice. Thus far, we had gotten along fine without needing to resort to that. In Richard's past hitchhiking travels, he wasn't homeless or dead broke. He was simply getting from his mom's place in Oregon to his dad's place in California, and back again.

Social services had often helped us so far when we asked for it. But when we could, we avoided them. They usually required something in return, whether showing ID, passing a screening test, or attending a church service beforehand—or as we called it, "sing for your dinner."

It's normal for homeless folks to be expected to sing hymns to Jesus before eating at a soup kitchen. Homeless shelters are also commonly set up to separate genders, and for good reason, however, many couples lose their sense of security when separated from their loved one.

After watching the woman with the sign a little while longer, she looked over at us, smiled, then relaxed her arm and left her post.

Richard smiled back. She crossed the street and walked up to us. "Hi, how are you guys doing?"

I ran my fingers through my hair to try to tidy my look. It had been days since we had clean tap water to bathe with. Richard did the talking for us, explaining our situation.

She pointed down the street and said to us, "My husband and I are staying in a room at that motel. I make enough working the sign to keep us in a room." She shifted her look and asked me, "You ever work the sign?"

I blushed. "No."

She said, "Oh girl, you got to work the sign. But you have to work it. Not fly it or hold it but work it. I'll show you how." She looked back at Richard. "You good with that? If I show you guys how she can work it?"

Richard turned his head to face me. "It's up to you."

Looking at Richard, then her, I answered, "Sure."

With a black marker from our supplies and a piece of used cardboard we found, she had me write out in big fat letters: *Homeless, Hungry. Please Help. God Bless.*

You might think there's nothing to it—stand there, hold the sign, rake in the money. But to work it, you have to know where to find the hotspots, where to stand, and when to stop. You need to know which direction to face, plus the best way to reply to any number of crazy comments. Long past Albany, a lady brought me two loaded hotdogs, two donuts, and hot coffee. She kindly told me, "Oprah told me to do this."

Food, cash, and clothing were among the items I'd go on to receive as I continued to work the sign in our travels. Some items were stranger than others. In Paducah, Kentucky, a woman dropped off two huge forty-gallon trash bags full of clothes as if I were the local thrift store. In Mississippi I was offered a joint, but turned it down. Money from working the sign kept us stocked in supplies like toothpaste, deodorant, razors, tobacco, candles, and batteries for our radio and flashlight.

If I had an especially profitable day working the sign, and if it had been a while since our last shower, we'd spend twenty-five dollars on a cheap single motel room. That let us kick back, relax, enjoy TV and a soft bed to sleep in—what normal folks took for granted.

But on that day in Albany, our newfound friend set me up in her spot on the interstate. She explained, "My husband and I are moving on to Atlanta tomorrow, so this spot is yours for the taking."

That afternoon, I stood and faced the traffic as it left the interstate. They had a stop sign before turning onto the main drag. My disheveled hair and dirty fingernails could only support my homeless claim. I stared ahead at the interstate. A car drove down the off-ramp. The driver turned his head, looked at me, then looked back at the road in front of him. Shame engulfed me.

Another car drove down the ramp, and this time, the driver stared at me while missing his turn at the stop sign. I looked back at the driver and held my sign tight, turning my body to show him what my sign said. A third car was coming my way, so I turned my body to face the new car. It stopped. The passenger rolled down the window and reached her arm out to me. I approached her. She handed me a dollar bill. "God bless you."

Taking the money, I said, "Thank you." Stepping backward, I returned to my post. The car drove on. I couldn't smile. I had to look pitiful. There was nothing to smile about. Over the next two hours, I watched as some cars passed me by, and I thanked those who stopped and gave me money. After several handouts I lost count of the cash I was reeling in. I still wasn't smiling though. I was pitiful.

I jonesed for a cigarette but didn't dare light up. I didn't want people to think I could afford to smoke. They weren't even real cigarettes. We were always scraping together cash to buy a seven-dollar bag of tobacco and papers to last both of us for a couple weeks or more.

At the end of my full afternoon, we bought a bottle of Night Train and sandwiches from the convenience store. At camp, we counted out my cash. I had made $240 for us. It reminded me of my early days with Jim, when I had raked in $8,000 from the stolen ATM card. But like it was with that first haul with Jim, my afternoon working the sign must have been beginner's luck. Any day thereafter, it brought us less than fifty dollars, and usually closer to thirty. Sometimes I made less than ten bucks.

Thanks to my take-in from working the sign, we washed a load of clothes at the laundromat. Our socks and underclothes were especially in need of a good washing. Our socks could be turned inside out only so many times before we had no choice but to retire them to the dirty clothes bag. Our jeans hadn't been washed since we left Terry's motel back in Pennsylvania. That was months before, or literally the year before. Our jeans were soiled to holes in the knees from the daily grind of dust and dirt on the open highway.

We repacked our bags to hitchhike out of Albany. That was our plan. Hooked on the money I could make, I told Richard, "Let me work the sign an hour before we head out."

Back at my post on the interstate off-ramp, I stayed alert to my surroundings. A man got out of his pickup truck at the convenience store. He walked up to me. I wasn't scared. Richard was watching from under the overpass. "Hi there, young lady. I have a warehouse, and if you'd be willing to help me out, I'd be willing to help you out."

I kept holding my sign upright, facing traffic. This man hadn't given me anything yet, and any time lost to talking was time lost that could be spent on cars stopping to give me money. He continued, "My warehouse is overstocked. Insurance doesn't cover the back room unless I have security in place."

I looked away from the traffic and faced him to listen to his story.

"It will be a week before I can get that stock moved out," he said.

I relaxed my arm, lowering my sign to give him my full attention, then waved Richard over. It would take him a few minutes to cross the street and get to me.

The man looked behind him to see why I was waving, then kept talking. "I'm there during the day. So are my workers. Night is different. There's an empty room you could sleep in during the day if you'd stay awake and guard that extra stock at night. I could pay you. My insurance carrier will cover that back room if I have a guard on duty."

Richard walked up to us. "I'm her husband."

With an all-business attitude, we discussed his offer. He explained further, "I have no problem with both of you helping me, but I can only pay one of you."

On a handshake, we agreed to meet up with him at his warehouse at six, later that day. We were familiar with walking the industrial side of town. That's where we had found the truck with the blade where we'd slept.

Our job lasted ten days, well, actually ten nights. We slept during day hours while workers were on site. Our sleeping room was a dark, square, windowless room, situated smack in the middle of a huge warehouse. If the room hadn't been near airtight, forklifts and commotion would have kept me awake. Workers left at six each day, which was our time to start our guard duty. When the job was over, our boss wrote out a $300 check. On our way to the interstate, Richard cashed it.

Leaving Georgia, our rides took us through the bayous of Alabama, Mississippi, Louisiana, and into Texas. On I-10, we were let out at a Dallas truck stop. Arriving after dark, we didn't see much of Dallas, save for the beautiful sunrise the next morning.

It had been a clear night when we laid our bedrolls out on the lawn at the farthest edge of that lot. We had fallen asleep sober under a blanket of countless bright stars. Come morning, the night sky was replaced by the sun, which rose ever so gallantly with streams of golden orange light outstretched as far as we could see, promising a warm March day.

Out of Dallas, our next two rides moved us along US-75 North, across a wide corner of Oklahoma. We pushed on and straddled state lines all the way up I-29. At a drop-off point in Fargo, North Dakota, we thanked our driver and set off on foot along a main drag.

Our eyes scanned both sides of the street. We needed to make camp somewhere for the night. And we had no idea where the next day's travel would lead us, other than we couldn't keep going north into Canada. A white cop car with local city markings passed us, right alongside drivers who seemed to mosey. He pulled into a driveway entry on our side of the street, then got out of his car and approached us. "Hello there," he said.

We stopped walking. Richard tugged at the weight of his pack and said, "Hi."

The cop bobbed his head toward Richard's pack. "You two are quite the travelers."

"Yeah, we're just passing through." I could hear in Richard's voice that he wasn't in the mood for chitchat.

The cop scratched his head, looked Richard up and down, and then suggested dinner. "Have you two eaten yet tonight?"

"No," Richard answered for us.

"Let me buy you dinner. There's a place down the road," he said as he pointed his finger.

Richard turned his head to look at me with a blank stare. I smiled back at Richard.

The cop said, "Come on, let me give you a lift, buy you both dinner, and see if we can find you a place to sleep for the night."

The cop took us to a diner and we sat down together at a booth. The cop ordered coffee for all of us and then the waitress took our order. While we waited, the cop asked, "If you have ID I can see, I'll get you lined up with a place to sleep tonight."

We showed him our IDs. The cop called into his office from a two-way radio that was clipped to his belt. "I have two people here, a Mr. Richard E. Park, DOB six—twenty-one—nineteen fifty-nine, and a Ms. Samantha Ann Mills, DOB eight—seven-teen—nineteen seventy-three, who need shelter tonight." A few minutes later, a reply came in, giving him an address. After dinner, he drove us to the house.

An older lady answered the door when the cop rang the doorbell. "Hello, I'm Mrs. Carver. You two need to rest up for the night?"

"Please. I'm Richard and this is my wife, Samantha."

"Come in out of the cold." She let us in and showed us the spare bedroom. We unloaded our packs on the bed. I washed my face and hands and combed my windblown hair. Joining our host in the front living room, it was as if I had stepped back into Nana's White Room, except for the splash of pink. White lace and hints of rosy pinks adorned Mrs. Carver's living room.

Mrs. Carver smiled at us. Richard spoke up first. As they chatted in small talk, she interrupted him, looking my way. "Honey, you must be tired. Why don't you sit and relax? There are some magazines on the coffee table if you like to read."

I sat down. She turned on a lamp for me. I could see fine, though, with the open drapes behind the couch I was sitting on. I thumbed through a glossy magazine. Richard and Mrs. Carver kept talking. Two magazines later, the cop pulled back into her driveway. Richard looked at me with a cold, hard stare. There was nothing we could do except find out what he wanted. She opened her door. "Mrs. Carver, I'm sorry, but it's best these folks don't stay with you."

The cop looked at Richard. "Mr. Park, we ran your ID. You have quite a history. I need you two to get your packs and please leave." The cop waited while we gathered our stuff, then stepped outside on the porch. The cop pointed to the right end of the street and said, "If you walk that way, you'll get back to town. You need to find your own place to stay. I'm sorry. I hope you understand that with your criminal history, we can't let you stay with Mrs. Carver."

The cop said nothing about a warrant for Richard, or his absconsion from parole. In that era, information sharing across police jurisdictions was limited. Usually they had to be specific in their request, unless it was a state neighboring the origin state from which the warrant was issued.

We did as the cop said and walked away. The cop stayed behind, talking with Mrs. Carver. We found ourselves an overnight camp spot, buying a quart of beer on our way. We pitched our tent but didn't bother with any card games. Instead, we sat cross-legged just outside our tent, our backs to it. The sun was setting. We passed the beer back and forth, taking turns drinking.

I stared into Richard's left eye. I could usually fake it well when looking into people's eyes, although I have but one good eye to look with. That time was different. I was not about to fake anything. Focused on my stare down, I said, "That was not good."

Richard looked at me with the teddy bear softness he was good at giving. "I know."

"I mean it. That was not good," I insisted. "I refuse to go back to prison."

Richard handed me the beer. "Yeah, but we got out of it okay."

I waited to take a swallow. "So what? What if they dig deeper into your ID? He could be pulling up more stuff right now. What if he comes looking for us and finds us?"

I shivered. To put anything or anyone before my freedom was not good. My secret had to be most important in my life. I took a swallow. Nana would agree with me. She never let anyone or anything come before herself. When back in the Arkansas Tent City camp, I couldn't survive without Richard as my partner in such a dejected existence. That was before I had ID.

I handed the bottle back to Richard and waited for a reply. He didn't say anything. His eyes no longer rested where I could affix my line of sight. I reemphasized my plea. "Never again will we let a cop talk us into such a thing."

"Okay. Are you going to be all right?" he asked me. He added, "You look stiff as a board. Here, have another drink."

He skipped his turn at taking a drink while I took the quart of beer from him. My only answer to his question was to remind him, "I refuse to go back to prison." I turned my head the other way and gulped. I gave him the bottle back and swatted at some flying insect. I looked out ahead of me and away from him.

Moments passed before he said anything. "Hey, let's get out of here for a while. Go for a walk."

"Where to?" It wasn't like us to leave camp after dark. Once settled, we were settled in for the night.

He answered, "That lady said the carnival is in town, over by the grocery store."

Our quart of beer was gone anyway. We got up and ventured into the carnival. I envied the Ferris wheel high in the sky, all alit with yellow and bright blue bulbs. The rides were too expensive on our homeless budget. People shrieked over their fun.

Richard tried his luck at darts for a prize, only to lose. *What am I going to do with a tall stuffed giraffe?* I thought.

At some ring-toss game, Richard worked his way into a conversation with the person who ran that booth. Looking at Richard, he told us, "We could use help running the carnival. Show up tomorrow morning, help us break down, and then you can hitch a ride from one of the workers to the next place we set up. Pay is twenty dollars cash a day."

"Hey, thanks for the tip. Maybe we will. It was nice talking with you," Richard said. He took my hand and we walked down the lane. Other games were going on. He tightened his grip on my hand and said, "It's an idea."

"That's what we need to do. Join the carnival. I don't want to be standing on the on-ramp tomorrow like a sitting duck for the cop to find us before we get a ride out of town," I said.

The next morning, we broke camp early and joined the carnival crew, helping to break down rides and booths. It hurt in a good way to pull down poles that held the booths up. The food concession manager told me, "You have a job with me."

Meanwhile, Richard was recruited to run one of the kiddie rides, which was a perfect match with his good wit and smile. We went where the carnival took us. Another couple who also worked the carnival gave us a ride to each new spot. They lived out of a small trailer, which they hauled behind their car. At each new spot, we pitched our tent on the pavement or gravel next to their trailer.

In the beginning, it didn't matter much to Richard and me where our next town was. From the Dakotas, our carnival traveled through Michigan, but then we turned the corner and worked our way back west and into Montana. Montana was full of casinos and bars. That's where we'd all gather after breaking down rides in one town, to get ready to travel to the next town. Montana was also awfully close to Oregon.

It was the spring of 1994 and my new birthdate meant I would turn twenty-one in August. Yet I never got carded at any one of the many casinos when I was just one in a crowd of carnies. In one casino visit, I drank more than I should have. Or the alcohol hit me harder than usual. My demeanor shifted from casual friendliness. I slobbered to Richard, "Are we in Montana?"

He answered, "Yeah, baby, we're in Montana."

I whined, "We shouldn't be in Montana. We gotta get far away." I slammed another gulp, then yelled at Richard, "What the fuck are we doin' here? Why ya bring me here?"

The more I drank, the more irked I became over the loss of our eastward journey. I wasn't angry at Richard but expressed my anger at him. When I came to the next morning after my outlandish behavior, I looked at Richard, demoralized. "That was stupid of me last night, huh?"

He rubbed his eyes, waking up the same as me. "You did make a scene."

I said, "I don't like being this close to Oregon—"

"Yeah, your screaming and crying made the others wonder what you were hollerin' about."

"I know, I know." Only mere days after promising myself I would do anything and everything to keep from going back to prison, my secret had been subjected to my risky behavior. While I nursed my hangover in my self-made rude awakening, I said to Richard, "Remember what you said to me, back in our apartment, just before we left Salem?"

"What?" he asked.

"Remember?" I looked out at the carnival equipment that needed to be set up. "You said there's gotta be a better place for you and me. Let's get out of here and go find that place."

CHAPTER 15

SAMANTHA MOTT

"Let me buy you coffee at McDonald's—we don't see your kind out here often," a cop told me.

Facing oncoming traffic on a business spur in Marshfield, Missouri, I stood on the sidewalk and held my homeless sign for everyone to see. McDonald's was close by, encouraging a few handouts at a dollar apiece that morning, but my next ogler had been that traffic cop. I had no room to argue with a cop, so I relaxed my stance.

Watching from afar, Richard walked over to us when the cop showed up. "Hello, I'm her husband," Richard told him.

The officer said, "Hi, like I told your wife, let me buy you some coffee."

Richard answered, "Thank you. I should wait out here with our packs. Sometimes places don't like it when we walk in with our backpacks."

"Fine, fine," the cop replied.

Richard put my pack on an outdoor picnic table and stood nearby while the cop and I went in for our coffee. Back at the table, our cop told us, "Sit. Enjoy your coffee."

We sat down to our coffee as the cop kept standing. Richard's pack leaned against the picnic table, too big to place on the table. Akin to a somewhat grouchy grumble, Richard drew a breath that sounded like a sigh of relief, although I knew better. I knew he knew what was coming next.

The cop opened his clipboard and pulled out a pen. "What are your names?"

But I didn't foresee what came after that. Richard replied, "Joshua Mott and this is my wife, Samantha." That was the first time he had ever used his alias with an authority figure.

The cop asked, "And do you have some ID I can see?"

Richard, now Josh, reached for his wallet from his back pocket. It was battered and stained and held more photos than ID. He handed over the ID card I'd made him back in Moosic. I did the same with my ID.

The cop went about his business while we sat and sipped ever so slowly on our coffee. It wasn't that we wanted to dawdle, but the McDonald's coffee was scalding hot and I feared I'd burn my tongue on it. A couple spoonfuls of instant coffee in a mug of stale water from our jug was what we were used to in the morning.

The cop wrote our names down on his pad, then handed our IDs back. "Sit, enjoy your coffee. Take a break. After that, though, I need you to move on. We have a city ordinance against panhandling. You ought to try your luck in Springfield. It's a much bigger city and they're set up with places to help."

As he closed his clipboard, we nodded our heads yes, and then heard, "Uh, excuse me."

It was a young man in blue jeans, a buttoned blue-checkered shirt, and a necktie who interjected as he approached us. "Hi, I'm Mr. Fairchild and I'm with the *Marshfield Mail*."

Mr. Fairchild sounded out of breath to me, as if the walk across the parking lot was too much for him. Our cop looked up and smiled at him. They exchanged handshakes, as if the cop was gladly handing us off to him. The new person then asked our cop, "Is it okay if I talk to them a bit? I'm hoping to understand their situation, that is if you're done talking with them."

The cop looked down at us and smiled. "By all means, they're all yours."

Mr. Fairchild asked, "May I sit?"

"Sure," Richard replied.

The cop said, "Have a good day," as he waved goodbye to us and walked off.

We answered Mr. Fairchild's questions to satisfy his curiosity about our homeless life. He then took a picture of me holding my sign. To get both of us in the picture, I had to stay seated. I didn't like that. I never worked my sign sitting down. That would show laziness. Later, our article appeared in their weekly newspaper, but with a few inaccuracies.

After we parted ways with Mr. Fairchild, Richard and I headed to the interstate on-ramp. As we passed time, waiting for a ride out of Marshfield, I asked Richard, "Springfield?"

He answered, "I know, we've been there before."

The time before we'd come from the south, up out of Arkansas. This time, we were working our way through Missouri after leaving the southwest corner of Kentucky. This time we could stay.

"The cop had a point," I said to Richard. Then, seeing an opportunity for persuasion, I added, "They do have The Missouri Hotel there. You did great showing the cop your Joshua ID. You can do that again. Maybe we could get a place there."

Richard said, "Your ID shows your maiden name of Mills, not my name of Mott. Remember, we have to prove we're married to get a free room there."

"No problem, we'll show them the copy of the marriage certificate I made," I said.

"I know, but I don't know. Are you sure that's what you want to do?" he asked me.

With more coaxing than obvious enthusiasm, I answered him, "Sure, yeah, don't you want to? I mean, aren't you getting tired? We could use a long rest."

Richard repeated himself, "Yeah, I guess, but I don't know."

"Hey, you got to enjoy the Sturgis Bike Rally and I got to touch the Atlantic Ocean. We've done a lot," I said.

I let him stew in silence. A car slowed in front of us, but the driver raised his hand in a gesture that meant, *I'm only going some short ways.*

I broke the silence. "We're halfway across the country, far from Oregon. We'd be safe here in Missouri. I'd like us to try settling down for a while. The Missouri Hotel could really help us with that."

"I'm not ready for a shelter. Let's just see what happens," Richard said.

"Okay." I conceded to him, but not to myself.

We stood silently, thumbs erect. Several minutes later, Richard turned his head away from traffic, looked at me, and said, "I mean, if you really want to try settling down, cool, but not in a shelter yet. So let's just—" But before he could finish, a mid-sized car pulled over, about ten yards from where we stood. We ran for it and Richard opened the passenger door.

"Hi, how far are you going?" the driver asked us.

"Springfield," Richard answered.

A few hours later, our driver let us out where I-44 and State Highway 160 intersected. The Missouri Hotel was on the east side of town. Our driver was headed west. Underneath the highway intersection was a deep crevice of dense woods and a creek. We set up camp there.

The next day, we came up out of our holler, bound for a two-mile walk to downtown where The Missouri Hotel sat. Our walk was cut short in panic as the air filled with tornado sirens that rang nonstop. People urged us to get somewhere safe quickly, blurting at us in passing, "A tornado is coming."

We didn't have tornados in Oregon. What I knew of tornados

was what I learned from Dorothy in *The Wizard of Oz*. I knew munchkins weren't real, but the beginning of the movie was what I remembered well. I had a frightening memory etched in me of a bicycle and Toto the dog flying in dizzying circles, helpless and lost in the eye of a tornado. I was scared.

Following a quick stop at a corner store, the clerk telling us, "Careful out there," we returned to the safety of our camp. Richard opened the forty-ounce Olde English Ale we had bought at the store. Below the deafening blow of sirens, we sat stunned and downed our beer. The more I drank, the more scared I got. I thought only pot made me scared—not alcohol. Usually I got brazenly courageous when drinking. Not so with visions of Toto the dog.

Above us, through the treetops, I saw the sky darkening to a deep grey with a competing array of indescribable colors. Richard took the last gulp, and wiping his lips with his hands, said, "Let's find out what's going on."

To appease his curiosity, we steadfastly climbed up and out, to the backside of a Waffle House. People still went about their business. I guess people still needed to eat.

We walked in and sat down to some coffee and a little something to eat. There, we found safety in numbers and solace in others, both diners and waitresses. They explained it wasn't a tornado, but a bad storm with the possibility of a tornado. "Oh-h-h," I said.

◆ ❖ ◆

The next day we made it to The Missouri Hotel and were interviewed by a caseworker who was a nun, although it wasn't a religious place. She photocopied our IDs as Joshua Mott and Samantha Mills, along with our marriage certificate, and placed them in her file on us. She assigned us a room where we'd share a bathroom with the adjoining room.

Without hesitation, I moved into action the next day. The Missouri Hotel was in the bad part of town, but it couldn't compare to some parts of the country we'd been through—New York City, or that city in North Carolina with the abandoned Section Eight apartment building. Those places were bad. Commercial Street in Springfield was a poppy field compared to those places. Self-assured, I was brave if not anxious to navigate my way to a new history and new future as a new woman. I was Samantha.

For starters, I used the public library to photocopy a page I found in a book, and then altered it, same as I had altered the marriage certificate. If asked for my Social Security card, I could show this document. It showed my Social Security number as Samantha, and that I had applied for a duplicate Social Security card, which needed to be mailed to me.

Before Springfield, many times as I worked the sign, people had yelled, "Get a job."

But getting a job, a real job, requires proving one's identity. That is federal law, supported by state laws. A contact phone number boosts your employability, yet that was before people carried cell phones. Many homeless people don't have ID, and for reasons other than my reason. A homeless person is at greater risk of theft, of possessions being ruined in a rainstorm, or being damaged by rough handling from not having any place for safekeeping. Also, homeless people are not as likely to renew or update expired documents. That costs money. Facing these hurdles, it can be challenging for a homeless person to get a legit job.

Over lunch in the soup kitchen, a young woman who sat across from us at the end of a table said, "Tyson's is hiring. It's a turkey plant. You need to have your own boots, though. See, like these." She brought her leg out from under the table and showed me her rubber rain boots.

I went to our caseworker, the nun, and she assured me I'd receive boots if hired by Tyson's. That same afternoon, I went to Tyson's. It was a twenty-block walk in warm weather. After completing the application and showing my Pennsylvania ID and supporting documents to prove my identity, I was hired.

Each day on the job was the same routine, with little variety. Standing in an assembly line with a conveyor belt going by, I'd reach for a dead turkey. It was already plucked and skinless. My job was to use my scalpel to scrape fat off that turkey, then put it back on the conveyor belt to send down to the next person, then reach for the next turkey. I wore rubber gloves, and over those, metal gloves to protect me from the scalpel.

While outside temperatures climbed into the eighties in that month of May, inside was a freeze zone. Long johns under my jeans were a must for me, and every other day I switched to my other sweatshirt. A heavy plastic apron covered my whole front side, and the rubber boots my caseworker gave me completed my outfit.

At the end of each work day, I hosed turkey guts off my apron and boots and then put those in my locker. Then I had my twenty-block walk back to our hotel, where I'd meet Richard in line for dinner. Soon after, I'd fall fast asleep.

The work was hard, but I was determined to make it work. If I could make a pleasant moment, I did. In lunch breaks shared with some of my coworkers, we sat outside to soak up the sunshine. I'd eat my packed sandwich and apple or orange, provided by The Missouri Hotel, while we laughed at turkeys who escaped their demise to run free on the sidewalk. Sometimes, a confused headless turkey would join us, running in circles.

Payday was every Friday at an hourly salary of $7.25. Most other jobs in the area paid four or five dollars an hour, but this hard work paid well. When I got my first paycheck, Richard wanted to see it. I showed it to him and said, "I'm not ready to cash it yet. We have everything we need here at the hotel and we need to save our money to get our own place."

"Whatever," was his only reply.

The only thing he needed money for, and it was more of a want than a need, was more beer. He had money coming in from donating plasma, so if he had to drink, he could do it with his own money. I worked hard, very hard, for my money. All I did was work, soak in the tub, and sleep. The work was exhausting. I'd survive this work. I was going to get a life. I was perfectly okay with the hard work and walking twenty blocks home with turkey guts all over me. In the end it would pay off.

Walking back to the hotel from work each day, I chatted with anyone I saw out on front porches. Inside the week of my second paycheck, I saw a "For Rent" sign on an old house that had been converted into four apartments. I checked it out and said I'd be back on Friday, payday.

On Friday, Richard met me at work so I could show him the apartment I found. Spacious, it was much bigger than the place we had back in Salem. It came with a back porch and a shared front porch. The front door needed a padlock to lock it. Splotches of yellow plaster and red paint covered nail holes and dents throughout. Otherwise, it was painted green, I think. I didn't mind the different colors. It seemed perfect to me. Richard, who was now going by the name of Josh everywhere, agreed as we talked with our new landlord.

Our partially furnished apartment came with a bed, dresser, kitchen table and a couch. To add class to our colorful walls, we got free throwaway promotional posters from several music stores. Joe Cocker, Kurt Cobain, Elvis Costello, and Axl Rose adorned our walls.

My weekly paychecks continued to pay our rent, month after month. Each night I came home dog-tired. I'd take a bath to wash off turkey juice that permeated my skin, then ate dinner and drank a beer as I watched *Jeopardy* and *Wheel of Fortune* on TV.

The central time zone put all primetime TV shows on an hour

earlier than the rest of the country. My two favorite shows, the only shows I watched, were on during the six to seven hour. Ten minutes after, I was asleep. In the mornings, I woke up early, splashed water on my face, brushed my teeth, got dressed, and did it all over again. There was no point in a daily shower. By first break, I'd reek of turkey guts. Richard was in his own world—a drunk.

I had no energy to do anything other than my tiring routine, and yet at times I came home to find I had to deal with Richard's drunkenness. My only reprieve was when he'd go to jail overnight on a PI charge. That meant he was out and about, but too drunk to be out, and got picked up for drunken disorderliness, or PI—public intoxication.

I soon quit wondering where he was when he didn't come home for the night. I knew he was in jail again. We didn't have a phone for him to call home to tell me. We figured we didn't need a phone since we didn't have any friends to call. Thankfully, he stayed true to his identity as Joshua Axl Mott in everything he did, jail time included.

When our six-month apartment lease was up, we moved into a nicer apartment. And I traded in my job for a new one. It was only $5.15 an hour, but the turkey job had done its job. I had pulled us up out of homelessness and I welcomed my new sit-down job on swing shift at Buyer's File, a market research firm.

I had fudged my way through the doors of Tyson's without a Social Security card. At Buyer's File I did the same. By that time, I had acquired a Missouri State ID card, letting go of the unofficial Pennsylvania ID. I showed my ID, which was barely glanced at. I wasn't asked for my Social Security card. Instead, I was waved to my assigned desk.

Our new apartment was in a better neighborhood, one without liquor stores on every corner. Richard kept drinking, though, and when he disappeared overnight, he didn't come home the next day. He was gone three or four nights in a row until he'd finally pop back in. After a few rounds of this, he came home on a Saturday afternoon. Casually strolling in, he said, "Hi."

"Hi," I said, "where have you been?"

"Sorry," he said, "we should talk." He sounded sober.

"Let's go to the kitchen table. You want some coffee?" I asked.

Richard took his coat off and tossed it on a chair. "I'll take a soda if we have any."

We settled in at the table. I lit a cigarette, took a sip of my coffee, and looked across the table at him.

Richard said, "You've probably been wondering where I've been all these nights."

"Yes, are you having an affair?" I asked.

"Her name is Grace," Richard said as he ran his fingers through his hair. He didn't have it pulled back in a rubber band this time. His hair looked clean, like he had just got out of a shower. Usually it was greasy.

"I came home to get my stuff. I can show you where she lives so you know where to find me. She's a block over," Richard said.

With his arm bent at the elbow, he pointed to the street behind our apartment complex.

"She doesn't know you as Richard, does she?" I asked.

"No." He lit his cigarette and then exhaled. "Grace knows me as Josh. I know you're scared shitless of getting found out. I wouldn't do that to you. Shit, with as many PIs that I'm racking up, I have to stay Josh. If the cops find out who I am, I'm on the next plane back to Oregon in handcuffs. Like you, no one needs to know about us." Richard smiled his teddy bear look at me. "It's our secret. I promise you that."

"I'll be okay," I said. "I'm so used to you being gone anyway."

Richard patted the top of my hand as I reached for the ashtray. "We'll stay friends. I care about you."

I brought my cigarette up to my mouth, letting his hand fall away. He said, "I want the best for you. You got what it takes. Me, I can't keep up with you. You do what you need to do. Me, I need to move in with Grace."

A year earlier we had sat on a Florida beach together over Christmas dinner. He'd be with his girlfriend, Grace, for Christmas 1994. I kept the last name Mott. It had been difficult enough to build my identity around that last name, and it was a fine name. There was no need for me to try to take back the name Mills.

I was Samantha Ann Mott, twenty-one years old. I was originally from Pennsylvania. I repeated my story so many times that it became my truth. Life was wide open for me.

◆ ❖ ◆

In early May that next spring, 1995, I was on a morning walk. Two guys were in a yard, pulling weeds or flinging worms or something like that. I stopped and watched. We chatted before I continued on my way. Where I lived must have come up in conversation. Only a few mornings later, one of the two guys showed up at my doorstep. I opened the door. It was the good-looking one of the two. He combed his fingers through his sandy-blond hair, letting his hair feather to the side. He smiled and said, "Hi, remember me?"

"Yes," I said, "you're the guy who was picking worms."

He laughed. His smile widened. "It's John, and I was helping my friend get fishing worms."

His smile seemed catchy. I smiled back. "I remember. You want to come in for coffee?"

"Sure, coffee sounds good," he said.

We settled into the living room, him in a chair and me on the couch. He was young, probably in his late twenties. Good-looking, too. Handing him his coffee, I asked, "So, is there good fishing around here?"

John answered, "On the James River. You're not from around here, are you?"

"I've been here a year now." I stopped short in my answer and took a sip of my coffee.

"Where from?" John asked.

"PA. Pennsylvania, that is. I like my job here, though. You work?"

John spooned more sugar into his coffee. I had probably made it too strong. Anything I drank had to be strong. "No, don't work. I help folks out whenever I can. I'm on Social Security and I can't pull in an income to get my checks. I have bipolar disorder."

"What's that?" I asked.

"It's a fancy word," John explained. "It has something to do with my moods. Usually, I'm fine. Supposed to be on meds, too, but I don't need them, so I don't take them."

Good thing my coffee was on the coffee table. A buzzing sound startled me. John looked down at his hip. He was wearing clean, neat jeans. He pushed a button on something he was wearing on his waist and the beeping stopped. "It's my pager," John said. "It's how my family gets ahold of me if they need me to call. It's a friend of mine. I told him I'd help him with some stuff today."

Looking up from his pager, John asked me, "You got plans Friday night?"

"No. No plans," I answered. He had such a baby face, smooth skinned, freshly shaven.

"Let's go out," John said. "Friday night, for dinner or anything else you'd like to do."

John and I hung out often, at his place or mine, or out and about. I met his mom and his friends. The tighter John and I got in getting to know each other, the more I turned to wine. Drinking gave me an escape from my facade. I could be anyone I wanted to be when lightly buzzed. Less than two weeks after we met, John and I spent one Sunday afternoon hanging out at his place, waiting on his pot connection. He was also expected at his folks' place later that day. It was Mother's Day. It was also my twenty-eighth birthday, but that was my secret.

While John toked on his pot that he finally got that day, I drowned my secret in a bottle of wine. As Samantha, I had to wait until August 17 for my birthday, at that time turning twenty-two. John was younger than me at twenty-seven, turning twenty-eight in September. It was my secret that he was younger than me. In this life, there was nothing ironic about our age difference. He was four months shy of twenty-eight years old. I was three months shy of twenty-two.

On the first Monday in June, John stopped by my apartment in the morning. We had spent all day Saturday with each other, waking up together the day before, Sunday. I had work later that day, Monday. "Hi, sweetie, this is a sweet surprise," I said.

He stepped in. I shut the door and he pulled me into his hug. It started out as a typical morning with him. He turned down coffee, but took a soda from my fridge. I'd had my share of coffee for the day, too. So I opted for a glass of wine. Only one glass wouldn't hurt. I had several hours before my afternoon starting time at my job.

I turned on the radio and we snuggled together on the couch, talking about stuff.

John asked, "Tell me more about why you ended up in Missouruh."

"I already told you," I said. I'd need another glass of wine for this talk. I went to the kitchen and poured another glass of wine. Returning to him, I could see the look on his face meant he was still waiting for my answer. I swallowed a gulp, wiped my lips, and said, "Remember? I told you, I moved out here with Josh after my folks died."

"Sorry," John said. "I can't imagine losing my mom. You want a hug?"

Before I could decide between a hug or another gulp of wine, his pager beeped again. He checked it. "It's my cousin, Ronnie. You want to meet him?"

"Sure," I answered. "Call him." That would get me out of this awkward moment. John called his cousin from my phone. Soon he showed up to meet me.

Strolling into my place, Cousin Ronnie gave me a hug. I didn't even know this guy. His cologne was heavy. After his hug, he slapped his hand on John's shoulder. "So, little cousin, is this the pretty thing you've been hiding from me?"

John said, "Ronnie, this is Samantha."

"Baby, this is my cousin, Ronnie."

Ronnie plopped his heavyset body into a chair. His Hawaiian button-down shirt was untucked, falling into his lap, with an open neckline showing his hair high up on his chest. I turned toward the kitchen. "Let me get us something to drink. Ronnie, you want Coke, same as John?"

I saw John sit back down, and Ronnie slapped his knee. "You lucky little cousin, you."

I got two sodas from the kitchen for them and refilled my wine glass while I was in there. Ronnie asked, "Why haven't I met you before, little lady?"

I answered, "John and I only just met."

"And she's from Pennsylvania originally," John piped in.

"Only just met, huh?" Ronnie leaned forward, his fat legs taking up all his leg room. "You two seem to be in love, to me."

John blushed, "Yep, Cousin, she's a keeper."

We listened to the radio and fell into a conversation together. After much back and forth chitchat, Ronnie piped up, "A keeper, huh. I agree, little Johnny. Let's make sure you keep her. We need to get you two married."

My glass was empty. I excused myself to the kitchen. This time, I pulled down my bottle of dry vermouth from the cupboard. I hadn't been able to find my preferred brand, Lyon's, but at only 18 percent, this was good stuff. I was going to open it two days before, on Saturday. When I ended up at John's, though, I stuck to wine. I didn't need to overdo it. On Saturday, that is. With Cousin Ronnie here, I needed this stiff drink. I took more sodas to them. They didn't seem to notice I had switched from dry white wine to vermouth.

As I handed John his soda, he said, "Thanks, baby. Hey, you're drinking a lot. You sure you want to go into work?"

John was right. I'd had too much to drink. Before I could reply one way or the other, Ronnie jumped into our talk. "Tell you what, cousins. Can I call you cousin, Samantha?"

Ronnie didn't let me answer. He kept talking. "Let me call your boss for you. I'll tell him you won't make it in to work today."

I dialed the number for him and listened to him do the talking when he got my boss on the phone. "I'm Samantha's dad."

I have a dad? I must be real to have a dad.

Luckily, I never talked about family at work.

Ronnie kept yakking. "I'm sorry, but Samantha won't be coming to work today. I'm in town visiting and I'm driving her and her boyfriend, Johnny, to Oklahoma to get married."

Huh? Did I have one too many drinks?

That caught me off guard.

Or do I need another drink?

I needed another drink. And then some. I filled up a carafe with the last of my vermouth, then the three of us headed out to Ronnie's car.

We were in love while a lunatic cousin drove us to Miami, Oklahoma. It was the closest place around to get married the same day, and only a two-hour drive from Springfield. Our ostentatious trip became surreal as we pulled into a little town.

Hot pink neon signs flashed, competing with bright sunshine. Ronnie hit the brakes hard, swerving his car into a parking space. We got out. Ronnie draped an arm over each of us. My euphoric drunkenness caused me to depend on this cousin to lead us into the wedding chapel.

We were legally married, and soon after found ourselves at a bar to celebrate. In commemoration of our day, we played darts. I joined Cousin Ronnie in whiskey shots and beer backs. John was in his own oblivion, manically fueled by his bipolar disorder.

Too drunk to drive, Cousin Ronnie checked us into a motel. Waking up from my drunken slumber early the next morning, the sobering jolt sparked me fully awake. On the nightstand lay the legal marriage certificate. It was Tuesday. We had married on Monday, June 5, 1995. Ronnie's arms came up from under the sheets. He was still wearing that gaudy Hawaiian shirt. He stretched and mumbled, "Uh, I have to drive us home."

I rolled over to face John. Only one question remained unanswered. Facing John, I asked, "Cousin Ronnie, which home?"

John glanced at our marriage certificate and then looked up at the ceiling. "We have two homes."

I had questions for my new husband, my fourth husband, but as far as John knew, this was only my second time getting married. I asked him, "Do we live at your place? Or my place?"

PART FOUR

CHAPTER 16

SAMANTHA ANN

In my new persona, I ignored my May 14 birthday in favor of August 17. John and his family saw me grow up through my twenties, not knowing I was already thirty years old the year I blew out twenty-four candles on my cake. He had a younger brother and sister and they had spouses. This tight-knit family gave me four older brothers and sisters. I accepted my place as baby of the family. Not to be confused with his sister, Samantha Lea, I was Samantha Ann.

One morning at breakfast with John, when we were not quite five months married, he asked, "You're eating that crap again? For breakfast?"

I pressed my fork into my eggs, letting the over-easy yolk soak into my mashed potatoes. Then I scraped a dollop of peanut butter from the side of my bowl and added it to my potatoes, right on top of the eggs. I took a big bite then reached into the fridge, which was close to our table, pulled out the carton of milk and handed it to John.

"Thanks, baby," John said. "You should drink some milk too."

When he said "milk," I grabbed my stomach and curled my lips. "Milk hasn't been agreeing with me lately."

John let his spoon drop in his bowl. He brought my wrist up from under the table and held it. "Samantha, baby, I think you're pregnant."

Oh, how I hated anyone or anything grabbing my wrists. That's why I never wore bracelets. They felt like handcuffs. I scowled. "I'm not pregnant."

He petted my hand. "Yes, babe, I think you are."

"Stop it, nonsense." I got up from the table and poured myself a glass of wine, then sat back down to my mashed potatoes and eggs with peanut butter. He could be right, though. Had he made this claim a few months before, when off his meds, then I would have had every reason not to believe him. When we were first married, he had been in and out of seventy-two-hour psychiatric holds until his bipolar disorder had been stabilized. These days he wasn't crazy like he had been in the beginning.

John said, "I can't even eat, watching you. And wine, now, too?"

"Today's Saturday. No work." I took a swallow of wine.

John said, "I know today is Saturday. It's just you shouldn't drink this early in the day."

I went about eating and drinking. John shook his head and said, "When you get to be my age, you'll understand."

When he said "my age" I threw back the rest of the wine, got up, and poured a second glass.

◆ ❖ ◆

At John's insistence, I got a pregnancy test at the medical center later that week. It was positive. He was my fourth husband, and this was a first for me. The doctor expressed her concern with my smoking and drinking habits, both of which I downplayed. She implored me to cut back my smoking to no more than five cigarettes a day, and not to drink any alcohol whatsoever. I left her exam room with serious intentions to adhere to her advice.

Willpower alone wasn't going to suffice to moderate my drinking. Out of opportunity, more so than out of want, I looked to my mother-in-law, Linda, to fill the void left when not drinking. Like John, she relied on disability income. Hers was from an on-the-job factory accident, which had left her hand deformed. For her to hold a pen or to chain smoke, her little finger and thumb had to pinch it just right, while her three middle fingers protruded out in a contrived manner. She chose little cigars over cigarettes, and I followed her habit to curb my nicotine use.

Shopping and spending time with Linda gave me the chance to show her I was worthy of her son. I also fought her motherly role, out of respect for Nana. Linda's patience with my spunky attitude won out as we melded our relationship into a mother-daughter friendship.

I wasn't convinced I wanted to be a mother. I had stuck close to John in his crazy times when first married, reasoning that two were stronger than one. Being married could help my alias. Now that motherhood presented itself to me, I reasoned that this too could only strengthen my new life as Samantha Ann. In juxtapose, I questioned if this could come back to haunt me. Our child, Lee-Ann if a girl, would have my alias name and age on his or her birth certificate.

Inside the new year, 1996, John and I went out to hear music at a neighborhood bar. It had been a long time since we had gone out for fun. Ignoring our rules, his not to drink on meds, and mine not to drink when pregnant, we ordered whiskey shots with our beer. John said, "Don't worry, Samantha, remember we walked here. I'm not driving."

So, another round of whiskey shots and beer came to our table. And another round. I lost count. So did John.

Staggering home, John took my hand. We giggled from giddiness. I helped him get back on solid footing when he started teetering. A few steps later, our laughter got the best of us and we dropped to the ground. It was a soft landing though, with sidewalks blanketed from the last snowfall. I packed some snow in my hand and started a snowball fight.

"Samantha, babe, I'm too tired to play. Let's get home."

I threw one last snowball at him, then stood up, took his hand back, and followed along.

We made it all the way home before falling again. Our apartment home was one of five in an old converted house with a shared, steep front yard. It was the smallest apartment, and the only one with a front porch.

Using all my energy, I didn't make it up the steps on my own. The first step was a doozy as I stumbled. John scooped me up and took me under his arm. He was trying to help me, not hug me.

Still, I couldn't resist hugging his 150-pound, five-foot-ten build. His build was a perfect match to mine.

With little will to embark up the step, it was John's strength, not mine, that pulled me up. That got us a little closer to our door. Over trivial laughter, we fell again. John pushed himself up, while I sat still and looked up at him. He broke his laughter to say, "Babe, I'm too wasted to get you. Come on, get up. It's cold out here."

I complied and soon we were inside, couch pulled out into our bed, as we cuddled into a stupefied slumber. When I woke up the next morning, I knew all wasn't well with me. My doctor's on-call nurse instructed me to stay in bed all day, and then to come in first thing Monday morning. I had miscarried.

As 1996 gave way to '97 and the start of '98, life with John and his family was as normal as any other family. Sliding into mainstream society, people believed I was who I said I was. It was the era before internet surfing and advancing information technology. Little, if anything, could challenge my claim as Samantha Ann. If only I didn't have to drink to cool my angst from my bubbling secret.

John blindly took charge as the sole account holder on any contract or legal agreement we entered. My income, at little more than five dollars an hour, wasn't worthy of a bank account or doing the IRS tax filing each year. John, too, saw no reason to voluntarily file taxes. For a while, his only income was his Social Security Disability Insurance.

When John got a responsible career position with his sister's mother-in-law, his salary went unreported. Otherwise, his disability government benefits would have been at risk. I didn't argue. And his boss, Shirley, who owned several mobile home parks, agreed with John's non-disclosure. Shady business practices were nothing new to her.

Through Shirley, we bought a mobile home. Only John's name went on the mortgage. Buying furniture on credit went the same way. With banks tied in nationally through the FDIC, I avoided anything bank related other than cashing my paychecks.

We worked during the week, and at first, many of our evenings and weekends were spent closely tied to his family. As my drinking increased, those visits became less frequent. Joining a Baptist church, we thought it would curb my problem drinking. And I thought our church membership would show I didn't have any problems. With my God concept dating back to that childhood morning when Nana told me Grandpa had gone to Heaven, God was just God. He always had been and always would be, same as the sun was yellow and the sky was blue.

John's mom, Linda, called us one evening to say, "Sam came home early. He's in the hospital with what's probably pneumonia."

John's stepdad, Sam, was a long-haul truck driver, gone often, and we had never known him to come home early from his routes. Linda stayed close to his hospital bedside and we stayed close to her. The gravity of his illness proved to be worse than pneumonia. Extensive medical tests revealed why. Linda called the family together to explain.

John, his brother and sister, their spouses, and I met his mom at Sam's bedside. Sam seemed to be feeling okay, alert and watching TV. He wasn't smiling, though. Linda turned the TV off. "Kids, your step-daddy, Sam—" she stopped mid-sentence, reached for a Kleenex and wiped her eyes.

Samantha Lea took her mom's hand and held it for support. Linda tried again to talk. "Sam, are you going to tell them, or do I have to?"

Sam looked around the room at all of us but didn't say a word. "Damn it, Sam," Linda said. She wasn't sniffling anymore. Her voice seemed stronger as she said, "Kids, what we need to tell you stays between us. No one can know. No one. Not even Grandpa Marty or Grandma. This has to stay a secret between us."

I saw Samantha Lea squeeze her mom's hand. Linda's hand was bony, and not from its deformity. Linda had lost a lot of weight lately. Try as she might, she couldn't seem to stay at a healthy weight. Only sixteen years older than John, her wrinkled skin and frail condition made her look much older.

John said, "We won't tell anyone, Mom. Tell us what's going on."

His mom looked up at John, then at Sam. "Your step-daddy, Sam, has HIV."

"What?" John's brother asked.

Linda stood up. "I said your step—"

"I heard you, Mom," he said, walking over to Linda and putting his arm around her. "I just..." His voice trailed off. If he said anything more, I couldn't make out his mumble.

After regaining her composure, Linda told us more. "Sam is bisexual. That, too, no one can find out. I mean it, kids. No one can know he is sick with HIV."

Sam spoke up. "Linda, calm down. Kids, Grandpa Marty and your grandma...as far as they know I came down with pneumonia. We don't need to make a big deal of it. I'm getting treatment and the doctors say—"

"Not make a big deal of it?" Linda interrupted. "You've been sleeping around. When you sleep with men, you have to use condoms. How could you be so careless, Sam? Never mind, don't answer. Keep staring at the TV. I'm not turning it back on for you. You piece of shit, Sam. How could you?"

Linda ran out of the room, crying. Samantha Lea followed her.

Sam didn't have anything to add other than to remind us this was top secret. Leaving his room, John put his arm around me. "How do you feel about all this?"

I answered, "It's tough to say. Your mom is hurting big time." What I wanted to say, was that, while Sam's behavior was inexcusable, I could understand. Society discouraged same-sex relations. That was part of why I had been married many times. There was no one right man for me.

John ran his fingers through my hair, pulling it back from my face. "We need to be there for Mom. It will get easier once she's over the shock. I thought Sam might be bisexual. I wasn't sure, though."

"John, sweetie. Let's stop at the store on the way home." I needed a drink.

"You're strong, Samantha, babe. I know it's hard to understand all this crap between my folks. When you get to be my age, things will make more sense to you."

Now I really need a drink. He said those words again, "my age."

I got my drink and then some. Days melted into weeks as I didn't like facing what was happening to my mother-in-law. With Sam's HIV diagnosis, Linda got tested. She had AIDS. Linda's treatment was rigid. It had to be. She had a death sentence hanging over her.

Several times a day, Linda took more pills than she could count in one hand. Sam was prescribed a simple medication, released to return home, but with an immediate termination from his job. Any time John and I went to their place, tension was thick. Their anger and hatred toward each other went unresolved, yet somehow, they stayed married as friends. And they kept reminding us to keep their secret. No one was to find out about his HIV or her AIDS.

I could keep their secret. Secrets were the norm for me. What wasn't normal for me was to be a hoarder of secrets. I had John's secret—no government official could know he was working; Linda's secret—she had AIDS; Sam's secret—he was bisexual; and my big secret. Remorse over my miscarriage only added to my baggage. And in all of that, I seldom thought of Nana. I didn't think Nana had ever had so many secrets. She had been outspoken.

Me, I drank.

◆ ❖ ◆

I habitually hid my bottles so John wouldn't discover my stock-pile, but then I'd get too drunk to remember where I hid them. John would try to comfort me. I'd try to make John understand, which was impossible. Without telling him my secret, he couldn't understand. Unlike a normal drinker, alcohol had its grip on me. To avoid the strangulation of being wrought with angst, alcohol gave me the freedom to breathe, and to be who I wanted to be at any given moment in time. When drunk, I forgot my secrets. I was Samantha Ann.

Drinking came with risks, but I drank without thought of what the next moment could entail. John became increasingly used to my debacles, but always pleaded with me to gain control. I'd yell, "You don't understand!"

Usually John and I got along fine. Sometimes, though, we had disagreements, and when we did, my alcoholic reasoning took over. My delusional reasoning only made things worse. In one such argu-ment, I accused him of buying another mobile home from his boss, Shirley. I believed he was leaving me. "No, Samantha. You got it all wrong. I tried to tell you that yesterday. I'm not going anywhere."

I didn't believe him. I poured another drink. John got up from the couch and said, "This is stupid, what you're saying. I'm going to work."

It was the middle of the day on Saturday. That fueled my rea-soning, which I didn't recognize as illogical at the time. He walked out, got in his truck, and drove off. I went in the bedroom, got some clothes, and threw them in the trunk of my car. This was normal for me.

I had run out on him many times before. It was normal for me to pile a bunch of clothes and dry foods, like peanut butter and bread, into my car trunk and drive off into the sunset, literally. Then I'd come-to the next morning, often far from home. I'd return home, apologizing to John, swearing it wouldn't happen again. Try as I might, I couldn't keep my promise. Still, he always forgave me.

On this Saturday, with him off to work, and me with a loaded car, I drove off into the sunset again. I didn't get far. South of us was the Hootentown Campground. Situated on the James River for canoeing, we had often enjoyed camping and live outdoor concerts there during the summer months. Privately owned, John and I knew the couple who ran it. I pulled in, saw one of them, and rolled down my window to talk to him. He was doing something with a stack of docked canoes.

After slobbering to him about my troubles with John, he pointed to their shed. "Sure, go ahead and stay in there. We have it set up with a bed and other stuff for overnight guests."

I had found my refuge. The next morning, I didn't return home. That wasn't normal for me. Instead, I had befriended a young man named Rusty. He was a drifter who camped one night at a time. Like me, he liked to drink hard and heavy. We stuck together all that day. And the next day. Whenever we ran low on booze, he'd borrow my car to run up to the liquor store on the main highway, close by. He had my okay to borrow it, and I always kept my keys in the ignition. It was safe at that campground and I didn't want to lose my keys, so the ignition was the best spot to keep them.

John showed up one day. The campground owners must have called him. Getting out of his truck, he ran up to Rusty and me, waving his fist. "So, are you with him now?"

John expected an immediate answer from me. I couldn't think, let alone answer him. "Well?" John asked again.

I wasn't really with that guy, but John wanted an answer. "Yeah, I'm with him."

John's flying fist punched Rusty. Rusty hit back, which catapulted them into a brawl. At one point they fell to the ground where they tried to suffocate each other in the dirt. Rusty barely knew me, so why he'd have a stake on me was a wonder. And John was on the verge of divorcing me, so that too was a wonder. As they jumped up from yet another roll in the dirt, Rusty yelled to me, "I'm outta here. I've had enough of this! You with me?"

Rusty pointed at the passenger side of my car. "Get in," he yelled.

I got in the car. Rusty grabbed his backpack and jumped in the driver's seat, throwing his pack over the side to the back seat. He squealed out of the lot and we drove off into the unknown, or as was common for me, into the sunset yet again. He had his pack. I had nothing other than my wallet in my pocket.

His backpack had some essentials and his sentimental stuff, but some items got left behind. He reasoned out loud that he could always get another sleeping bag. Rusty also told me he was wanted for murder. He was out of there, with no intention to return, and I was with him.

I have little recollection of our time drunk on the road. Of my foggy memories, we fished together on a river in Kentucky at their Land Between Lakes resort area, and later, were at a hot tub party at some woman's home in the backwoods of Minnesota.

And I remember a big city with Rusty sitting in my car in a parking lot close by, while I stood on a street corner working the sign. I couldn't fake humiliation. I had pulled Richard and me up out of homelessness. This sign working shouldn't be happening again.

I stared at traffic. My thoughts drifted to Nana. It had been a long time since I let myself be subject to her disapproval. However long gone she was, she was with me. In that moment, I realized my choices were not something to be proud of. I pushed those thoughts aside and shifted gears to a new goal. I had to get myself back home to John.

Back home?

Yes, I had to get back home. I had to quiet my urge to run. I had to make my life right again. With a few dollars in hand from those who passed by, I left my corner and handed Rusty my cash. We would need it for gas and beer and whiskey. I had no idea where I was or how I was going to get back home, but I was determined to figure it out.

When drunk again, I had no recollection of my goal. Then, in the heat of a yelling match with Rusty, I snapped back to reality. That's how alcoholic blackouts went for me. If my emotions or body became overly stressed, my brain shook me sober, yet still inebriated. Rusty and I were standing on a rocky beach.

What seemed like muffled noises to me were families barbecuing. Smoke mixed with roasting meat was all I could smell. Campsites were compacted all around us, without a hint of grass. I remembered my goal to find home. Some distance away behind Rusty was a lake with waves rolling in and crashing. I faced him and believed I was angry at him, but I didn't know why.

I stepped backward, almost skipping. My car was right behind us, but I didn't remember how I knew that. I remembered nothing about that day, up until the smell of hamburgers and hotdogs. I opened the driver's side door of my car and got in. Good, the keys were in the ignition as usual. I locked all the doors. I pulled my car out of our parking spot in reverse as Rusty ran after me, banging on the car's hood.

I turned the wheel, drove forward, and looked in my rearview mirror. Rusty stopped running. He yelled, "No, come back. No, not my pack. No, don't leave me here. No-oo."

Driving off into the sunset again, before the sun had set, I drove into oblivion.

I found myself parked in a vacant gravel lot, and had no idea what time it was, save for the hint from the rapidly rising sun. The sun's seething rays stabbed at my already pounding head. I forced my eyes open and peeled my cheek from my driver's side window. A crossroads with a long barren stretch of rural highway gave me no clue as to where I was. Only a convenience store, which sat across the highway, was in sight. Thankfully, it faced away from me. I must have been an eyesore. I was thirsty, and I had to use the bathroom.

In the glove box, I found my little cigars. Rusty hated that I smoked little cigars instead of cigarettes. It didn't matter. He was in the dust. To validate he was gone, I looked in my back seat and saw his huge backpack. I had to work hard to piece my brain cells back together. My brainpower, which was foggy at best, had to be put toward survival. That's what I had to do—*survive.*

Smoking, I counted my money. It wasn't much. A wadded one-dollar bill and a bunch of change brought it up to a few dollars.

My throat was scratchy from thirst. Not for a stiff drink, though. No amount of beer or whiskey could wipe away the complex disgust for myself. In my newfound reality, I had to focus on my goal to get home to John.

Of the roads in front of me, it was clear I had four choices. Even if I used the rising sun to determine which direction was west, east, north or south, it would do me no good. Missouri was right smack dab in the middle of the country.

Where am I?

First, I had to pee something awful. I had to drive across the street to that convenience store for a bathroom. Starting the car, I noticed the turn signal switch on the steering column was jimmy-rigged—superglued in.

Huh? Okay, survive, Samantha, survive.

Without further ado, and with all the courage I could muster up, I made it to the store. But in my short jaunt, I saw my front windshield had some cracks. The bathroom doors were on the outside of the building. I went in and got the key, used the bathroom, and returning to the front door of the store, I saw a phone booth at the far corner, close to the highway. I returned the bathroom keys, then walked across the lot to the phone booth.

I was too ashamed to call John. Fumbling in my wallet, I tried to find a phone number for someone, anyone, it would be okay to call. I found Ruth's number. Her husband was an elder in our church and I was on friendly terms with her. I didn't want to call anyone, but I had to. I had no earthly idea how to get out of my mess, or which direction to take on that crossroads.

"Hello," she answered the phone.

"Hi, um, it's Samantha. I don't know what to do."

"Oh Samantha, we've been so worried about you. Where are you?"

"I don't know. Not anywhere near Springfield."

As if instinctually, Ruth said, "Tell me what you see."

I told her. Ruth's first set of instructions directed me to go into the convenience store and ask where I was. I had to admit I needed orange juice. Before going inside, I searched Rusty's pack for more money. There wasn't any. All he had in there was clothes and crap and a handmade birthday card with his son's hair lock. I had no idea he had a son.

Nearly all my money would go to orange juice and a package of rolling tobacco with papers. Under the alias of Samantha, I did not have the dubious luxury of bank cards or credit cards like most normal folks. Normal folks could solve their problems with a credit card. I was not normal.

I faked a smile at the store clerk, smoothed out my one-dollar bill, and handed him my money. I watched the money as he put it in the cash register. I was broke.

"Will this be all for you?" he asked.

"Yeah, but I'm a little turned around. Which way should I go to get to Springfield?"

He scratched his forehead. "Uh, Spreengfield?"

"Yeah, Springfield, Missouruh," I clarified, looking back at him.

He looked out the window at the highways, then back at me. "Oh, you probably just crossed the state line from South Dakota. This is Wyoming. You need Eighteen East." He scratched his head again. "Eighteen East will take you all the way to where you can drop down into Missouri." He looked back at the sparse highway stretch and pointed to the right. "That road there, that's Eighteen. Take that road. You want to stay east on it."

"Okay, thank you," I said, unscrewing the lid on my juice.

He handed me a book of matches to go with my tobacco. "Sure, no problem. How'd you get so turned around?"

"It was late and dark when I got tired from driving so I stopped and rested but fell asleep."

He looked into my eyes, but I quickly glanced away. "Yeah, just stay on that road. It'll get you to where you're going."

"Okay, thanks."

As I walked out I told myself, "That wasn't so bad."

But then I recanted my spoken thought at my first real eyeful of my car, parked front and center of me. My windshield was spiderwebbed with cracks, and not just a little cracked as I had first pictured. My passenger door was beat in to a pulp. I tried its door handle to find it still opened, but then I looked down. My tire looked way too low. I vaguely remembered that Rusty and I had sometimes pumped it up with an air pump. I knew I had to find the air pump, which was likely somewhere in the strewn about clothes and canned food.

As I scavenged the back seat, I discovered a huge burn hole. Not small like a cigarette type of burn, but deep enough it revealed the springs. I held the air pump and sat dazed.

How long have I been gone? What all did Rusty and I do? Oh yeah, we bought a BBQ at a Walmart. Oh yeah, somehow, the BBQ or its gas or something caught on fire. I remember billowing flames that Rusty smothered with blankets or clothes or something. Did I get new clothes at Walmart to have something else to wear other than what I left with?

I must have. Three summer blouses were in the clothing mess.

After I filled the tire with air from the hand pump, I called Ruth back. I heard her fumble in what sounded like a drawer. "Hang on, let me get a map."

Ruth informed me I was on the right road, but that it could be a three-day drive for me. If my vision were better, I could drive straight through in less time, but as it was I had lost my glasses, and just couldn't see well enough to drive in the dark. We ended our phone call with a prayer for my safe return and my promise to call her each night.

I had to return to survival mode, away from any interrupting thoughts, to stay focused on my present moment. I reasoned I could do nothing about the window or turn signal. I also couldn't use my seat belt. It was in a tangled knot. Of all the things wrong with the car, no seat belt scared me the most. I remembered the stick that protruded through the window in the triple rollover with Jim years before. My seat belt had saved me then.

I had to get down the road on what gas I had in the tank. *How far do I have to go? How far will this gas last me at a little over a half a tank?*

I rolled my window down to let in a cool breeze. The sun was no longer on the horizon line and it was a hot day. Air-conditioning would eat my gas. When the gas tank got to just below a quarter full, I pulled into a hick town.

What am I going to do?

And then I answered myself aloud, "Survive."

At the post office, I bellied up to the counter and asked, "Is there anywhere around here I could get some help with gas? I'm leaving a bad situation and trying to get home to Springfield, Missouri, but I'm running low on gas."

The postal worker sympathized with my sob story and referred me to a church, who then gave me a ten-dollar voucher for the gas station. It was the first of several stops like it to get me down the road. I had to stop every two hours anyway, just to pump the bad tire back up. My overnight stays were spent at rest stops, from sundown until sunup, ignoring any posted signs stating no overnight parking.

While I had gas taken care of through my sheer determination to hide my pride and ask for help—150 miles at a time—I was not enthused about driving long hours without a drink, or limiting my smoking. Furthermore, I didn't like being alone with my self-hatred. Remembering the hopes I had when hitchhiking cross-country, I picked up hitchhikers four times during my trip.

Through the rides I offered, I was friendly—not overtly friendly, but instead, in a kittenish way—and pleaded for beer and smokes. It worked every time. Nana had once shown me the fine art of how to acquire favors from simple friendliness.

But as I talked with my hitchhikers, I couldn't articulate my words well. It wasn't a problem of not knowing what to say, but the inability to clearly pronounce my words. My spoken vowels came out as different vowels. Instead of "tired," my vocal chords would say "toured." I shrugged off my acute problem as stress. I had to keep going.

By late morning of my third day, I was a few miles shy of Springfield when I stopped to call Ruth again, to let her know I was almost home.

"Oh good, I knew our prayers were working," she said.

I looked over at the highway. Weather was clear for driving. "I should get home to John."

"No, Samantha, wait. John's not ready to see you yet. It really hurt him this time. Paul and I will be happy to have you stay with us until John's ready to see you again."

I spent the next three weeks at their home, camped out in their living room. They had four kids who were on summer break from school, and I must have been in their playroom. My boss took me back and a coworker helped me with money until my next paycheck.

In my stay with the church family, I had to smoke outside, which gave me my hidden chance to drink. I drank only a few beers a day, from a suitcase of beer in the warm trunk of my car. I had to stay off the hard stuff. Beer took the edge off, and thus, it sufficed.

My problem drinking slowed down to intermittent havoc from then on into the next year, 1999. Our church family helped as best they could, but all the prayer chains in the world weren't going to save me. John was relieved when I called the hotline for Alcoholics Anonymous. I called several times. I found those phone calls with the AA women helpful. John also must have seen some hope.

Throughout the summer of '99, my weekend drunkenness intensified nearly to the level it had been the summer before. The Saturday night of Labor Day weekend, I drank myself into a stupor, which was normal for me. I passed out, again, normalcy for me.

I came to at about 4:30 in the morning. John was still asleep. I wanted to sleep too, but couldn't. I drank the last of some whiskey. It wasn't enough. I finished off what little was left at the bottom of a wine bottle from the kitchen cabinet, but that wasn't enough. I was waking up, not going back to sleep.

I next rummaged through some clothes on the floor of our bedroom closet. Somewhere, I had a bottle hidden. I found it, just a little bit left from a fifth of vodka. I also grabbed a pair of jeans and a bra and shirt from the closet floor. I figured I may as well get dressed. As I backed out of our closet, John rolled over and ducked under the covers. I tucked my vodka bottle under my jeans and left the bedroom, shutting the door behind me. He must have gone back to sleep.

On the kitchen table, I saw the AA meeting schedule. One of the women I had talked to on the AA hotline had mailed it to me. I thumbed through it and noticed that Springfield had a lot of meetings to choose from around the clock.

I looked at the clock on the wall. It was going on 5:30. A morning meeting was scheduled for 6:00 at a clubhouse out on James River Highway. I knew that road. It was on the way to the mobile home park where John worked. It was an easy drive. I grabbed the car keys and hurried out the door.

At just shy of 6:00 a.m., I walked into that AA meeting. About ten people, nearly all men, sat at both sides of a long conference table. Coffee repulsed my nostrils. I saw AA Big Books on their table. I knew what Big Books were. One man looked up at me as I approached them. "Good morning, welcome," he said, taking a drag from his cigarette.

I didn't hold back in my response. "Hi, I need help. I need to get sober."

They deviated from their normal routine in their hour-long meeting to address my needs. The only requirement for AA membership is a desire to stop drinking, and I had that desire without a doubt. I hated myself for who I had become. I was ashamed of what Nana would see in me if she were still alive. I had changed my identity. Now, I needed to change my life.

CHAPTER 17

SAM', I

Treatment following a three-day hospital stay involved group counseling and education. Hospital staff said my best chance to beat my alcoholism was in their outpatient recovery program, as was standard practice. Discharged three days later, I joined about twenty other clients for six weeks, at six full days each week. John fully supported my endeavor, however only time would tell if it would fix our troubled marriage.

In our sessions, I had to tune out anything unrelated to alcoholism. Food, drugs, sex, gambling, and shoplifting were not my problems. Two people I clicked with were also in for alcoholism. One was a young woman, and we'd support each other in our early months with AA as we were encouraged to join. The other was a guy named Jim.

Fridays were field trip days. One trip was to the Springfield Conservation Center, a deeply wooded park with hiking trails. While others split off onto different hikes, Jim and I held back to talk freely—like old friends in a place where it did not seem easy to make friends. I told him I once knew a Jim and didn't want to be reminded of that time when I heard his name. He chuckled his usual loud half of a laugh, which sounded more like the neigh of a horse. "Okay, let's think of a nickname for me."

I studied his physical appearance to see if I could come up with something. He was tall at well over six feet, and lanky. He had a protruding forehead with balding hair greased neatly back. His skin was pale white without a hint of sun. His facial features were firm and not flawed, like my crooked nose. He was dressed in blue jeans like me, but always wore clunky black dress shoes that polished his casual attire. No, I couldn't gather a nickname from his appearance. I said, "Well, I think of you as my buddy in this place."

He asked, "My buddy?"

I said, "Yeah, I mean, I really can't relate to any of them and you are great to be buds with."

We looked over the deck at others who were lost in their own conversations. I looked back at him. "I know. You're my bud, right?"

He answered, "Yes...I..." He chuckled his neigh again instead of finishing his sentence.

"You're Bud," I told him.

He didn't laugh again. He quietly assumed his name. From then on, he was Bud. Sadly, as I write my story today, he's no longer alive. In June 2014, a car hit him as he walked home from his neighborhood liquor store. He succumbed to his injuries. He was fifty-two years old.

◆ ❖ ◆

Willing to do anything suggested for the sake of my recovery, I immediately latched onto a sponsor, Christine. In most any Twelve-Step Program, a sponsor serves in the role of mentor and is an integral part of the social support system. Within six months, I exhaustively worked the twelve steps through prayer, written self-inventory, unloading secrets to my sponsor, open discussion in group meetings, and where I could, restitution.

I righted one wrong through my restitution efforts by returning Rusty's backpack. It had been sitting in a storage shed for more than a year. I had found his mother's address in it. I handwrote a letter of apology, spent money on postage for such a bulky package, and mailed it to him at his mother's place. I knew what it was like to lose stuff and believed he'd like to have his son's hair lock returned, still tucked in a side pocket.

In each of the twelve AA steps, I followed Christine's lead as we adhered exactly to the directions from the AA Big Book. With Step Three, we knelt in prayer for release from the disease. Ritualistic praying felt awkward to me. I didn't understand the whole God concept, even though John and I had been going to church. I couldn't wholeheartedly believe in a god without understanding why society proclaimed his existence as true. For the sake of my recovery, I did it.

Step Five was my confessional step. It put me into a catch-22. I could stay a drunk, but that would jeopardize my secret. Or, I could get sober so I could move past my difficult secret keeping. But to do that, I had to let go of my secret. I still couldn't wholly trust anyone, not even Christine as my sponsor.

Christine and I set aside a full afternoon and evening at her place to get through that step. Arriving at her place, we settled in on her porch for a smoke and coffee. She asked me, "Are you ready for this?"

I answered, "I have to be. I can't keep drinking. And I know why I keep drinking, but I can't tell anyone, not even you. So, I wrote you a letter to tell you."

I handed her my letter. When done reading, she looked at me. I said, "Now do you understand why this is so hard? My name is not Samantha and I am not twenty-six years old."

Christine's reply was to share in confidence a similar situation, and although it wasn't quite my story, apparently she had once been on the run. Although she hadn't changed her identity, her experience told me she knew what it was like to hold a secret. Without any real understanding of God, I considered our similarities a "God thing."

As we proceeded through the remaining AA steps, Christine saw me through viable solutions. For one, I received treatment for my speech impediment, which stemmed from my '98 parking lot episode. Sober, my speech worsened. Three minutes into whatever I said, my dialogue became riddled with poor enunciation. I cared less about my impediment and more about sobriety. Through treatment, my clumsy speech became right again—almost. To this day, I talk fine unless I'm overly tired or stressed out, then it flares up until I regain my well-being.

Christine also encouraged me to retain a criminal lawyer to make right my legal wrongs. If I didn't have that secret to run from, the higher my chances were I wouldn't run to the booze. Of course, it made sense if I first told my husband, John, about this. I didn't have money or resources to retain legal counsel. Besides, whatever the outcome, John would be affected. A well-known AA motto is *"To thine own self, be true."* I had to be truthful in my life to keep my sobriety. For me, truth meant setting the secrets free.

After stewing in my decision-making process for a few days, I told John, "We need to talk about something serious."

John said, "Now's a good enough time as any."

We sat down at our kitchen table, across from each other. I fiddled with my coffee and lit a little cigar, then fiddled with my smoking. John said, "I'm listening."

I said, "You know how I often tell you that you don't understand?"

John took my hand and held it gently. "I know you had a rough life with Josh and had to leave Pennsylvania when your folks died."

I said, "You still don't understand. I must tell you something. I'm older than you. My name is not Samantha Ann. My name is Kym and I'm four months older than you. I'm not the frickin' baby of the family."

"What?" John asked. He let go of my hand and leaned back from the table. "What are you talking about?"

I spilled my secrets. He was calm and attentive to my revelations. Through our discussion, we agreed not to run uninformed to an attorney. That could cause immediate apprehension.

John had a close friend who had recently been released from prison and was on parole. This friend had experience with how the criminal system currently worked. We looked to him for answers.

At our scheduled visit, his friend listened to my story, asked me questions, and laid out the probability of repercussions and how to avoid them. From our talk, we learned I had to get a damn good reputable attorney to handle everything on my behalf. That sounded expensive. Our emergency savings account wasn't that bulky.

John let his boss, Shirley, know he needed her help in a confidential problem. Financially well-off and Samantha Lea's mother-in-law, Shirley had already proven herself when it came to keeping secrets from the government by employing John without reporting it. Like with John's friend, we sat down behind closed doors to share my secret with her. She called an attorney friend who specialized in criminal matters in Missouri, with practicing privileges in three other states—Oregon, for one. Shirley wrote out a check for $1,000 for his retainer fee.

My attorney attended court appearances on my behalf. Each time, I waited at home for a phone call to find out how it went. He diligently fought for me, even when Oregon threatened extradition to serve three years for failing to fulfill my parole. Through my attorney's advice and recommendation, we brought a second lawyer into my case. This lawyer handled the specific wrongs relating to my fraudulent use of a Social Security number.

By proving I was a contributing member of society, my attorneys won my case. I was released from parole with no warrants pending. To finalize the matter, my first attorney also petitioned the Missouri courts to recognize my name change. No longer living under an alias, I was legally Samantha Ann with John's last name.

John and my attorney questioned my choice to retain John's last name, advising me I could instead go back to my birth name, or Mott, the alias name I held prior to him. I saw no need to do that. We were married.

That was May 2000, the month of my true thirty-third birthday. As days melted away into summer heat, John and I resumed our usual life as best we could, but our relationship was forevermore strained. By mid-summer, John told me he wanted a divorce. I fought his decision, but his decision was final.

Again, like five years earlier, I had to fill up my life with something. Two things consumed my otherwise lonely hours. One was AA, and the other was Saturday Scrabble games with my friend Bud and his dad.

I also tried the dating game during the winter holidays. On my first Valentine's Day without John, I gave Bud an elaborate Hallmark card. Bud pointed out that it was a friendship card, then questioned, "Why won't you go out with me, Sam'?"

In my single life, I had dropped my family name of Samantha Ann in favor of Sam'. Not "Sam" as in a guy's name, but with an apostrophe placed at the end of my name, showing it was short for something. I replied to his question. "Because, Bud, you're my best friend."

Six months after John and I parted, I was struggling with rent and other expenses. So I gave in to Bud's pleas by moving in with him. Although I wasn't in love with him, I had grown to love him. I found I liked playing house with him and his rottweiler. But where I had loved AA life, Bud lagged. He was a wallflower sort of guy. I had to be okay with him as he was. That is, until he drank again. Unlike his Al-Anon mom, I didn't enable him.

I refused to clean up after him when he parked his butt on the couch for the long haul. Only taxi rides to the liquor store got him up. I let him be while I moved from our shared bedroom into the spare bedroom. I had to separate myself from his life as a drunk.

As days passed, crap cluttered the front room floor not far from where he lay drinking. With a broom, I swept clothes, empty fifths, dog feces, and an exploded ketchup bottle into his bedroom. Before shutting his bedroom door, I took one last look at that mess and questioned what Nana would have done.

You can't live like this. John is gone. Your secret is gone. Nothing is holding you back. Make me proud.

Could I make Nana proud? From Missouri? Now, in the legal clear, I had choices. I had seen many beautiful places in my year of homelessness, and weather without tornadoes. Had I been drunk, I'd have thrown stuff in my car and driven off into the sunset. I was not drunk. I was sober and in AA. Unlike before, I could get a job anywhere, now that I had a Social Security card.

◆ ❖ ◆

Four hundred dollars cash moved me hassle-free into a rooming house. It was my first day in Savannah, Georgia, not counting when hitchhiking through in '93. The hallway had fresh paint; if only it wasn't that familiar institutional green. The shared bathroom and kitchenette were close to my room. The place smelled clean with Lysol.

Palm trees divided traffic lanes seen from my window, which spanned the full length of my back wall. Across the street, a park followed the roadside farther than my eye could see. Oak trees hung their moss over its paved walking trails. Some people walked their dogs, while others seemed intent to get somewhere important.

I interviewed with temporary employment agencies, but the responses didn't vary. "You did well on your filing and typing tests, but I'm sorry, we don't have anything available right now. Please stay in touch for when something opens up."

Each day I called the agencies from a nearby pay phone, but at a quarter a call, I didn't want to run out of what little money I had. I then turned to the State Employment Office. All they could offer me was a job at Wendy's fast food restaurant.

Wendy's was on the same street I lived, but twenty blocks farther out. I walked in that day and asked for the manager. My wait gave me time to look around, only to feel dwarfed. I was the only white person. I needed a job, though, and always thought of people as people, no matter what their ethnicity. The manager came to the counter to greet me. Ornamental combs piled her long hair on top of her head. She appeared to be about my age, and attractive if not for her straight face. Without a hint of a smile or a frown, she told me, "We're not hiring now."

I handed her my referral slip. "The Employment Office sent me here."

She read my small six-inch piece of paper. It was signed by my intake worker and had my name and their office stamp. She then reached for an application and gave it to me. "Here, fill this out. When you're done, let me know and we'll talk."

"Thank you," I replied.

My rent got paid on time from my part-time Wendy's income. After that, I was left with barely enough money for tobacco and laundry. I couldn't afford both rent and food, turning to the food stamp program. I also looked for other work with more pay, even if that meant working more hours at the same minimum wage, but no job was to be had for me.

Homelife was simple with quiet moments to read or people watch out the window. My neighborhood had plenty of free touristy sites and I fell in love with the city's historical beauty. Coworkers were friendly, but nothing substantial beyond the job level. I had no one to play weekend Scrabble with. Neighbors, like the guy who lived in the room next door to me, were friendly. He often passed me in the hall, headed to our community bathroom as I was leaving. We were on the same shower schedule.

My car began to act up. It would need new brakes before long, but with no money for such expenditures, I limited its use to get to and from work. Otherwise, I walked everywhere. I needed to be patient while I worked through my financial difficulties. I knew what it was like to be outright homeless and I wasn't homeless. I had a job and a roof over my head.

Into my second month in Savannah, life was routine for me. After working the lunch shift one afternoon, I came home to rest. Reading a book on my bed, I fell into a nap. I was jolted awake when someone banged on my door. "Get out, get out now! Fire!"

I sat up and looked around to see what I could grab.

Then my door was hit again. "Get out, get out now! FIRE!" It was my landlord's voice.

Okay. All I could do was grab my shoes that lay by my bed. I chose my Converse high-top tennies over my work shoes. My keys and wallet were still in my pockets. I was still dressed in my Wendy's polyester uniform.

I opened my door and stepped out, locking my door as I shut it behind me. Savannah wasn't that safe of a city, and I didn't want to be robbed of what little I owned.

This can't be that serious.

I had lived through the fire when living on my own for the first time ever, back when I left Steve. That apartment fire wasn't that big of a deal. Surely, this one wasn't either.

I didn't see any fire, but my lungs tensed up to what smelled like burnt toast. Walking to the door that led out of the apartment building, I didn't stop to look around. A cutting odor scratched my throat. When I stepped outside, humidity and the high afternoon sun hit me. I rubbed my watery eyes and didn't bother to check for oncoming traffic as I followed others to the front lawn of a house across the side street.

Curiosity caused me to look back at what I smelled. The floor above my apartment glowed bright orange from every window. The room right above mine also had blue flames. My next-door neighbor, the friendly shower guy, was soon right beside me. We stood to face what was once our home. I heard a loud pop, and then like a colorful firecracker, flames rose from the rooftop. Then, more pops. And more flames, erratic, as if they too had to escape. Then the roof was gone, which made way for flames to stretch high into the sky. I'd forgotten how tall fire could be, rarely thinking about the arson in my past.

Firefighters rushed around our building with their water hoses. I tried to understand the gravity of our dilemma from their walkie-talkies, but it sounded more like garbled radio interruptions. One fireman was up on a ladder with his hose pointed at the rooftop flames. We watched in amazement as he seemed determined to bring the blaze down. Finally, the sky-high flames he fought shrank, turning from red to a dark orange ball of fire, engulfed by colorful gray puffs. It wasn't anything like the fire I had been in before.

Shower guy—the guy who lived next door to me—tried to comfort me. He stood next to me and said, "It will be okay. We'll be okay."

How?

I heard another pop with crackles as our first-floor bathroom window exploded. Shards of glass spit out of it to make way for swirls of light gray smoke that bounced in and out of its window frame. A green curtain blew in the breeze and fell to the street. It too was on fire, but succumbed to a smoldering damp death.

Black smoke swept through cars parked curbside but stopped before it reached us. Firemen were shooting their water hoses at anything that moved. I was too numb to know what to do about my car, so I let it sit parked alongside other cars. It had bad brakes anyway. I held tight onto my tennies. They were now all that I owned. Shower guy spoke up again. "You can put your shoes on now if you want."

I couldn't have answered him even if I knew what to say. Sirens deafened our ears. Fire trucks and more fire trucks kept arriving on the scene. I sat down on the curb, stunned speechless. I put my shoes on and tied my laces. TV crew people were next on the scene, and the Red Cross. My landlord, with his assistant next to him, quieted us down. I was already quiet.

My landlord's assistant spoke as loud as he could to make sure we could all hear him. "I'm as shocked as all of you are. Someone was cooking dinner on the third floor when his hot plate started the fire."

A big dark-skinned guy in our group spoke up, interrupting him. "I'm sorry." He rubbed his eyes then turned to someone beside him and buried himself into a hug.

My landlord's assistant continued explaining the situation to us. "The fire department is doing all they can but it's not safe to go back in now."

Duh.

He opened his arms out as if to show an empty hug. "I know a lot of you don't have anywhere else to go. We have other places to help you move to if you want. But for tonight, the Red Cross is here, and if you will form a line, they will take your name and help you. We'll let you know more when we can."

It took more than an hour for the Red Cross to process us, but in the meantime, they offered coffee and fed us hotdogs and juice. Despite my preference for coffee, I chose juice to quench my raw throat.

By nightfall, many of us were taken by van to a motel on the other side of Savannah where we could stay for as long as we needed, up to ten days. The Red Cross also gave each of us a $100 Kmart gift certificate. And for those who needed it, twenty single-use bus passes. I needed it. I was clueless about how to get to work from the motel, and my car was a no-go.

At a Kmart close to my work, I got jeans, underclothes, T-shirts, hygiene items, and a cheap comb on that gift certificate. In my third day at the motel, my landlord came to me. "We need you to move your car. It's in the way of the clean-up crew."

I responded, "It has bad brakes. Where am I going to take it? It's not safe to drive out this far."

"There's an empty lot not far from the apartment building. If you want, I'll move it there for you. I have to go there today anyway."

I handed him the keys and told him to bring them back to me. When he returned my keys, he informed me they were getting another place ready for us to move into. He explained, "The rent is five hundred dollars, but you won't be sharing a bathroom." I couldn't afford that. My monthly income was only about $480.

Shower guy, whose name I learned was Patrick, was as poor as me in his waiter job. So we joined forces to accept one studio apartment. It was one single room with twin beds, an open kitchenette, and a locking bathroom. It was a safe roof over us.

In the meantime, my car got stolen from its new parking space. Broken glass on black pavement was all that was left of it. I filed a police report, but for lack of insurance, it was a loss to me. Weeks later, my car would be recovered from a police chase. Two guys had used it as their getaway car in an armed robbery at a convenience store. My mushy brakes completely failed when cop cars chased after them. They crashed. Cops wanted them and had no need for my car. It was towed to the back parking lot of my place, where it sat unused. I eventually sold it as-is for $200 cash.

I walked to work, rather than taking the bus, so I could save money. Savannah weather was warm, and our apartment was on the same street as before, same street as my job, so it was easy enough to walk the seventeen blocks. On nights I worked closing duty, my manager gave me a ride home for my safety.

Our roommate situation was simple. We didn't see much of each other, however, when we did cross paths, I saw he displayed a slight drinking problem. I'd sometimes find an eight-ounce beer or two in our fridge and let them sit next to what sparse food we had in there. But Saturday nights were different. He'd go out and then return home drunker than a skunk.

One Saturday night, or more like early Sunday morning, Patrick returned home same as usual, but couldn't keep his pants on. He wasn't sexually overt, but in his drunkenness, he walked circles butt naked. The next morning after he sobered up, I told him about his inappropriate behavior. Likely out of embarrassment, he said we couldn't live together anymore. "It's not going to work out, you and me."

I shrugged him off. I wasn't going anywhere. I had nowhere else to go. I simply wanted him to keep his pants on and not show me his penis again. A few days later, Patrick stayed true to his word and he moved out. I could stay as long as I could afford it. I couldn't afford it. At month's end, I couldn't stay. I knew that. And my measly paycheck wasn't going to get me into another place, with or without my landlord.

Following a landlord notice to pay up in full or move on, I kept my latest paycheck. My money couldn't even come close to covering rent. Thirty dollars of it went to a small two-man tent from Kmart, and a few dollars were spent on survival essentials from a thrift store. I pitched my tent in an overgrown field far behind Kmart and on the other side of some railroad tracks. Each day I padlocked my tent before my walk to work. Each night after work,

I returned home to my camp. After washing fast-food grease off me with water I stored in a jug, I'd fall asleep with a paperback book. *What else can I do? What would Nana have done?*

Nana would never have gotten into such a predicament in the first place. When she was a young woman, long before I was born, she opened her home to unwed pregnant women who had nowhere else to go. Few homeless shelters existed back then. Savannah had shelters downtown. But I felt safer and less stressed by myself. Besides, it was a shorter walk to work.

The Red Cross had been an immediate lifesaver, but proved help is temporary. To be at the mercy and whim of others meant loss of control for me. The independence found in my homestead made me feel strong. I figured I could live like that for a few months while I pulled myself up into a normal existence. That was Option A.

Option B was to admit defeat in my move to Savannah. I called Bud to ask him what to do. He told me he had sobered up. He also suggested Option B when he said, "Sam, come home."

CHAPTER 18

SAM', II

My bus traveled through one terminal after another with one layover after another until it finally got me home a week later—to Springfield, to Bud. It was a starting point, yet again. I started a new job, amped up my AA meeting attendance, and put up with Bud's shit. Sometimes Bud was softhearted. Other times, he was a drunken nuisance.

Soon I moved out and into a duplex apartment. In my new neighborhood I discovered the Westside Center, a clubhouse with AA meetings. There I reconnected with Don. I had met him back in my early recovery days. Don was an older gentleman, witty and spry. He and a young handsome guy, Billy, helped manage this clubhouse, which was owned by Catfish Tom.

Going into the year 2002, Billy was my new love. In June of that year, Don was his best man as we professed our relationship. Catfish Tom assumed the fatherly role and gave me away to Billy. As we waited for the procession march to start, Catfish Tom, with gray hair and a face of wisdom, smiled at me. "You look beautiful. Billy should be so lucky."

We had transformed the clubhouse with dark purple and gold decorations. Like a country-western star, Billy wore a button-down purple shirt with gold fringes. Contrary to wedding norms, my dress was black, and I felt glamorous in it. Like Nana who had met society in her challenging way, so did I, in my black country-western gown and lace.

A honeymoon trip to Branson sealed our love, and once back home, we settled into a rented house. We returned to work, family, and friends. He had his job at the Westside Center, and I worked with Edco, scanning medical record documents onto microfilm. While Billy was husband number five, with Vance, Jim, Richard, and John before him, my commitment to number five couldn't wane, or so I thought.

At five weeks married, my worldly truth turned upside down. It had been a typical day for us with nothing askew. Returning home from my swing shift job shortly after midnight, I walked into an eerie space. I reached to turn the lamp on, but it was gone. I flipped the overhead light switch, but no lights came on. As I adjusted to see by streetlights that shone through our front window, I saw our living room furniture was gone. It was a starkly empty shell of a house. On the bathroom counter sat my toothbrush. Billy's toothbrush was gone.

The phone, still plugged into the wall, sat on the floor. In utter confusion, I called Catfish Tom, despite the ungodly hour of the night. All he could tell me was that Billy's uncle, Clyde, helped him move, but that Billy wasn't at Clyde's, nor with him. Catfish Tom didn't know where he was. I stayed awake for the last few hours of darkness. *What the heck?*

Once daylight came, I took stock of what little Billy had left me. I first noticed I had no toilet paper to start my day. Cheese was the only food left behind in the kitchen. Two pieces of furniture were still there: our bed, and a huge, five-foot-long desk. My clothes from the dresser were in a big heaping pile on the floor. Most of my personal effects were unscathed, but my box of legal documents was nowhere to be found anywhere in the house. My anger and confusion escalated to panic and fear.

That box held proof I was free from parole or other criminal wrongs out of Oregon. That box held my birth certificate and supporting documentation explaining how I got from my birth name to my current legal name. Those documents kept me out of prison should cops ever question my history. I refused to go back to prison over a misunderstanding. Those documents allowed me to survive without harboring a secret. I was scared. Very scared. Those legal papers were my life. I had to get my documents back.

In under ten minutes, I was at Westside Center pleading with Catfish Tom to help me find it. I also pleaded with Don, whom I thought of as a dear friend. They were as confused as I was, with no answers to offer me.

I couldn't move forward as my new self without legal proof to support my life. My life had stagnated when I'd been with John, stuck in the same job for years, unable to open bank accounts, and so on. I'd got my life back, but lost it again with my papers gone.

The day turned into night. I had no choice but to rest after pounding the pavement in my fervent search. My predicament heightened during the next day of searching. I had loved Billy. Now I hated him. I had felt safe and secure. Now I felt confused. Mentally anguished, I was physically depressed.

In AA meetings I shared little, mostly listening. Folks said they understood, yet I questioned how they could grasp my fear when my documents were lost. I was a real basket case, full of shame, remorse, sadness, and anger, intermixed with determination instilled by Nana's expectations.

Under the kitchen sink were cleaning solutions. Billy hadn't bothered taking those. Countless times I held an open bottle of poison and dared myself to drink it, to get it over with. But I couldn't go through with it. I didn't have the guts to kill myself as much as I wanted to. Not only did I fail to drink the poisons, but I refused to drink alcohol. I had to prove, as an AA member, that I didn't have to drink. Nana had picked herself up when her first husband had left her. With a newborn baby to take care of back in 1926, my great-grandmother did what she had to do. She survived. That's what I had to do. *Survive.*

Three days after Billy's departure, Catfish Tom called me. "Your box of stuff is here. Billy just dropped it off. He wouldn't tell me anything else but showed me a bus ticket."

"Huh?" My knees buckled. I fell to the carpeted floor. "I just want my box. I don't care about anything else. I'll be right there."

I hurried to Westside Center. Don handed me my box. "You know I care about you? If you need anything, let me know."

Catfish Tom stood next to Don. "Billy wouldn't tell me why. He's on his way to his dad's, up in Michigan. I don't know where the other stuff is he took, but it's probably with Clyde."

Consumed with the shame of what Billy and Clyde had done, I couldn't tell the difference between embarrassment and hurt. It was as if I should have known better than to get involved with him, let alone fall in love with and marry him. Or maybe what people said about wearing black on your wedding day was true—it brings bad luck.

The next day, and for several days afterward, I woke up to a miserable existence. I was swallowed whole in my loneliness and depression without the man I had fallen in love with, only to come to hate him. Don came by to check on me daily. "I don't like to see you so depressed, Sam'. Let me help you."

Every day, Don helped me choose clothes to wear, and then put his arm around my back and shoulders to walk me to the bathroom to shower and brush my teeth. At first, I had no appetite for anything except cheese and crackers, but over time, Don worked me up to a cheese sandwich, and then a full meal.

I wouldn't let go of my suicide option, but lacked courage for that act. Drinking was also an option. But there too, I refused to succumb. Unlike with my suicidal thoughts, it wasn't a lack of courage, but stubbornness that kept me from drinking. At nearly three years sober and with hurdles behind me to reach my milestone, I had an aggressive attitude in my recovery. I refused to drink no matter fuckin' what.

I kept going to AA. I had to. I wanted to stay sober through this crap. AA was my only choice to stay sober. AA is completely self-run at the meeting level with elected officers to represent its area-wide groups. Clyde, Billy's uncle who helped him leave, came up for election. I attended the business meeting for choosing our officers. At the appointed time for discussion, I expressed why he was not to be trusted with a high-ranking service position. I then cast my nay vote for him. He won the election.

Betrayed by my AA community, I boycotted the geographic region Clyde served. I've never again returned to an AA meeting in that region. As usual, Don supported me in my choice, but he didn't want to see me go without an AA meeting. I hadn't rejected AA. I respected that AA had saved my life, but I wasn't about to lose my life through my support of wrongdoing. Each Saturday night, Don drove two hours or more so we could attend an AA meeting outside of Clyde's district.

Don was my support person, reminding me I wasn't to blame for what Billy and Clyde had done. As my health strengthened, my newfound hatred of Springfield didn't break. I was resigned to leave Springfield. I had tried it once before, only to fail, but had learned from that mistake. Surely, there was a better way to go about it, a financially secure way.

Don understood and told me, "If you want someone to help you, I can be that man for you. I can support you in anything you do. It was totally wrong what Billy did, and I'd never do that to you."

Clinging to Don's words with serious consideration, I had a chance to start life anew. Springfield had quit working for me. Legally free and clear, I decided to go west, not east as I had in my failed Savannah move. But farther west than Oregon, to Alaska. I couldn't fail in this relocation. Nana had made me aware we were to use whatever means necessary to make life better. And I felt something more for Don. I believed I could reciprocate his devotion.

Six and a half months out from the day I married Billy, Don and I drove an hour south to Harrison, Arkansas. Our plan was to marry on December 24, but a blizzard was on the horizon so we left a day early. We checked into a cheesy motel room and woke up the next morning to a snowed-in town. Highways were shut down. Main streets had yet to have their snow plowed. While our car wasn't moving, we could still walk the snowy sidewalks. We had a 9:00 a.m. appointment at the courthouse, and it was only a few blocks away from the motel.

Warm clothes were a must for the walk. Dressing in our finest clothes was also a must for our appointment. Don wore corduroy dress pants over his long johns, along with a matching suit jacket and overcoat. I wore a white satin gown that fell into a full ballerina skirt at knee length, with a white long john shirt underneath. White wool tights with tulle lace that peeked out from the ankles of my pure white snow boots added warmth. I put on my white jacket and took Don's hand. We ventured out into the snow for our walk.

When we arrived at the courthouse a news reporter approached us. "Is it okay if I take pictures of your ceremony to put in our paper? It's not every day we marry a couple in our courtyard, and in a blizzard, no less."

I gripped Don's hand. Don smiled and answered her, "Yes, that's okay."

"Great. Tell me your names and ages for this article," the reporter asked.

Don answered her, giving her our names, then said, "I'm fifty-three and Samantha is thirty-five."

A court clerk approached us, wearing a heavy coat and hat. "Ready?" she asked us.

We followed her and another clerk and the judge outside. The reporter followed behind, snapping pictures. Blowing snow had trickled down to a light falling. The roof on the open gazebo added to our shelter from the wind as Don and I put our overcoats on the side railing. Fraser fir and pine trees dotted the courtyard, caked with snow all around us.

The judge opened our ceremony with words about love and commitment. I then placed a silver band on Don's ring finger as he placed an amethyst solitaire ring on mine. The judge told us to kiss. We kissed. The reporter snapped another picture. Court clerks signed our license. We were Mr. and Mrs. Birran, married on the morning of Christmas Eve, 2002.

Don was husband number six, but he didn't mind. He was along for the ride of my life, including our intended embarkment to Alaska the following spring. The apartment lease would be up April 1, which gave us three months from our wedding day to prepare for our relocation. We finished out our winter months in Springfield with extra hours at our jobs, all the while filling up our joint bank account. Seeing dollar signs increase was beyond rewarding, in comparison to the days I illegally held a net worth of a million dollars.

Aside from his job with Catfish Tom, Don got Social Security disability payments. He was from an older generation, having grown up in Kansas with farm duties that took precedence over school. That rendered him at a third-grade reading level. Illiteracy qualified him for his monies from Social Security. This fixed income would give us a cushion to fall back on once we arrived in Alaska with its higher cost of living.

In our remaining days in Springfield, we liquidated as best we could, and earned pocket cash from yard sales. We bought a secondhand S10 Chevy pickup truck and camper shell. We stocked up on wool blankets, warm clothes, and lots of maps for travel due north out of Missouri and into Canada, westbound to Alaska.

Come the early daylight hours of a warm April day in 2003, we finished loading our truck and Don tightened the packing straps to keep our camper secure. "Any last goodbyes to Springfield before we leave?" Don asked me.

"Nope."

CHAPTER 19

SAM', III

Our trip up I-35 North would be a twelve-hour drive, not counting stops for gas and meals. From there, it was another three hours on a rural highway, US-53, to the Canadian border crossing. At an overnight stop in a lakefront campground, falling asleep in awe under our starry night was the only thing on our minds. The big city of St. Paul was behind us, and all that remained between us and Canada were tiny towns.

We talked about our travels ahead. Winnipeg, Manitoba in Canada was on our schedule for the next morning, and from there, two weeks tromping through Saskatchewan, Alberta, and British Columbia, then into White Horse, and then down around the corner of Alaska to drop into the Kenai Peninsula. We were Alaska-bound and fell asleep tired from our excitement.

Don woke me up as he complained about stomach pains. I wasn't yet ready to wake up. It was the middle of the night.

"Go back to sleep," I told him.

Don exhaled another whine. "I can't. My stomach hurts."

I rolled away from him. "Well, don't pass gas."

"Oh, Sam', it hu-uu-rts."

"You ate too much. Tomorrow morning you can walk down to the bathroom," I said.

He hugged his stomach. "My stomach hurts nowww."

"Go back to sleep and you won't notice it."

"Sam', my stomach hurts."

"Go back to sleep."

"I can't. You have to take me to the hospital."

I lifted my head up from my pillow. "Huh? Go back to sleep."

He hugged his stomach again. "I can't."

I was tired. Not just sleepy-tired, but tired of our argument. "Let me get dressed first."

I drove him thirty miles back south, to the hospital we had passed on our way to the campground. I couldn't drive fast. With vision in only one eye, I had never been a reliable driver in the dark when in unknown territory.

It was an unusually small hospital with no traffic in its parking lot. I walked Don to the ER door. The door was locked but it had a buzzer, which I pushed. Once inside, medical personnel stabilized and medicated him for his pain. The doctor told me, "Your husband has a kidney stone that needs to pass. He needs treatment that we don't have here."

I rode in the ambulance as they took him back north and west of US-53, to a larger hospital. We stayed long enough for him to pass his stone. On our first day there, arrangements were made through hospital support services to take me to our campground spot to pack up our belongings, and then to retrieve our truck from the first hospital.

On the second day of his hospital stay he passed the stone, and the next morning, was released. Our medical ordeal ended in an unrelenting rainstorm. We were only a short way from International Falls and reasoned we should head for the border that morning.

In a heavy downpour of rain, we approached the gate to the border crossing in our hillbilly truck, our ill-fitting camper shell bungee-corded to it. We stopped under a carport to hand our IDs through the window. A man in a uniform slid open the window he sat behind. "Your ID."

Don handed the Canadian guard his Missouri driver's license and Kansas birth certificate. I handed Don my Missouri driver's license, my Arkansas birth certificate, and supporting documentation for my legal name change. Don passed my documents to the guard, saying, "These are my wife's papers."

The guard told us to wait. He left his window to approach other guards nearby. I don't know if they were bored on that rainy morning, perplexed by our vehicle of choice, or confused by who I was when I asked to be let into their country. Either way, they didn't wave us through. Instead, a different guard came to the window. "I need you to pull over to that carport," he said as he pointed ahead.

Don pulled in as instructed and parked, then rolled down his window. The same guard who had told us to park walked up to our truck. He stepped up to Don's side and said, "We need to search your truck before you cross."

Stepping out, we agreed, and Don handed the guard the truck keys. Our only choice was to comply. The inconvenience didn't worry us. We knew the rules, what we could and couldn't transport across the border, and the only things we had against the rules were three cartons of cigarettes and little cigars. We had those packed deep in our luggage, several layers back, likely to go unnoticed. Tobacco products in Canada were an outrageous price.

Judging by the look on the guard's face, he wasn't pleased with his duties. As he proceeded, he found a small box of memorabilia items in our cab. It had photographs of Don's two young nieces, playing with balloons at a birthday party. The guard held the pictures and looked at Don. "Child pornography is not allowed at our border crossing."

Don started to laugh but cut his giggle short. He explained, "Those are my nieces."

The guard's eyes narrowed. The skin on his forehead tightened. He shook his head, tossed the pictures back in Don's box, and then rummaged through the passenger side of the cab. He pulled out my manila envelope from under the seat. It held all my legal documents.

Not waiting for the guard to question me as he flipped through the papers in the envelope, I said, "Those are mine. I keep them safe under the seat, so they don't get lost or damaged. My name has been legally changed more than once, and those papers show why my name is different from the name on my birth certificate."

The guard gave me a half smile, put the papers on the seat, picked one out of the middle of the stack, and read it to himself. He then tossed it on top of the pile and again picked another document at random and read that one. He then grabbed the pile and started flipping through them again. "How many times have you been married?"

I started to answer him. "Don is—"

The guard interrupted me, "You're a bad person, being married so many times."

I crossed my arms, took a deep breath, and started to explain. "I—"

The guard interrupted me. "I need to check your camper." He tossed the papers that were in his hands onto the pile he had left on my seat, then walked to the back of our truck.

Our guard next opened the hatch door to our camper shell. He shook his head, opened a bag, and looked inside it. He then pulled another bag closer to him and did the same. He shook his head again, stepped back a few steps, and looked intently at the inside of our camper shell. We had a lot of crap crammed into our truck bed. We were moving to Alaska.

"Follow me inside for an interview," he said.

The falling rain was relentless, but our walk was completely covered by the carport. Escorted to a desk and chairs, two guards stood close by. I sat down in one chair, and Don sat in the other. I remained quiet. The interviewing officer who sat across from us said, "Sir, judging from these pictures in your truck, are you a child molester?"

Don answered, "No, those are my nieces. What? You guys think I'm a child molester?"

Our interviewer looked up from the folder he held. "Yes, are you? And you, ma'am, are you married to him?"

I gave my one-word answer, "Yes."

"Why so many names?" he asked, as he thumbed through our file of, what was to them, incriminating evidence. To me, it was more like a monkey trial. I knew what a real investigation was, and that was far from it. But we couldn't just stand up and walk out. We were locked in between two border gates and the Canadian side had my documents. We had to put up with their bullshit.

I explained, "I've been married before and—"

The interviewing guard interrupted me. "How many times married?"

I let him sift through the documentation, rather than answering him directly. He didn't prod for an answer, instead shifting to a different question. He looked at me, then Don, then back at me, and then asked, "Have you ever been convicted of a felony?"

I didn't break my blank stare. To answer truthfully wouldn't be in our favor, but to answer falsely could prove a lack of cooperation should they discover my lie. So far, we hadn't lied about anything. Surely Nana hadn't had this dilemma, when at age seventeen, she and her boyfriend and two friends crossed the same state for a weekend vacation in Canada. Don, who was usually wordy, didn't say anything and I kept silent.

The guard prodded for an answer. "You may as well tell us. We will find out anyway."

I said, "Yes, in 1990."

The guard asked, "For what?"

I answered, "Burglary."

He shut our file with a slam. "We can't let convicted felons cross our border, and don't go trying to cross the border from another state or we will have you arrested."

A guard standing nearby instructed us in how to take the circular drive to return to the United States. We left and drove the circle, but at the American side of the border crossing window, we were again questioned.

Don turned the ignition off. We were subjected to a twenty-minute interview from the cab of our truck. After a lengthy back and forth rebuttal, the American guard repeated what he had already said, "You can't cross here. Best if you go back through Canada and find another place to cross back into America."

Don flung his arms. His voice weakened. "We tried. They won't let us cross."

"You can't cross our American border. Your wife has felony convictions."

We were stuck between two borders. Don didn't bother to turn the ignition back on. We had nowhere to drive to, forward or backward. We sat still. Finally, a higher-ranking guard walked outside and approached Don to intervene. In the end, we could cross through their gate into the United States.

As Don drove southwest, off US-53 and onto US-71, we were at a loss of where to go next, other than certainly not back to Missouri. We discussed crossing the border out of Washington state, only to finally discard that idea. Fearing we were on a blacklist at every border crossing, we didn't want to waste our energy, time, and money risking it.

In our drive to who knows where, we defaulted to choosing a part of the country neither of us had seen before. When I had hitchhiked the country I'd never made it to Maine, but that was too far off the beaten track. That only left the desert area of Arizona and New Mexico.

Our wanderlust spirit overshadowed our riled letdown. Instead, and like perfect tourists, we took in all the sights we could. Don had a special pass card through the Federal Park System. It gave us free admittance to many state and federal touristy spots, camping included. With the burden of lodging expenses lifted, we freely meandered. Historical monuments, small town museums, and stops at hole-in-the-wall diners placated our dilemma. Views at overlook points gave us shared moments of reflection. Springfield was behind us and a new life awaited us.

With snow falling in the surrounding hills, we spent my thirty-sixth birthday at Yellowstone National Park in Wyoming. Warm weather followed with a trip to the Grand Canyon, and even warmer weather hit us as we traveled the wine country of California. Heat engulfed us in 125 degree terrain in southwest Arizona. Come mid-June, we tried camping at Elephant Butte, New Mexico.

I soon came to call it Elephant Butt, without the long "u" sound.

It wasn't pretty enough to call it a butte, or even a beaut. Each tent space had a cement shelter with slabs that stood to protect campers from wind gusts, but did a poor job of it. In an afternoon high wind gale, we draped our tarp over our picnic table inside our shelter and ducked under. We had experienced rainstorms, snow, scorching heat, canyon depth, and now, extreme wind. Surely there had to be somewhere livable, somewhere in our big country to call home.

From Elephant Butt, we stopped in at nearby Truth or Consequences, "T or C" as locals called it. We tried out their AA meeting and checked out their small city. I liked it but found it too small for working opportunities. While there, I read the newspaper out of nearby Las Cruces. It was a city with 100,000 people and had a major medical center and other worthwhile amenities. I told Don, "I want to try Las Cruces."

Settling into our community, the language barrier was my only disappointment. Otherwise, I came to love Las Cruces. Businesses and houses didn't crowd one another. It was spacious. Weather was beautiful, clear, and arid. Nestled below mountain ranges, it sits at a high altitude. The Rio Grande River runs through Las Cruces to the Mexican border, however shallow. Summers were hot but dry, not sticky wet. Winters brought cooler temperatures, but not too cold for an outdoor picnic in a T-shirt and jeans. Our local TV news also covered El Paso, Texas, and Ciudad Juarez in Chihuahua, Mexico.

We'd been living in Las Cruces for six months when in March

2004, we received a flyer advertising a neighborhood church. It wasn't an invitation to their worship services as much as it was an invitation to a special series of religious education they offered. A visiting pastor from Texas had been invited to give the lecture series.

I had dabbled in church before, like when John and I were members of the Baptist church. And Don and I had previously attended an informational dinner with an Episcopalian church. My need for church was less about fellowship. Rather, it stemmed from a need to understand the God concept.

Nana had instilled in me the notion of making sense of my community and a purpose behind everything I did. The advertisement promised fact-based wisdom, not social fluff. In AA I was expected to depend on God, but my dependency was false when I questioned my belief.

On the opening night of this event, a friend went with Don and me as we walked into the Seventh-day Adventist church. Two people stood in the foyer and greeted us. The man shook Don's hand and the lady handed me some papers. We found a seat up front in their cushioned velvet pews. I wanted to be close enough to hear every word in their message.

A well-dressed man boisterously took the microphone and kindly shouted, "The conflict between our great religions of the world will shake our very foundation of life as we know it, erupting into a cataclysmic climax that will destroy everything we think we know."

A month later, I was baptized. I didn't want to be left behind during the end times of Christ's second coming. Fully immersed in their teachings, which were based on historical context, I learned about the biblical commandments, the Sabbath, the calendar change to the Julian era, the book of Revelations. I wholeheartedly believed I was part of the remnant church.

In early 2006, departmental restructuring at work caused strife in my Sabbath keeping. With my church's help, I argued for my religious rights, and when we reached a higher level with my employer, I won. Through my fight, I took a closer look at my job choice. It was a housekeeping position. It was gainful employment, but it didn't offer me an opportunity to use my skills.

I enrolled at the community college with New Mexico State University, and left the housekeeping job in favor of a flexible employer. I took only one class my first semester, a basic computer class, which taught me what a mouse was, and what to do with a mouse. I had no experience whatsoever with computers, but understood the world was changing technologically.

Don and I were living twenty minutes south in Vado on a one-acre rented lot. Our house was actually an RV we owned, but it had everything we needed. Our living room, like any typical American home, had a couch and chairs, a TV, phone, bookshelves with books, and knickknacks. However, ours was outside in a gazebo with desert sand as our floor.

Year round, warm air with little rain gave us a full view of beautiful sunrises and colorful sunsets against the backdrop of orange-tipped mountains. Those mountains were the perfect view when working through my homework. Later, we traded in the RV for an Airstream trailer.

My new employer was with Home Instead Senior Care, through which I provided non-clinical care for the elderly and disabled in their homes. Assigned shifts ranged from a few hours to an overnight stay, all in consideration of my class schedule. Among my regular clients was Mr. Beuhler. At eighty years old, he had dementia. Mrs. Beuhler, who was in her seventies and energetic, went out a couple afternoons a week, leaving me to care for her husband.

In their upper-middle-class home, Mr. Beuhler liked to rock in his rocking chair and tell me stories. Tall windows and skylights lit up the living room as we sat and talked. He'd often pinch his eyes shut, remembering a time in his life he wanted to share with me. I took those moments to look out their windows. Their place was sparsely decorated, but the outside view with tall trees nearby and golden mesas far off made up for it.

Mr. Beuhler reminded me of Grandpa. Pondering the workings of our universe, I was easily swept up in his simple words explaining the meaning of life, all in an intelligent manner.

Shortly after my tenure with the Beuhlers started, so did my time with Mrs. Overton. She was an older woman, slow in her movements and afflicted with dementia. Her daughter, Madilyn, had recently moved her into a semi-independent retirement apartment complex.

My times with Mrs. Overton were challenging, as her confusion never abated. But Madilyn caused me to fall in love with my commitment to Mrs. Overton. Aside from my hourly pay from Home Instead, she showered me with spending money and often took her mom and me out to lunch at Red Lobster. She even sold me her six-year-old car, a 2000 Ford Taurus, at a great deal.

As I fixed Mr. Buehler's lunch one day, I gave him his glass of wine. He was allowed one glass of red wine a day, but no more, no matter how often he was forgetful that he'd already had his limit. Mr. Buehler asked, "You want one too?"

He asked me that every time, and every time I had answered him with a, "No, thank you."

He knew I didn't drink, but his dementia kept him from remembering.

I was just short of seven years sober. Drinking was not an option for me. I was active in AA, active in church, gainfully employed, a college student, and proud to be married to Don. That's when it hit me. I was carefree and worry free.

AA told me the disease centered in the mind. I errantly took that to mean that if I had problems, I would drink problematically, but if I was free from problems, there would be no problems. No longer a troubled young woman, I errantly believed I was immune to problem drinking.

I opened their cupboard and answered, "Sure, I'll have a glass with you."

I poured myself a glass of wine and carried it with his plate to the table. We sat down together. He didn't say anything and bit into his sandwich. He never talked when he ate his lunch. I drank my wine. When he took the last bite of his sandwich, he pushed his plate to me, then washed his meal down with the last sip of his wine.

I got up from the table and carried our dishes to the sink. I put his plate in the soapy water but held back on putting our glasses in the sink. I poured each of us another glass of wine and turned to him. He was already up from the table and watching me. He reached his hand out to take his glass and said, "I was wondering where my glass of wine was. You know, Sam', I'm supposed to have one glass of red wine with my lunch."

I smiled. He had forgotten he'd already had his one glass. I took a drink from my glass and washed his plate. He drank his down quickly, as if it were only water, and as I was rubbing a towel over his clean plate, he handed me his empty glass. I gulped the rest of the wine in my glass, then washed both of our glasses, dried them, and returned them to the cupboard.

My job was important to me. I couldn't over-imbibe. With a giggly rapport, we finished our afternoon in a shared attempt at a jigsaw puzzle.

Then there was my relationship to Mrs. Overton and her daughter, Madilyn. At our next luncheon, Madilyn ordered the first of her two martinis. Every time we went out to eat, Marilyn drank two. She looked at me and asked, "Do you want one? I know you're not supposed to drink when working, but I don't mind."

Mrs. Overton interjected. Sitting across from her daughter, she leaned forward and stretched her arms on the table toward Madilyn. "Honey, I'd like one too."

Madilyn said, "No, Mom. You know you can't drink on your medication. Sam, martini?"

I answered, "Yes, please."

Madilyn never let her mom drink, but the medication part was an excuse. She had often explained to me in private that her mom had a bad drinking problem before she came down with dementia.

I limited myself to one martini over lunch. I didn't want to appear irresponsible with her mother. It was understood that after lunch I'd drive her mom home, then spend time with her. My assignments with Mrs. Overton increased, and Madilyn let go of other caregivers, always asking for me by name when requesting service with Home Instead.

At times my duties included us dining out together. At other times, my responsibility was to watch TV or visit in Madilyn's home. Unlike the caregivers who had come before me, Madilyn didn't have to hide how much she drank. I drank right alongside her. I had slipped into a life of two lives. One life was with Don, from whom I hid my inebriation. My other life was wrapped around Madilyn, the bored alcoholic housewife.

My relapse lasted four months. In early November, I came home too drunk to bother hiding it from Don. I suppose it didn't help I had wrecked the back-passenger door on the car from Madilyn, with no recollection of how. It took me three weeks to patch together more than a few days of sobriety.

I went back to AA and had Don's support. I resumed my serious intentions with college classes. And I had one less thing to hide from my church. But I had to hide my wrecked car from Madilyn. So, for the sanity of my recovery, I cut ties to her.

Spring 2007 brought me new awareness in an array of ways. For starters, I attended a new weekly study through my church. My life had become their life, solidified wholly in their hands and direction. Knowledge gave me the assurance I needed to make sense of life, and then death afterward.

As my loyalty to church intensified, so did my thirst for answers to questions that had lain dormant in me. I questioned our study leader and church elders and tested their answers by fact-checking in scientific journals and library books, some on anthropology, some on the historicity centering around the first century, A.D. The complexity of religious development uncovered discrepancies in the answers my church elders had given me.

Surely they wouldn't have lied to me, would they?

I pushed my doubts aside and tried to fit in with the spiritual side of AA. College kept my mind off my doubts. Classes in computers and math had to be conquered in my part-time schedules before going into a full schedule based on a degree program.

Open to career possibilities, I became aware of an emerging career field in allied health sciences. With my clerical skills, I could study toward a degree and lucrative salary as a medical coder or biller. The one catch was a requirement to eventually sit for the national credentialing exam, and neither the community college nor NMSU met the requirements as set by its exam board.

Through my research, I discovered only a few colleges held the credentials with their allied health degrees that satisfied the credentialing board. I applied and was accepted for a September 2007 start date at Shoreline Community College. At full-time attendance, I had a 2009 graduation date with an associate degree to look forward to.

That college was near Seattle, which meant moving away from the city I'd come to love. Again, Don was willing to follow me to the ends of the earth. But I also hungered for change and new direction. I loved Don but wasn't sure I wanted him to follow me to Seattle. He had been there for me when I needed him most, back when I wanted out of Springfield. I was stronger now, not needy. The drifter in my blood would win.

I felt a tug-of-war in my heartstrings. Preparing to relocate, I was concerned with how Don would get along without me. I helped him with reading, writing, bill paying, and understanding contracts. When I expressed my concern to a friend, she replied, "How did he get by before you came along?"

Her question was rhetorical. Don would be fine, and I had to be true to myself.

I next went to Don and told him what my decision was. He said, "Okay. I meant what I said when I told you I'd always support you. Seattle might be good for you. I wish I had gone to college. Don't worry about me. I will be fine. And I'll always love you and I want you to keep in touch with me."

Dissolving a marriage came all too easily for me. To ease the feeling that I had disrespected our vows and commitment, I prepared documents to contractually divvy our property. Notarized by the county clerk, Don would retain full rights to keep the trailer home, with the car left to me. Don and I each kept a legal copy to protect our individual interests. To this day, Don and I remain legally separated and fully supportive of each other with frequent phone calls to keep in touch.

On a Tuesday morning, I hit Seattle's rainy rush hour traffic on the interstate from the east side. I took my first exit to Shoreline for an AA meeting that was listed in my AA schedule. Coincidentally, it was at a Seventh-day Adventist church. Just a few minutes off the interstate, I had located two lifelines.

The AA meeting was a women-only meeting. When it ended, a woman approached me. "Welcome. Do you have time for lunch? I know the best coffee place, and it's close by."

During our coffeehouse visit we discussed my plans, and she suggested two newspapers I could look to for rental ideas. I called one number to leave a voicemail. The second number I called was for a woman who rented out rooms in a house she owned in Lynnwood. That was a little farther north than I wanted, but still part of Seattle's greater metropolitan span, and close to the Aurora Avenue main drag, which led everywhere. Later that same day, I moved into one of her three basement rooms.

Far from beautiful orange and red mesas, Shoreline Community College, or SCC for short, showed me another side of beauty. At more than eighty acres, evergreen trees were its majestic canopy. Red maple and pink magnolias dotted green grass. Ornamental landscaping in a Japanese design could swallow one up in its beauty.

Sidewalks meandered through campus leading to each academic building. Wooden signs in white lettering on green directed me along its paths. There was even an espresso bar to be found. With an innate drive to become involved, everything would soon become familiar territory and my everyday stomping ground.

Like twenty-some years before when I was at Job Corps, wallflower status was not for me. When at Job Corps, I had succeeded as one of the youngest students. At SCC, I was determined to succeed as one of the oldest students. Other nontraditional students attended SCC, but most of them had other responsibilities, such as children and families and work. I had none of that, only SCC to make my life into something worthwhile.

Ignoring my age of forty, I merged into social circles with classmates who were young enough to be my kids, open to their guidance and wisdom. I committed myself to campus involvement and activism. Leadership roles, club participations, and a year on Student Government as Student Advocate gave me an outlet for my compulsive drive, but in a good way this time around.

Coursework in the Health Information Technology Program, or

HIT for short, jump-started my thirst for knowledge. My second semester in, I dropped from a full course load to three classes per semester, ensuring a rounded balance between classes and college activities. My new graduation date was set for June 2010.

Work came through the college library, and it was my first working experience in a library. However, my office clerical skills and understanding of filing systems were in my favor, and I quickly caught on to the Dewey decimal system. My working hours were scheduled around my class schedule at a few hours a day. And not willing to break my Sabbath-keeping, I pulled another six hours each Sunday. Saturday, for church, was my one scheduled day off from anything campus related.

Each day, I started with an early morning AA meeting. There I met Krista, who became my AA sponsor and good friend. Younger, but astute in her worldly views and smart in her tenacity for life, I wanted what she had. Her smile evoked confidence and happiness, no matter what difficulties gave her a bumpy history.

I attended my sister church in Shoreline twice but didn't transfer my membership. At first I fell into a state of aloofness, but then my fear of Hell pushed me to resolve my confusion with religion. I needed real answers to questions I had put forth to my church when back in Las Cruces. I discussed religion with other classmates and listened to alternate views, some supported with reason. I added to my understanding through elective classes and other means of discovery.

As my skepticism grew, the AA message to "Let go and let God" became difficult for me. With plenty of evidence, I doubted I still believed in God. Without God, there couldn't be Hell. If only Nana had given me some sort of clue about God, other than to plainly insinuate His existence. Silent on that topic, she had been focused on life, and not on what came before or after. I filed my ever-developing breakdown over the concept or ideology of God somewhere in the back of my brain and turned my attention elsewhere.

In my occasional phone calls with Don, I couldn't bring myself to share any of that with him. I was ashamed to have believed in God, or ashamed I no longer believed. Either way, I held more shame than confidence, and I didn't want to crush his belief in God.

Don had moved to Wichita, Kansas to be close to his mom. There, he settled well into a trailer park. He also connected with a community program, Christy Hope, which gave him a support system that I was no longer able to provide for him. We mutually supported each other in our new paths.

PART FIVE

CHAPTER 20

SAMUELLE

Campus life was not only my love, but also my escape from living under my landlord's thumb. I had moved closer to campus in my second year, renting a mother-in-law apartment. My landlord, Ahmad, and his family lived in a big family house, situated with a garage between us. My AA home group changed, partly for its closer location, and partly for its comparatively relaxed view on the God concept.

My morning routine started with the 7:00 a.m. Broadview AA meeting, which led me to the campus foothills and my library job for my 8:30 start time. A gentleman friend from my Broadview group, Dennis, often walked with me and then browsed the library. Spry as a fifty-year-old, but older than eighty, he earned his nickname, "Schoolboy." When I struggled with the Christian undercurrent at Christmastime, he suggested, "Sam', try celebrating it the American way for now. Forget about that religious crap."

My landlord's wife, Marjou, worked full time. Ahmad didn't, and was instead home with some disability. When my landlord and

I had first met, he was impressed with my scholastic endeavors. Like Nana being proud for me, Ahmad was proud in a fatherly way. That should have been clue number one for me. I don't function well under parental-like authorities. The apartment's proximity to school and the privacy of my quarters were my incentives to rent from him.

Like my relationship with Nana had been, trying to live up to his many expectations became exhausting. My apartment also had a back door, which led to a patio for my use. On warmer days I'd sit outside, do homework, and smoke freely. I couldn't smoke inside.

Deep in thought over the page in my textbook, I was on my patio when Ahmad startled me. "Your smoke is drifting up to my open window. I was trying to take a nap."

He stood facing me with a disgruntled look, pointing above me to their second floor.

I put my little cigar out in my ashtray and said, "Sorry."

He turned around and pointed to the house next door. "I don't want the neighbors to see you smoking."

With my smoke out, he walked away. Later that day, I walked out to the street to have another smoke. It was early evening. Ahmad and his family should have been busy with their dinner. I faced the street. Behind me, I heard Ahmad as he walked out to me. "Sam, the neighbors will see you here. I told you I don't want the neighbors seeing you smoke."

I relaxed my arm but held on to my little cigar.

He said, "Follow me."

As I followed him, he pointed to a corner in our shared yard, where tall bushes edged the neighboring yard. "If you must smoke, smoke there." He turned around and walked away.

My final year of coursework stretched my intelligence through advanced classes applying medical billing and coding principles. Sometimes when I turned in my homework assignments, my teachers would mark them up with red writing in all caps.

Our instructors had to set high standards for us. Our program of study had to comply with accreditation standards, as set by the American Health Information Management Association, known as AHIMA. Credentialing as a Registered Health Information Technician was our goal, but to sit for the national exam to earn our credentials we had to first meet those accrediting standards.

Aside from learning how to do the work, I also learned about the professional responsibilities that came with this career path. I had been attracted to college to get out of a rut of low-wage jobs. This degree had seemed appealing because it let me advance the clerical skills I already had. The legal responsibilities of this career work detracted from my passion for this career. Where I was once excited for this degree, I now disliked some of what I had learned in three years.

I tried to set my dissatisfaction aside through commitment to my immediate classmates and by spending less time in other campus activities. We celebrated when someone was offered a job, and we cried together when someone didn't do well on a test. We discussed plans after college. Our optimism was sometimes disillusioned. An offer for a career job relied on more than our degree. It often demanded work experience in the field.

In my final semester, a classmate and I got into a heated argument in our online discussion board. It was over something trivial. After the backlash of several comments to each other, she retorted, "You will never get a job as an RHIT in Seattle. I know people, and when I'm done spreading the word, no one will want to hire you."

Our instructor intervened, deleted our online correspondence, and put us on academic probation. After we each completed an additional assignment, an essay on problem resolution, our probation was lifted. Graduation was right around the corner.

My classmate's threat left a scar. I half believed her and gave credit to its potential validity. She was already working in the professional field. She was a strong student, self-assured as someone who knew intricate nuances of medical law backward and forward. Her threats and my insecurities incited my lack of productivity, as if it were useless to figure out where to go when my campus life ended.

Left feeling like I had little control over where I'd be next, I took control over who I'd be. Three years of separation from Don was long enough for me to let go of his last name. While I no longer had a secret identity to protect, I abstained from telling others about my prior last names. Letting go of Don's last name, and without ties to any other last name, I defaulted to the prior alias name of Mott.

For my first name, I liked that people called me Sam', but didn't like when they used my full name Samantha. After toying with alternatives, I settled on Samuelle instead of Samantha. Not to be confused with Samuel, my new choice elicited a feminine long "l" sound, like Danielle compared to Daniel. With a fondness for the reasons I had first chosen my middle name, Ann was the one name I couldn't part with.

In my third and last year of college, I petitioned the judge at my county courthouse for a legal name change. The next step was to change my ID. Stepping up to the counter at the Social Security Office, I let the clerk know I needed a new card. He started my application, then looked up at me and said, "You are nearing your lifetime limit of name changes."

"What?" I asked.

He said, "You're allowed ten name changes. This is your eighth."

In my responsibility to inform state and federal agencies of my name change, I hadn't before been aware of any limits. Then again, it was nothing new to me to do something again, and again, from four high schools to becoming a career criminal with thirteen cats, to hitchhiking through forty-some states, to being married six times. One of anything was never enough for me.

My name change was finalized in May, near my forty-third birthday, and less than a month before graduation. I was still Sam'.

Legally, Samuelle. Although I had named myself, I wasn't convinced I knew who I was. And I certainly had no idea where I was going, without any serious thought to life after campus life.

Clusters of classmates stood in circles, each well-defined by our program of study or degree. Molly stood silently right by my side. I felt pressured to hold enough confidence for both Molly and me. We had studied hard together and shared our short internship. Like me, she questioned if we truly had what it took to succeed as allied health professionals. Unlike me, Molly admitted her doubts when we studied together.

I wanted to crawl back into my world of denial rather than be there in that green graduation gown, feeling strangled by the yellow honor sash as it crossed my body. Well dressed, if only to rise above standards of my own style, all that showed from under my graduation garb was my paisley necktie, tightly knotted where revealed by a v-neckline. Paisley may have gone out of style years before, but I liked the individuality and nonconformity it suggested, even though my choice might have dated me as I waited with classmates half my age for the procession.

The year prior I could have passed as barely older than them, but on that day the youth in my face was gone, weathered by sweat and tears I had poured into my campus life for three years. Nor was I a scrawny teenager, but buff with a buzz haircut as if to make a political statement with my five-foot-one stature. Other than my necktie, my black patent oxfords showed. They were polished, should someone bother to look down.

If it wasn't for the cap and gown I wore, same as other students, I could easily have been mistaken for a teacher in Fine Arts, or maybe even Phys. Ed. Certainly not a professor. They were easy to pick out with their greyed hair, wrinkles, and reading glasses that either dangled lopsided off their noses or on chains at their full bosoms. Many glances were thrown my way, smiles lingering before gazes were redirected elsewhere.

I remembered the heartfelt eagerness I held on my first day on campus. That was nearly three years prior to graduation day. On this day, I stood with my peers, waiting for our official send-off. Campus was no longer my place. New students, fresh faces, and a rush of eighteen-year-olds would call that land their land come the new semester. Where I had once proved my presence worthy of the campus community, it would be up to the new faces to make their mark.

Our Project Pride Club had existed before me, but with another name. We changed its name, brought it up from its stale standing, and made a positive difference on campus and in the community through our activism. Matthew was gone, no longer motivating the club, and now I had to leave. *Would it be stale again?*

My year on student government was the year they tested it out without ambassadors. It was the year our college's student government went from a bicameral body with executive and legislative branches to a parliament. As Student Advocate, classmates and campus peers came to me over problems with grades, teachers, and rules. We presented a new way of doing things, and as such, operated as one team and not two as before. *Did we make a difference?*

I looked around. I saw Yasu. He was smiling and talking with several girls who circled around him. He stood tall as he always did. Yasu had come to this college from Japan. I had volunteered as a mentor in the International Student Program. It was one-on-one time for students who were brand new, not only to our campus, but to our country. Likened to my club activism for an all-inclusive campus community, I learned from those I mentored. They taught me their foreign customs and values and enlarged my friendship circle. *Did I touch them as they had touched me?*

My program of study was still in its infancy as a fully online program. The confrontation between Debbie and me set a precedent for how our professors dealt with problems from then on out. Hopefully it wasn't the only mark I had left them with. I had to believe in myself, same as Molly trusted in me.

And surely, had Nana still been alive, she'd have been proud of me. I was a college graduate. More so, I had completed coursework from one of only a small number of colleges nationwide respected by AHIMA for its rigorous coursework. I went from marking my homeless pleas on cardboard signs sixteen years earlier, to marking my answers on college exams, and to marking my place in the history of our campus community.

The mere thought that I was a college graduate was overwhelming. It meant I had to go on, to prove myself in a brand-new way.

And I had been so caught up in campus life, in denial that it had to end, I hadn't given any thought to what came next for me.

Perhaps if I'd been at a normal college age, troubling thoughts wouldn't have prevailed. But as it was, I was in my early forties, significantly older than those I had melded with for three years. I should have looked forward to a career, but no longer desired my degree choice, and I had no job lined up. In my matriculation, even my campus library job was no more.

My classmates had spent spring semester job interviewing for their new lives, whereas I had barely touched a job application. Instead, spring semester for me had been one of complacency. I didn't want to face the fact that my world as I knew it had to end. I looked over and smiled at Molly, who was still standing next to me. I didn't dare show my sadness. My peers looked up to me and always had, no matter what my role. I couldn't let them down. Never had before, and wouldn't on our final day together.

My memories were interrupted as a classmate jumped out of her group and into mine. She gave me a big hug and said, "Congratulations, we did it."

Yes, "did," as in past tense. I saw the gymnasium door swing open and everyone fell back into their respective clusters as the procession into the auditorium began. I stepped in line and followed.

I took my seat and looked to the sidelines. Krista whistled kisses to me. I knew many of my classmates had moms and dads in the audience. I had Krista, my AA sponsor and friend, and two other gal friends. My older gentleman friend from my AA group, Schoolboy, was in the overflow room. Tickets for the gymnasium seating were limited, but others could watch from the viewing room.

Schoolboy had once walked beside me from our AA meeting onto campus. He now sat with Mike-Bike to watch me graduate. Mike wasn't at the top of my list, but I had asked him to escort Schoolboy. I hadn't wanted Schoolboy to sit alone, nor did I want him to get lost or confused. Before Mike bought a used car, he rode his bicycle everywhere, giving him his nickname.

Mr. Backes spoke into the microphone and welcomed everyone. He was the campus Vice President of Academic Affairs, the overseer of all deans, and a familiar face to me. We had talked countless times, sometimes in seriousness when in my Student Advocate role. Often, though, we had talked over nothing more than the rainy weather or the recent presidential campaign between Obama and McCain.

My attention drifted from his monotone voice. I thought to myself, *It's a good thing teachers can't poke at my brain now. They'd discover me deep in thought, far from this moment in time.* If I could have spoken aloud, what I wanted to say was, "Poof, whoosh, vamoose, no more. It's done and gone, forevermore."

Reality hit me like a ton of bricks on that summer day in 2010, Monday, June 7—I didn't have my campus life. I needed a career job. That was what I went to college to obtain. I looked to my older gentleman friend, Schoolboy, to help me navigate Seattle for interviews.

Several times weekly, Schoolboy rode the bus with me to downtown. Otherwise I'd easily get lost. Disjointed streets swallowed towering buildings with courtyards and lobbies that spanned full street blocks. To be lost in their concrete jungle, in the few times I went by myself, only heightened my grudging feat to find work. On a day he couldn't go with me, the city's visitor center helped me with directions to get home.

While my college degree was outstanding, time and again I was told in interviews, "We need someone with several years of experience."

Disappointing interviews and threats from my former classmate Debbie hung in my head, feeding my depression. Apprehension over legal responsibilities my career choice demanded also loomed in my head. I was more frightful than excited. I'd rather have been back on campus than anywhere else.

A viable working opportunity came through a temporary employment agency. The job could end at any time. It was with a company that did medical billing. I took it, however grudgingly. The metropolis commute was atrociously long.

It meant leaving my home professionally dressed at 5:05 a.m. to walk fifteen minutes for a 5:25 a.m. bus to Renton, a suburb south of Seattle. It was a direct route to Renton, but an hour long. After a twenty-minute layover at a bus stop in what seemed like the middle of nowhere, I transferred onto the crosstown bus. That put me at work at 7:45 a.m. for my 8:00 a.m. start time. My return commute was via the same two buses, which dropped me off at my original bus stop close to 7:30 p.m.

It also meant forgoing my usual routine in waking up. Before this job, I'd wake up, grab a cup of coffee, a smoke, and a blanket to sit on and head out to my designated smoking corner in the yard. There, I'd sit cross-legged on the grass. Lingering in my smoke break, I'd look up at the sky and talk out loud, but quietly. "Thank you for everything and please be with me today. I doubt you exist, but AA says you do. I can't stay sober on my own. Please keep me sober today."

Those mornings were gone. In my new routine, I hurried from my bed to put myself together for the day. I could have turned down the job offer, but it was my only offer. Besides, it was only a temporary job. It was working experience, which I needed. Between that and my resentment over ex-classmate Debbie ever-pressing on my pea-brain, I chose to persevere. My forced perseverance threatened my serenity. And serenity was precious to my sobriety.

My department was busy with women at their desks inside their respective cubicles, each lost in their own responsibilities. One manager served as supervisor and had the only office. I didn't have my own cubicle, or even my own desk. I shared a cubicle with two other women. I shared my desk with Pam. We cozied up to our shared desk, side by side, each with our own assigned computer and stacks of paper to process.

I liked Pam. She evoked strength when she spoke. She was strikingly beautiful with auburn hair against her ebony skin. She wore boxy pantsuits and walked with purpose. Pam often compliment-ed me on my neckties. I had acquired many neckties in the year I served as Student Advocate. My favorite was the pink paisley one, but she favored my silk tie with a silver Egyptian pattern against a soft blue background. Pam and I clicked so well that our coworkers saw us as one. Soon, our coworkers merged our names, Sam' and Pam. We became the Spam-Team.

Shortly into my job assignment, I left work as usual, crossing the street to wait at the bus stop for ten minutes for my first bus ride. I shifted the weight on my shoulder from my black leath-er tote bag. I hated the bulky feel of purses. My wallet stayed in my back pocket—I always had to keep my valuables on me. But I needed my tote bag too. It carried my coffee thermos, lunch, and study materials for my RHIT exam scheduled for early August, two months out.

At my Renton layover between buses, I stood and watched traf-fic. If only I had a car, but that got sold a couple years before, when I couldn't afford the insurance and maintenance on a student in-come. The commute sucked. A small convenience store was across the street. Other than that, not much else was out here, except peo-ple driving by.

Campus life was gone. AA meetings were few and far between since I couldn't make it to my morning AA homegroup. *Why bother?*

I had another fifteen minutes to wait on the bus. I waited for the next line of cars to clear, then crossed the street. Inside the conve-nience store, I scanned the layout, then went to its cooler. I picked out a six-pack of fine dark ale, purchased it, and put it in my tote bag, pulling my lunch bag out. It didn't fit anymore.

Returning to my bus stop, I stopped and watched traffic some more. Finally, my bus showed up. I chose a back-row seat, settled in, and peeked in my tote bag. The beer looked good. Shit, I had over an hour to go before getting home. The bus turned a bend and then stopped, letting several people off. It was like that every day. Few people rode the bus in the next fifteen-minute stretch.

I looked back in my tote bag and started to pull out my book to study for that darn RHIT exam. Letting go of it, I pulled out my empty coffee thermos, then cracked open a beer and poured it into my thermos. Ignoring the cup with the thermos, I took a swallow out of the thermos bottle. It stung my throat. It warmed me going down. Under my breath I said, "I'll just nurse it."

But I'd always been a gulper, so that went all too quickly. The bus pulled up to my neighborhood stop, which was next to a park-and-ride lot for commuters. Only two beers were left, not worthy to stay in the box they came in. In the parking lot, I tucked the two beers under some study materials, and keeping the box in the plastic shopping bag it came in, I put it in a trash can.

My walk home led me through a residential area. Once home, instead of changing into my pajamas, I changed into jeans. The liquor store was not more than five blocks away on Aurora Avenue. The last two beers from my tote bag weren't going to be enough.

Over that weekend, I nursed what remained of my second six-pack of ale. It was a welcome respite to my stress and I was ready for work Monday morning—but for reasons other than work. Like a nerd in school can spot a troublemaker, I could always spot Pam. With her, I could let go of my stress daily as I fell in beside her and her sneaky wayward ways.

The Spam-Team retreated to her blazer during our lunch hour to kick off our shoes and down airplane bottles. On the job, we often excused ourselves to the supply room downstairs where we'd hide away together. Our torrid affair with each other and our airplane bottles would last only as long as the Spam-Team working relationship lasted.

In early August, I sat for my RHIT exam, paid for by a social service agency. It was on a Monday, and I had prescheduled the day off from work. It was a three-hour exam, but I finished in only two hours, even after double-checking my answers. I felt confident as I took the exam, but felt I could have done better if I hadn't been hungover.

At work the next day, Pam gave me a big hug in our office and exclaimed, "Congratulations, you did it."

Later, in the supply room, Pam gave me a big kiss that left the taste of coral lipstick melted on my lips. "See, I told you that you could do it. We're both smart women, don't ever forget that."

Her words sounded all too familiar, as if Nana were speaking to me. But Nana wouldn't have worn such provocative lipstick. Instead, Nana had always worn true red on her lips. Nana would have been proud of me. Perhaps I was finally moving forward in my life, discovering true purpose and meaning, away from the problems I'd once had. Then again, I couldn't see with any pride how a daily reprieve from the grind, as found in the Spam-Team, moved me forward to a well-adjusted life.

My AA sponsor, Krista, had beamed the evening before when I dropped by her house to share my great news. "I passed."

She pulled me into her space and squeezed me with a natural smile. I let her hug me, but my self-hatred that lay hidden in my secrets defused any shrieks of joy from me. I didn't dare let her know I had returned to problem drinking. I knew I'd pass but was disappointed in myself. The exam was more of an expectation than something I could feel excited about. My depressive drinking had left me drained of spiritual energy.

I forced a smile for Krista when she was done hugging me. Her accolades pierced my low self-worth. With her beaming smile, she said, "I'm jealous. Aren't you proud to have letters behind your name? You're Samuelle Mott, R-H-I-T."

CHAPTER 21

ELLIE, I

"Come get me out of this," I said in a phone call to Bike-Mike. I still called him that, even though he had a car now. We were friends. He had sat with my older gentleman friend at my graduation ceremony. A few months after graduating, it was a warm Saturday night and my landlady was setting out decorations in their driveway, right outside my door.

I hardly ever saw my landlady. It was her husband, Ahmad, my landlord, who was usually too close to my apartment. Earlier, Ahmad had told me, "We're having a party."

I got the gist that it was a family celebration or religious observation. I closed my drapes and downed another beer. I needed something stronger. I needed a smoke anyway, without being on display in my assigned smoking spot in the front corner of our yard. I walked to the liquor store, and when I returned, Marjou looked up from a well-dressed buffet table on their driveway, four feet from my door. "Hi Sam'. Once people start eating, please take some kufteh and kabobs."

Her kind words were more pretentious than genuine. I was a misfit in their space. Inside, I downed a shot of whiskey and threw back a gulp of beer. In my call to Mike, I said, "They're having a party and way too close to my door. I need out."

Mike showed up, coming up to my back door with his little twenty-pound dog in his arms. He knew better than to use my front door. My landlords didn't allow dogs and Mike's dog went everywhere with him. "You ready?" Mike asked me.

The door stood open and he waited for me as I grabbed my cellphone, took a gulp of whiskey, and put my bottle in my back waistband. My untucked shirt would hide it. Mike stared at me.

Shit, there goes that secret.

Daybreak and dogs barking outside snapped me back to reality. I was with Mike. In a surreal moment in his nine-by-eleven room in a rooming house, I had to piece together what had happened, all while wanting to puke over stale smells that drifted in his room from his shared hallway.

The night before, when my landlords were having their party, was the only time Mike had seen me drink. I was a sober AA member, or so I had pretended until then. I wanted to tell him I would never have done whatever it was we did, had I been sober.

Days added up without a solution to my messy life. Laid off from my job, I looked for work, yet the economy President Obama had stepped into left little hiring choices for employers. Threats of ex-classmate Debbie played ping-pong in my head, when after each interview I'd be reminded, "We need someone with years of experience."

I got sober again with AA meetings in a different neighborhood, but it didn't fix my problems. I had to somehow become the woman Nana had expected. My failed career start and awkward connection to Mike were my clues that Seattle wasn't the place to regroup.

My long-ago failed relocation to Savannah haunted me. I couldn't afford to leave Seattle on my own. Since Mike wanted to keep a grip on me, it was to my advantage to let his grip be a means to an end. I turned my head to Mike, who was again hovering over me, and said, "Let's leave Seattle."

A free Native American band played music from a bandstand in a city park in Springdale, Utah, at the foothills of Mt. Zion National Park. People played Frisbee. I crocheted while Mike worked a cross-word puzzle, and his dog, Manny, people watched from his leash. It was my forty-fourth birthday. I didn't get a birthday present, but being with Manny while listening to poetic flutes and pipes with a graceful harmony made up for it.

We had left Seattle a month earlier. Before leaving, we had sold what we could live without and Mike had traded in his little car for a Suburban wagon. Mike had driven us through Oregon to its Red-woods, down the coastline to San Francisco, then to Las Vegas and farther east. Nights were spent in his Suburban, usually in Walmart parking lots.

"Mike," I said, "I want a birthday cake. After the concert, let's stop at that little store down the road and see if they have a bakery. Not a whole cake. Just a slice for us."

"Oh yeah, it's your birthday. Happy birthday."

"Thanks, but you knew that."

"I need a seven-letter word for amphibian." He went back to the crossword puzzle in his newspaper. I watched Manny chew on a bone.

That evening, we went to the grocery store to buy my cake. Before going in, Mike and I talked about getting beer, too. "Are you sure?" Mike asked.

I was sober again but didn't see the point in it. "I'd like to have a beer for my birthday."

Mike asked, "Should we?"

I said, "If we can enjoy a beer without getting drunk, then yeah, let's have a beer." As an afterthought, I added, "Oh, this is probably a stupid idea. You'll lose your two years of sobriety if we do."

Right outside of town, Mike turned onto a dirt road and parked at a secluded spot to stay overnight. He opened our tailgate and rolled out our sleeping bag to make a makeshift couch. Cold sandwiches, two twelve-ounce Corona beers for each of us, and chocolate cake with a lit candle in my slice illuminated my respite from our countless nights in Walmart parking lots. I let the last remnants of Seattle stress roll off my shoulders.

Mike tipped his bottle of beer to clink with my bottle and said, "Happy birthday, Ellie."

That was my name, only it was a first that I hadn't named myself, not counting my birth name. Before we had left Seattle, Mike had exalted my legal name change from Samantha to Samuelle, by pronouncing it "Sam-You-Ell-ee." Then, he affectionately shortened it to Ellie, pronounced "El-ee." Others in Seattle had stayed true to Sam', but Mike was different. With Seattle in my past, Sam' was gone and Ellie remained.

Night fell to late darkness as we pretended to like each other. I was pretending. I had no idea if Mike liked me or not. I started talking about a UFO encounter Richard and I had when in Florida. Mike replied, "Oh, you don't really believe in UFOs, do you?"

"Of course I do. You do too. You told me."

Mike said, "I lied."

"What?" I asked.

Mike replied, "I wanted you to like me. So, I lied. What's the big deal?"

The next day, we climbed the mountainous road to the Grand Canyon. We were the first car in on that opening day. After that day trip, we went north to Salt Lake City, Utah. It was a chilly day for May with snowbanks left over from winter piled at the edges of parking lots.

We meandered in the Suburban at a city park. It was a place to let Manny out to relieve himself. People didn't seem to mind the cold. A group of older women practiced hula hooping. Mike suddenly said, "I'm going to call information and try to find a number for my Aunt Celeste. She's the one person I could always talk to and I miss her."

"Mike, you told me you don't have any family. That you were just like me."

He said, "I lied about that too."

I rolled my eyes, looked out my side window, then back at him and said, "Great."

"Of course I have family, Ellie. Everyone has family. I just haven't seen them in like more than ten years."

"It's been more like twenty years for me, and I don't have any family. They rejected me," I said.

He reached Celeste by phone. She told him she had been looking for him, posting messages online in her search. He also learned his folks were in Elko, Nevada. Indecisiveness was replaced by a drive to northern Nevada flatlands. Following several days with his folks, we went westward through dusty, dry Nevada plains. Our next long-term stop reconnected him with his uncle Joe, who lived on five acres in Brownsville, a rural area in north central California.

During our stay with Joe, we bought a small older trailer from his neighbor. I helped Mike and his uncle replace the flooring where it was rotting. They replaced the plumbing. The trailer was not only old, it was an antique from the sixties. Mike made a morning trip to Marysville, California for the license and tags for it. He also tried to show me how to hitch and unhitch the trailer to the Suburban, but it was a confusing concept to me. Besides, Mike did all the driving.

We left Joe's place on an old state highway, the safest route to pull an older trailer. The interstate was closer but had steep hills. We couldn't risk wearing out the brakes on the Suburban with the weight she pulled. On our chosen route, Klamath Falls, Oregon lay ahead. At normal interstate speed, a six-hour drive was plausible. With this trailer, it would take us much longer.

Long before we crossed the Oregon border, we pulled into Susanville, California, and Mike parked at Walmart. The sun was ready to set, and with darkness, Manny was ready for sleep. We hadn't drank since my birthday, careful to be on our best behavior around his family. To appease our thirst, we walked across the parking lot to a bowling alley, where a neon sign flashed the word "Bar."

After we arrived at the bar, as we downed a pitcher of beer, a group at a nearby table asked us to join them. Downing another pitcher, one of our new friends suggested, "Hey, Mike and Ellie, walk with us. There's a cool bar right down the street."

In our walk to the next bar, my cognition quickly became nonexistent.

Sobering consciousness returned as my right eye opened while my bad eye stayed squinted shut, pressed into a cold cement slab. Shivering cold, I pulled myself up into a sitting position, feeling goosebumps on my bare legs, and looked around.

A plastered half wall wrapped around a steel toilet, with an opening to get to it. That was all I could immediately see, aside from the tiny room I was in. Above, bars lined two of my four walls. I stood up to look out. A male guard sat at a desk in a guard shack encased in plexiglass across the hall. I was at the corner of two hallways and looked down both halls. The only things I saw were a desk and chair in the middle of one hallway.

I looked back at the guard shack, hoping to see a clock, but I didn't see one. Then, a woman guard came down one hall. I knocked heavily on my steel door as she started to pass by. She stopped and said, "You're being held on public intoxication as a courtesy to get you off the streets before you hurt anyone or yourself."

Duh.

She moved on, then later returned with a male guard beside her. She unlocked and opened my steel door, gripped my upper arm, and walked me to that desk in the hallway. The male guard took the seat at the desk as I stood shivering next to the woman guard. The only clothes I was wearing were my summer undershorts and tank top with a bra under that.

I shivered more as she stepped back and walked away. The male guard asked me questions about my identity and I answered him. She returned with a blanket and draped it over my shoulders, letting it hang down around me. She asked me, "Where are your pants?"

How am I supposed to know? I just came to from a blackout.

"I don't know," I said.

The male guard wrote something down on a form and then

closed it in a manila folder. The woman guard walked me back to my cell and told me I needed more time to sober up while they found my clothes.

No thank you to the first reason—but thank you for the second one.

I went back to the cold floor, curling up in my blanket. I drifted in and out of napping. Later, she returned and escorted me back to that same desk, with the same male guard who sat behind it. He handed me my jeans, belt, summer jacket, and sandals. I weaved my belt through the loops of my jeans. He then handed me my lighter, my wallet, and two cell phones—one was Mike's. He said, "That's all the property you were signed in with." He pushed a paper across the desk to me, which I signed.

The female guard then told me, "You're free to go."

As I put my jeans on, I asked, "Where's Mike Petrocchi who I came in with?" In my absent memory, I assumed he was also in jail.

She answered me, "He has at least another two hours to sober up before being released."

Next, I asked, "Where's Walmart from here?" I worried about Manny.

She gave me directions, which seemed sketchy to my pounding hangover. Outside, I pondered a moment, not knowing if I should wait for Mike. I looked at my discharge papers and saw the time was 7:05 a.m. Sunlight seemed awfully bright for this hour.

Jonesing for a smoke, I took off walking, throwing my summer jacket in someone's bushes. My jacket was stained with puke. Everywhere I stepped, I looked for a cigarette butt. Even though I preferred little cigars, a cigarette butt was a more likely find. I had no money for any convenience stores up ahead. My cash must have been spent at the bar. If only I had a credit card, but those were for people with money, something I hadn't had when a student or low-income graduate.

Baffled over where to turn on foot, I flagged down a car, but the driver thrashed her arms in front of her face refusing my plea to take me to Walmart. *I must look as sick as I feel.*

At the end of the long road, I came to a main drag that I recognized. Believing Walmart was to the left, my confidence peaked. I counted more than twenty blocks as my walk led me to the bowling alley where we had started. I hit the jackpot in their outdoor ashtray, but by then I could see Walmart. I lit a long cigarette butt and inhaled, letting its buzz swallow my headache.

When I stepped inside our trailer, Manny jumped up into my arms. He had pooped on the bed. That was a sign of his disappointment in us. I let him out to relieve himself, and when both of our bathroom breaks were over, reality sunk deep into me.

I wanted to drive away with Manny. I couldn't. I didn't have a gas tank key. Only Mike did. Besides, I had no earthly idea how to drive with a trailer hitched up. When Mike had tried to show me how to turn the ball and put the pin in, I reasoned it was too complicated to bother with since he never let me drive.

And if all that wasn't enough to keep me stuck in place, I had no financial means, nor could I call Mike since I had both phones. I had a big responsibility to Manny. I replenished his food and water bowls and felt hungry myself yet nauseated. A few bites of canned applesauce with crackers was all I could get down.

An open case with cans of pee-beer sat in the thawing fridge. Dry parked, we had no electricity. Low in alcohol content at only .03%, all it was good for was making you pee, which was why I called it pee-beer. We kept it to curb our problem drinking. I opened a beer and drank it slowly. There was no point in chugging, as weak as it was.

Impatiently, I waited for Mike. At 10:00 a.m., I called the jail, who informed me he hadn't been released yet. Then I called information to get his uncle Joe's number. I didn't call Joe, but knowing it was an option felt powerful. At twelve noon I called the jail back, only to be told he had been let go an hour earlier.

An hour later, at 1:00, I put Manny on a leash and we went outside to the grassy edge of the parking lot. I had to believe the sunshine would do us good, and I had to hope Mike would return soon. Two hours had passed since his release, twice as long as it had taken me to get back. *Where is he?*

I drifted into the what-ifs. What if Mike never returned. I had a roof over my head in a Walmart parking lot. I could go to work at Walmart to get money to work myself up out of my destitution. Or, I could work the homeless sign, which I had sworn never to do again.

I considered reaching out to a social service agency but shrugged that off. People behind a crisis line might take me in, but only to put Manny in some sort of dog pound, and I refused to let that happen. If only Manny wasn't in the picture, I'd bravely pack a bag and leave.

Mike has to return to take care of his dog. And me. I gave up on the sunshine idea and mind-fucking, then tugged at Manny's leash. We walked across the parking lot to the bowling alley to search for Mike, but no one there had seen him that day.

I proceeded down the main drag, not letting Manny slow me down. Disoriented in Susanville, I looked everywhere for that missing man. Whenever we passed someone on the sidewalk, I'd stop them to ask if they had seen him, giving a description. "White with dark complexion, six feet tall, heavyset with dark curly hair just starting to grow out, and a mustache. He's in jeans and a dark blue T-shirt...walks kind of funny with a limp."

Mike didn't turn up on our walk. We were damn near back to Walmart when we spotted him straight ahead at Burger King. And the cops. He was stumbling drunk with a bag of fast food in one hand and an open fifth of whiskey in the other. Manny and I rushed to the unfolding scene. A cop put his arm out to stop me from getting closer. I said, "That's my husband, Mike. He's been missing. I took our dog for a walk to try to find him."

In my fit of desperation, trying to sound serious, the husband part had to be added. A lieutenant approached me while two city cops put Mike in handcuffs. I was relieved to have found him, but angered he had got himself arrested again. I asked the lieutenant if Mike could give me some money or his bank card and the key to the gas tank. The lieutenant was kind as he interceded. He relayed my wishes to Mike, but Mike refused to give me anything. I handed Mike's cell phone to the lieutenant and asked if it could be added to his property. He told me, "Yes."

That Mike had a phone to call me when released, rather than getting lost and drunk again, boosted my power. As cops drove away with Mike, the lieutenant stayed to talk more. I had been too ashamed to call anyone for help and too afraid to call a crisis line, but opened up to the kind officer at my side. I was at a loss of what to do, and felt the more honest I was, the more helpful he could be.

The lieutenant handed me his business card, assuring me I was legally safe to stay parked, and added, "When he's released, he can call you."

Manny and I returned to the trailer. I couldn't sit still and let the unknown play out. Nor did any gods in the sky exist to magically manifest any miracles. I couldn't live out of a Walmart parking lot forever. Manny wouldn't stop walking from the door to the bed and back and forth again. His sniffing tactics weren't going to find his owner. I had to take control.

For starters, I took a good hard look at the hook-up between the Suburban and the trailer. They were attached but I didn't know if it was ready to drive. I played with a crank-like thing, but had no idea what I was doing. I resigned myself to crossing my fingers for luck. I looked away from the hook-up to see a young man return to his car, near our trailer. I said hi and he said hi back.

"Hey, can you tell me how to get to the jail from here? I need to help a friend."

"The jail?" he asked.

"Yeah, the jail. I'm from out of town and I'm here to help a friend. I need to pick him up at the jail. I'm not sure how to get there though."

He pointed to the exit near Burger King. "You take a left out of Walmart then go through several lights. You'll turn right but that's—"

An older man approached and introduced himself as the young man's dad. They drew me a map on a pad of paper while explaining directions. If I had a car instead of a Suburban and trailer, I could have driven in circles until I found it, but driving that apparatus obliterated that option. And I couldn't remember all the streets I took earlier from the jail, or if any were restricted to one-way traffic. I needed a beeline route, a direct drive to the jail with no problems.

I didn't know how to drive with a trailer in tow, but had no choice but to put my foot on the pedal and hope it wouldn't fall off or hit something. I didn't detour. The trailer didn't fall off and I didn't hit anything, plus I had enough gas. I made it to the jail, no problem. *Phew!*

So far, so good, but when I entered the parking lot, I shouldn't have driven right up to the front door. It wasn't the most clandestine parking spot, plus I was too big to navigate the marked parking spaces.

I put the gear in reverse. Thus far, my drive had been all forward, not backward. I backed up a few feet while I turned the steering wheel. Then I put it in park, got out, and looked at my progress. *Damn, I should have turned the wheel the other way.*

I got back in, drove forward a few feet, then put the gear back in reverse and turned the wheel the opposite way. After a few feet, I got out and looked again. It was better, but barely a start. I repeated my method several times, a few feet at a time.

Finally, I parked, situated parallel to a meadow bordering their parking lot. The full-sized Suburban and small trailer took up a good forty feet, far too long for even two parking spaces together. I went inside and let them know I was there to wait for Mike.

At 3:00 a.m., twelve hours after his arrest, Mike was released without his cell phone. We went back inside the jail lobby to claim it, but were told it was at the lieutenant's office downtown, and of course it was closed at that hour. I wanted to get out of Dodge, but Mike said he was too tired and still too drunk to drive. He rested another two hours. His last words to me before he drifted off to snore were, "You were so stupid, Ellie, to give them my cell phone."

Before Susanville, our plan had been to stay on the same highway, which led to Klamath Falls, Oregon. Detours put us in a quick succession of campground stays in July and August. Our traveling could be likened to my days with Richard, except that my tolerance for Mike had grown to pure unadulterated hatred. Penniless, I had to pretend I liked Mike while harboring my secret goal to gain independence. Nana had expected better from me.

I held no assurance we were headed for the city. Silently I repeated to myself, *I am a good person, I am smart, I am a good person, I am—* The horn sounded. Mike punched the steering wheel and demanded, "Ellie, why did you let me break the trailer door? Why?"

I didn't answer him. Our mutual communication had broken the day that happened. Mike had been outside, downing another beer with the neighbors who were having their morning coffee. When I stepped outside of our trailer, the door's slippery latch fell too fast for me to catch it from locking. I didn't have a key and Mike's key ring was on the table inside.

From the neighbor's fire pit, Mike had screamed, "What the fuck did you do? What the fuck! Ellie, no! Ellie, you are so fuckin' stupid."

He then ran to me, pushed me out of the way, and rammed his shoulder into the door. He busted it open, forever damaging its locking mechanism.

Potholes jerked me back to reality as Mike half-ass dodged them. Campground hosts back there had told us, "Don't come back."

I wouldn't have wanted to go back. Mike had been a maniac drunk. Sometimes I managed to pack a day bag and retreat to the backwoods for the afternoon. At other times, he was more successful in his control. When he blocked the trailer door to keep me from going in to use our bathroom, I'd hike off to the campground bathroom. During one of those bathroom trips, a woman had looked up from the sink and said, "Hey, if you want, my husband and I can take you to a women's shelter."

Shelters were temporary, and I couldn't leave Manny behind. I shook my head no and proceeded to a stall. Neighbors had noticed Mike's frequent outbursts as he threw his dinner plate and my books. I feared I'd be an object in his way. Cops had shown up one time, but after talking with him, left. As we had packed up to leave that place, our nearest neighbor told me, "Good luck, Ellie. You and your boyfriend have a good trip."

I had no idea how to define Mike, but nodded anyway at his comment.

Mike's driving jumped another pothole and he again questioned, "Why?"

His right arm swung at me. "Fine, fuckin' ignore me. I fuckin' hate you, Ellie."

His reaction scared me, but then his arm stopped in mid-air. He grabbed the steering wheel again for control as we bounced deeper into a graveled stretch of road. I hadn't noticed when or how we'd left the paved road. Cacti and pine trees kept the world out. He could have pulled over and killed me. He was mad enough. And strong enough.

We traveled much too fast for a sixteen-foot trailer on that road. We bounced in and out of another pocket of gravel and kicked up dust. I grabbed my door handle for leverage even though no other cars were around. Ever since my triple rollover accident, I often gripped something. Mike grabbed my arm and pulled it away from the door. "Stop that, Ellie. Now, look—you're upsetting Manny."

He screeched to a stop, turned the ignition off and pocketed his keys. He got out and Manny followed him with his tail wagging behind his twenty pounds of white matted fur. I tasted a dirty, salty grit from gravel dust that stirred in the air. I hated the name Ellie. I missed Sam.

I didn't have my cell phone to use to tell time—Mike had taken it when his got taken by the detective in Susanville. Moments spilled, one from another, like dripping molasses. I stayed seated. Should I walk off? He could kill me, but maybe not, I reasoned. Fear gripped me. If I ran, all my possessions would be left behind. I could part with jeans and toothpaste, but not my diploma and documents. A greater stronghold was my love and concern for Manny who was dependent on his adult caregivers.

I must convince Mike to get us moved into a Klamath Falls RV park. My excuse could be that winter travel isn't safe.

Manny jumped on the seat and licked my face. If Mike stayed put in Klamath Falls when I escaped, then Manny would be okay. That hope strengthened my willpower. Mike got up. "Ellie, stay put. We're leaving."

As Mike drove us forward, he approached our road at a safer speed. We came to a fork in the road. The turn to the left was also graveled. To the right, the road was paved. He turned right.

A car passed us. We were in traffic again. A highway sign read, "Klamath Falls, 10 miles." Right after that, a brown highway sign read, "Campground." Mike turned onto the road leading to the campground. It was dry and littered and had only a small patch of grass. Our gravel road dead-ended at a dirty riverbank, perhaps once good for local fishermen, but now stinky green stuff floated on it. Off to the side was a train track, situated between us and the state highway. A posted sign read, "Free Camping. 10-Day Limit."

We pitched our tent and settled in. By day two, Mike had set his unrelenting verbal attacks aside and returned to his old erratic self, which meant sometimes he was kind, sometimes not. With the same gumption Nana had once shown me, I reminded him of our goal. "It's time for me to go to work now that we've seen the Grand Canyon."

Mike said, "Yeah, when we left Joe's we were going to head to Klamath Falls to see if that's a good spot for us."

"So, what's stopping us?" I asked him.

"I don't like society. I don't like people. And I don't like the rat race of a city, but you're ready to go back to work, huh?"

"Yes, I need to do something with my college degree."

"Oh yeah, you're all important now with letters behind your name. You're not going to leave me, are you?"

"No, I'm not going to leave you."

"You love Manny. You don't love me."

"I love you, and think how nice it would be to have a home for us. Manny deserves a good home."

"Manny's just fine. Look at him. He's happy."

After watching Manny chase a green-winged insect, I added, "From the tourist magazines I've been picking up, I see Klamath Falls has jobs and stuff. Let's see what places to call about long-term RV stays."

I looked up and noticed two men setting up their homestead at the last tent space along the grass line, close to the public restrooms.

Mike looked up and said, "Huh, how about that? We're not the only ones here."

Before these men, we hadn't seen any regular people pitching tents. We hadn't seen any families cooking s'mores over an open campfire. What people we saw were stragglers with an occasional pup tent that went up for the night, then down the next morning. Most often, when we saw a car drive through, they hadn't stayed long.

We walked the grass line with Manny in tow, over to their site to introduce ourselves. Mike waved to the men and said, "Howdy, neighbors."

The white scrawny beanpole of a man said back, "Hi, how are you folks doing?"

Mike said, "Good, good. Just thought we'd be neighborly-like and come say hello."

"It's good you did. We don't get much folk around here."

The other man, also skinny, but older, stood up and exchanged a firm handshake with Mike. "I'm Tony, and this here is Fred."

"I'm Mike and this is my girlfriend, Ellie."

Wow. He called me his girlfriend and not his old lady, I thought to myself.

Tony asked, "You folks from around here?"

Mike answered, "No, no, we're just passing through, and tomorrow we might move on to Klamath Falls, see if there's a place for us to settle down at."

Fred pointed to their ice chest and said, "Get yourself a beer."

"Thank you. Don't mind if I do." Mike took out two beers and gave one to me.

All four of us bellied up to their battered wooden picnic table. Fred lit a joint, and after he took a hit, he handed it to Mike. I passed when it was my turn. A boom box in the background played soft rock from a Klamath Falls radio station, and their campfire glowed with orange sparks. It wasn't my idyllic daydream for a normal social life. But I welcomed distraction from the friendly banter I had to fake all day with Mike.

A small car pulled up, parked, and two people got out—a young man and a middle-aged woman. They dropped by to check on Tony and Fred but didn't join us. Our party spread out a bit. While Mike went about his own fun, I fell into informative talk with their visitors.

The young man declined a beer and explained to me he was active and sober in AA. He also told me his mom was a social worker who helped people. I casually worked my way over to her space to find out more. I revealed a little bit to her about my life with Mike and my hope to get away. She gave me her phone number. Our connection filled my lungs with hope.

The next day Mike and I poured over our travel magazines. Klamath Falls wouldn't normally be on my list of top ten places for relocation, but it was all I had to work with. Then, out of the blue, which really wasn't out of the blue considering Mike's character, he said, "What were their names again? Those two guys from last night?"

"I don't remember," I said. I didn't want Mike to think I cared enough about some other guy to remember his name.

Mike answered himself. "Fred. I think that was his name—the one you kept dancing with."

"I wasn't dancing with anyone. I was just having a good time, same as you."

"Fred was his name, and he wanted you."

"I don't think he wanted me, and I certainly didn't want him."

"Yeah, you kept flirting with him."

"Stop this. Let's make some calls to Klamath Falls, pick a spot to get moved to."

He dropped his head and stopped talking to me. A few minutes later he lifted his head back up, faced Manny and said, "Yeah right. Come on, Manny, let's go for a walk."

As they took their walk, I made a list of options for Klamath Falls. We needed long term, and secondly, we had a fifty-year-old trailer when most places wanted only newer models. When they returned, I shared my notes with Mike, and he handed me the phone. Several phone calls later, the park manager accepted us. That afternoon, we moved in.

The next day, I punched my courage up a notch. I told Mike, "I'd like to call Mary. You know, the woman we met a couple nights ago? Just to let her know how we're doing."

Mike asked, "Why would you want to do that? You just want to get together with Fred."

"Stop this with Fred—"

"You stop it. You're the one who was flirting with him."

"This has nothing to do with him. I need all the resources I can get in finding a good job. Mary actually has her head on straight, not drunk and homeless like the others, and maybe she can help me find a job. She gave me her number, and I want to check in with her."

"Fine. Whatever. Here's the phone."

I got her voicemail and had to think on the fly to get my real meaning across. I said, "Hi, this is Ellie. Thank you for your number. As you may remember, we met the night before when you visited the campsite. We're now at an RV park in Klamath Falls and doing fine. He's right here beside me. I'm hoping you'll give me a call back. Mike's cell phone number is..."

Later, I left another voicemail. She didn't return my call, which left me resigned to go it alone. On day two, I boarded the city bus from its stop at the RV park and rode it to downtown.

Inside the first week of our Klamath Falls relocation, I discovered my resources were the public library, the State Career Center, and the welfare office for food stamp benefits. The career center gave me free access to computers, a phone, and fax service. I needed those.

The last two days of that first week and early in the following week, I proved my accountability to Express Temporary Employment Agency. At minimum wage, I waved a sign on a street corner for two afternoons for a store's grand opening sale. Next, I worked two mornings for Express in the lobby of a veterinarian's office. That first paycheck paid for my own cell phone, considering Mike had confiscated the one phone we shared. Daily, I used my resources in search of a permanent job and a place to live.

Express next put me to work long term at Walmart in a production stocking position. While their offer came with a likely layoff at the close of the Christmas holiday, I couldn't say no to an income. Klamath Falls had been hit hard by the recession.

A Craigslist ad led me to a young guy who offered a spare bedroom for sublet out of his rented house. While I didn't have a permanent income, I was confident my three months of Walmart wages could carry me over until I secured other employment. He was asking only $200 a month. I had to grab it. While securing move-in arrangements with him, Mike called me. "Hey, when are you coming home?"

I answered him, "Sorry, I know it's late. I have a job interview at three and can go in jeans, so I'll be home as soon as I can."

Mike hung up on me.

It was close to 6:00 p.m. when I arrived back at the trailer to pack. As I got off the bus, I told the bus driver I'd be back at the stop, precisely on time for the next bus. I didn't want to be passed by in the dark. She gave me a reflective flashlight thing and said, "I won't be driving then, but we give these out to our riders to use so the drivers can see you in the dark."

The next bus was scheduled to arrive in thirty minutes. Surely, it would only take a few minutes to pack. I arrived at our trailer after walking the gravel drive from the bus stop and saw the Suburban was gone, which meant Mike and Manny were gone. His dog went everywhere with him, not counting jail. Likely pissed at me for staying out all day, he probably went to the liquor store. No matter, I had less than thirty minutes to get in and get out. I had topped that timing back when I was a burglar, so I knew I had it made with him gone.

I quickly packed up everything I could fit into two duffel bags. My diploma, legal papers, a few clothes, and even a ceramic fish from Krista made the cut. I swung two camping chairs, folded up, over my shoulder and got the hell out and back to my bus stop.

CHAPTER 22

SOWER NUMBER FIVE

Logan had left the porch light on for me. He was my new landlord and roommate and had told me he'd be at his girlfriend's place when I got back with my stuff. His Great Dane, Abby, greeted me with a big wave of her tail and followed me. I stepped into my room and dropped everything I owned. I plopped down on the hardwood floor and sniffled. I rummaged through my pocket for a Kleenex to wipe my nose again. I had an awful cold.

I'd set my camping chairs up later. For now, I took off my winter coat and spread it out on the floor. It had to do until I got to the thrift store for bedding. I let out a sigh and whispered out loud, "I'll be okay." Abby nudged her big wet nose to meet my equally wet nose. She must have agreed with me.

The next day started what would become routine for me. Three days a week, I went to a 7:00 a.m. AA meeting, then to work, then home to dinner and two tall, one-dollar cans of beer. In AA, I shared superficially, crowing for sympathy more so than offering or listening to any program-driven solutions. I've always equated relapse with shame, whether AA intends this or not. Beer calmed my intensifying shame and job hunting frustration.

Saturdays and Sundays were different. Buses didn't run to Walmart then. I'd bundle up in my winter gear, snow boots too, and brace myself for the forty-five-minute weekend walk to work. On those nights, I rewarded myself with an extra beer, which I bought midway on my way home, downing it in a darkened corner lot. Most days, snow came in the middle of the night but never seemed to melt away. By early October, Klamath Falls was buried in snow under its abundant sunshine. It was an unchanging winter scene.

Lunch breaks were spent with Eve in her older Ford truck. I had met her in our shared first day of work. Her name tag read "Yvonne," but when we settled into her truck for a smoke that first day, she told me, "Call me Eve."

I had let my name tag speak for itself. Choosing which name to use hadn't hit my priority list. Eve was a little older than me at forty-nine, had strawberry blonde hair cut butch short, and like Pam, walked with purpose. Like me, she was exhausted from job searches.

Each lunch break with Eve was much like the one before. Eve lit her cigarette and then handed me her lighter to use. She turned her truck's ignition on and cranked the heat up. She rolled her window down a little and blew out smoke. "I hate this job. They've got me working in the freezer with—" Shania Twain interrupted Eve as she turned her radio dial.

I nodded in agreement. "I'm going to probably lose my credentials. I worked so hard for them, but I don't have the money to renew them come December."

Eve also had professional credentials. Eve was a licensed phlebotomist yet was scraping by on minimum-wage jobs. Mutual disappointment prevailed as we agreed our current job situation kept us from advancement.

Walmart's district manager approached me as I stocked oranges in the produce department. I wiped my hands on my apron and then accepted his firm handshake. Lanky with neatly combed back hair, he looked directly at me and said, "I've heard good things about you. I'm impressed with your work. I guarantee you'll have a job here at the end of your assignment with Express—stop in at HR to do the paperwork, and the job is yours."

This relieved my financial worries. If only I could live up to Nana's standards. I'd gone to college to avoid menial jobs. I felt duped for trusting a college degree could help, only to be held back by our country's recession. Professional salaries made the difference between struggle and a real life. Pushing my disappointment aside, I completed the necessary paperwork. The office staff thanked me, saying, "We'll let you know more when we can."

A week later, when I came home, Logan had something to tell me. "You've been an awesome roommate, but my girlfriend and I are getting real close now."

I could see what his girlfriend saw in him. Logan had a lot going for him. He cared about his appearance and had a lucrative job with the utility company, fresh out of high school. "We want to live together," he said. "I'm letting the house go. Keep your money for next month's rent. Put it toward another place."

Life had been tough, but doable. My job wasn't what I wanted, but it was a job. My room in his house wasn't my own place and I smoked outside to please him, but it was what I could afford. Apartments didn't go for as cheap as $200. That was unthinkable.

His dog, Abby, brought me her ball. She had been my comfort in my separation from Manny. I wasn't in the mood to play. "When?" I asked.

Logan answered, "On your next day off from work, try to find another place."

Tuesdays and Wednesdays were my days off. Those were my days to look for a better job. This Tuesday, though, I also had to look for another place to live. After my morning job searching, I looked at an apartment on my way home, but it was too expensive. A half pint of cheap whiskey was usual after a full day of job searching. That day, I upgraded to a pint to chase down my two cans of beer. I had to take the edge off.

Logan was out that night. Abby followed me around, playing at my feet, as my afternoon imbibing moved me with energy. In my inebriation, I hunted for clues to explain his decision. My aimless wandering led me into his bedroom. If by chance he came home, I'd say I was using the laundry room—it was on the other side of his bedroom.

First, I found an open bottle of Crown Royal rum and took a sip. Later, I returned to his room for another sip. Then I saw his rifle. I knew he was a hunter. He had gone on a hunting trip with his dad and friends one long weekend after I had moved in.

I took another sip of his Crown Royal. I looked at his bed. It was full-sized, or that is, much bigger than my sleeping spot. It looked comfortable, not to sleep in, but to sleep in and never wake up. After shooing Abby out of his room and shutting the door behind her, I took his rifle from his gun rack above his headboard. Potential power glided in my hands. In that moment, I didn't want life. I wanted death.

Death would mean life with Nana. It was as if my blood flowed with tranquil warmth. It had been a long time since I had last known what peace felt like, and as I looked at his bed and felt control in my hands, a promise of peace swept over me. I didn't want Nana to see me in between life and death. Urgency became apparent. I had to end my life, right then and there, quick, fast.

I lay on his bed and hugged the rifle flat against me, its tip resting right above my chin. Long and slender, except for its beefy two-foot barrel, it was built differently than my guns of yesteryear. I missed my .22 Jennings, and then the bigger gun after it—they had been my lifeline. The power I embraced in his rifle was my new lifeline, to pass from one life to another. I shifted its weight to cradle it on my right side.

At the thought it likely wasn't loaded, I sprang up, took another sip of his Crown Royal, and began a fervent search for bullets. I found them. I held the box of bullets tightly in my left clenched fist, and held the rifle braced against me. It was huge at nearly five feet tall, almost as tall as me. I had handled countless rifles and other firearms back in my burglary days, but had never even tried to fire anything bigger than a .44-caliber handgun. Rifles had been nothing more than something to take, and then to sell. Even Jim hadn't bothered with them.

My feet were planted on his bedroom rug. I sat at the edge of his bed. The box of bullets sat beside me. I fingered every bump on that rifle, from sharp edges to smooth mechanisms. I played with every knob, but for the life of me, couldn't figure out how to load it. If only it were a handgun. Without a shadow of a doubt, had it been a handgun, I would not be alive today. I wanted to die and be with Nana forevermore. I had the power, but not the know-how to make that power work.

I returned his rifle to its case, put the box of bullets back where I had found them, and took another sip of his Crown Royal. Recoiling to the living room couch, I downed my beer. When Logan came home, I cried out to him, "I don't want to end up in a homeless shelter."

"It'll be all right," he said as he walked me to my bedroom.

The next morning, he assured me again, "Everything will work out. You'll see. I'll help you."

Before the week's end, Logan helped me move into an apartment closer to work, cutting my weekend walk time in half. He also bought me about thirty dollars' worth of cleaning supplies. I needed those. My limited income and cash on hand put me into no more than a slop of an apartment.

My routine continued. Returning home each day from job searching, I'd shiver walking in. My courtyard apartment was always drafty. I had to conserve electricity and keep my furnace knob low. The electric bill could come before another paycheck. In the evenings, I huddled under blankets in bed, watching my *Lost* DVD series for the umpteenth time on my seven-inch portable DVD player. I never bothered using the living room. My only furniture in there was an ugly beat-up couch that came with the place. It had a missing leg.

Eve was an occasional reprieve from that monotony. I'd tag along as she ran her errands. She owned a mobile home and had rented her space for twenty years from the same person, who let her slide on rent payment. It was out in the country, on the other side of Walmart.

In December, the Walmart district manager came to me. "Sorry, but budget restraints keep me from hiring you. This will be your last week here."

What the fuck? What, firm handshakes are a thing of the past?

A week later, Eve was also let go. In the first few days following our news, hope and Eve's belief in my hope left me believing things would get better. I'd find a job. I'd always been able to find a job.

More likely, the hope Eve instilled in me came from warm fuzzy feelings she got from pot smoking.

For lack of a job, my new full-time job was to find a job. I kept in daily contact with Express, sometimes by phone, but mostly through drop-in visits. My cell phone minutes came free through a low-income government program, but the minutes allotted per month were limited. Walking to Express was free. With absolutely no income to my name, I couldn't freely spend money on fifty-cent bus fares. Instead, I soon became accustomed to walking anywhere I had to go in that city, whether a few blocks away or two miles out.

Planning my route home from job searching was also important—for a beer break. Those breaks dropped in frequency as my money dwindled. I then turned to pruno. My prison time had taught me well how to get drunk, and I had no guards to hide it from.

Food stamp cards can't be used on alcohol, only food. My card bought my sugar, fruit, yeast packets, and other stuff I needed to make pruno. As angry as I was that no one would hire me, and as depressed as I was that my life sucked, I drank to escape. Two tall beers a day wasn't going to cut it, and when money ran out for beer, pruno became my best friend.

I needed work bad. I needed an income bad. Express kept telling me they were dried up. I stayed stocked in resumes, with free copies made at the State Career Center. I carried two versions of my resume. One showed my education and credentials. The other was dumbed down. From office jobs to fast-food work, the recession had hit Klamath Falls hard.

Through an AA contact, I worked a cash-under-the-table snow shoveling job. A city ordinance made people responsible for keeping their side of the sidewalk clear of snow. Twice a week, I walked from my morning AA meeting with my contact's shovel in hand to my clients downtown. People didn't pay much for snow shoveling. Each week I earned about twenty dollars.

While I lingered in the throes of destitution, Eve was given another assignment through Express as a housekeeper at an area resort. I don't know what I would have done, had it not been for her kleptomaniac gifts to me. Daily, she'd leave work with as much toilet paper, soap, toothpaste, and sample-sized deodorants as she could hide, and then shared with me. On occasion I did my laundry at Eve's house, but most often my two pairs of jeans, interview slacks, and shirts got worn over and over again before hitting her washing machine.

Then my first electric bill came. It was over one hundred dollars.

"What the fuck?"

I called the utility company for an explanation. Informed of delivery charges up front before any charges for electric use, my first month was set at a standard fee of sixty-some dollars. Then, it would be thirty-some dollars. Even by limiting my kilowatt usage to ten dollars' worth, my bill would be no less than forty dollars each month, not counting added taxes and surcharges. I couldn't afford that. I had no money.

◆ ❖ ◆

The end of that year, 2011, proved to be an ongoing struggle. Express gave me a few days of intermittent work at the condominium resort where Eve was on assignment. My depression made it physically challenging. As Eve drove us to and from work each day, we'd whine to each other about how we hated that job. I had to scrape together rent money by January 1, never mind my electricity would get shut off soon. Eve said, "You don't need to be homeless if you can't afford the rent. Stay with me."

I said, "My independence is important to me. I think I can make it. If I go long term in this assignment like you, then I'll make rent."

I withheld the whole truth from Eve. I didn't want to live in a house with illegal activity, namely her pot use. I refused to go back to prison. I remembered my cellmate who did time over her kids who kept pot in her home. I'd heard plenty of horror stories when inside, enough to understand that by living in an illegal situation, I'd be legally liable. I couldn't move in with her.

I had my first paycheck to expect in early January. I explained my situation to my landlord, José. "You need to apply my move-in deposit to January rent, and I'll give you the rest in cash when I get paid."

José said, "No bueno. No, no good. No bueno, no."

On my next free day, I went to a social service agency to ask for help in making my rent payment. I had less than two dollars, all in change, and a paycheck for my sporadically assigned days, about $120, to look forward to the next week. Rent was $375.

They informed me their funding had run out and suggested another place. The secretary kindly added, "You need to be there on Wednesday. They open at nine but be early. Only the first few people are seen."

My morning AA meeting ended at eight. By 8:15 I was in line as the thirteenth person. Two more people were soon behind me and I waited out the remaining hour, not knowing if I was too far back in line for help. Five minutes before nine, our line grew longer. At 9:05 their doors opened, and I was the last person let in. Those behind me were turned away.

We were escorted to a cafeteria-style room and told to sit. The person who had been first in line was seen first, while the rest of us waited. In the meantime, someone with a clipboard made the rounds, writing down names. My name went on the last line. I had to find permanent work to make a permanent fix for my situation, yet I had no choice but to sit tight in that cafeteria to wait out my turn. I whiled away the time by working on job applications I had with me. At 11:35, I was the last person in the room. I heard a woman's voice call, "Samuel Mott."

I stood up and said, "Samuelle Mott," emphasizing the long "L" sound at the end of my name. I followed her into a small conference room the size of a closet, and was directed to sit at a desk across from interviewers. They sat side by side. A woman in a floral dress and button-down sweater was on the left, and a man in a suit and tie on the right. In between, a man leaned forward and rested his chin on his hands with bent elbows. "How can we help you today?"

"I need help with rent money, please."

He said, "Can we talk to you about Jesus?"

I said, "I'd rather not."

"Then why are you here?"

"Because, I need help with rent. I was sent here. You help community members in need, and I need help."

I was too weak to tell them I already knew all about Jesus and no longer believed in that idea. I don't know which was more awkward—my weakened emotional capacity that rendered me incapable of a theological debate, or their surprise that I didn't yet have a seventy-two-hour notice from my landlord, but instead was being proactive to avoid a move-out notice.

Our discussion evolved and I made them aware I had a college education and professional credentials but was unable to find work. They were astonished they couldn't fix me, as if poor people were poor from not managing money. My problem was I had no money to manage. He looked at me point-blank and asked, "Have you ever accepted Jesus as your Savior?"

"Yes," I answered.

"As a child?" he asked.

"No, as an adult," I said.

"And you still don't want to talk about Jesus?"

"No, I don't. I'm not here to talk about Jesus. I'm here for help with rent money."

He opened a folder and pulled out a checkbook. Flashbacks of being interrogated by detectives haunted me as I chewed on the last words we exchanged.

He handwrote a check for one hundred dollars, payable to José.

That was almost $300 shy of what I needed. That's when they informed me it was their maximum allowable charity gift.

I gave José their check and again told him to use my deposit. He took the check, but again said, "No bueno."

From the State Career Center, I contacted AHIMA, the governing body for my professional credentials. In my economic hardship, AHIMA waived my annual certification fee. A staff member at the State Career Center then made me aware that I likely qualified for unemployment benefits. As advised, I completed the application and submitted it to Oregon state, only to be notified I first had to apply with Washington state. I did as advised, only for Washington state to inform me by letter that Oregon state had to handle it.

Neither state would budge on their stance, nor would either state communicate with the other state. The State Career Center was not staffed with representatives to handle unemployment claims. Using their resources, I faxed documentation from each state to the other state to show their stalemate. One day, several days out, a claims representative visited the office, but she played the same no-budge game. As a last-ditch plea, I told her, "I need an ombudsman."

She said, "We don't offer that service."

Days later, in mid-January, when Eve and I returned to my apartment after work, we stepped into my kitchen. While I opened my mail, she put a roll of paper towels and a cardboard can of granulated sugar on my stove, stockpiled from work supplies. I held a letter from the State Unemployment Office, either Oregon or Washington, I don't remember which.

The letter informed me I was to complete the enclosed paperwork and return it to them for a determination of benefits to be made. The letter did not begin with "Dear Samuelle Ann Mott." It was addressed to Samuel Lynn Mott, with a misspelled first name and wrong middle name. Worse yet, no papers accompanied their letter.

I was physically exhausted from work. I was emotionally downtrodden from my struggles. And I held a letter that made no sense to me. I screamed. My knees buckled. I fell to the floor and burst into tears. Eve turned around from the stove and took me into her arms. She read it for herself as she cradled me. One-handed, she crumpled their letter and threw it on the floor. After a five-minute embrace, she stood up as she pulled my weight close to her and said, "You're coming home with me tonight."

There was no need to pack my bags. Her car was already loaded to the gills with stolen hygiene items. And her clothes fit me. I didn't need anything but her. On our drive to her house, she stopped at a liquor store and bought me beer. We fell into our mutual evening routines. She smoked pot like there was no tomorrow, and I drank my beer. I told myself, *It's just for one night.*

As it turned out, the easier, softer thing to do was not leave her place and instead pack up my stuff. I was broken and beat down. I didn't like the idea of living in an illegal pot situation, but with so much uncertainty and a cold apartment with threatening letters from my landlord as the only alternative, I caved.

Emotionally challenged, I couldn't think of any viable solution. Then again, any possible solution was pointless. In early February, the resort management ended my work assignment while permanently hiring Eve. I was homebound at Eve's with no income, and too far out to pound the pavement in another job search.

To compound my financial difficulties, I didn't even have money from filing a tax return to look forward to, or at least not any time soon. It seemed it had been years since I left Seattle. Actually, it had been less than a year before when I had worked there. A W2 went to my old address, never forwarded, and thus I never got it. They were waiting until March to mail out W2 duplicates. The IRS told me I could file without that W2, but only after a certain future date.

Then, before the end of February, I got a phone call from a supervisor out of the Washington State Unemployment Office. She apologetically told me she had found my faxed papers in a problem pile and would look into it further. I gave her the riot act and in vivid detail described how I lost my apartment when they failed to process my application in a timely manner. Again, she apologized, "I'm sorry. Let me see what I can do about this."

Although I verbally blamed her, I inwardly blamed myself for being a failure. Normal people had money in savings to fall back on when the state fucked up, but I wasn't normal. I was a failure. Two days later, she called me back to let me know she had processed my claim. Weekly payments would be a little under eighty dollars.

I told Eve, "I need to be in a downtown location so I can go back to looking for work. I don't want to depend on you. I should have my own place."

I moved into a boarding house in downtown at a flat rate of $350 a month, with no move-in deposits and that month prorated. For a little more than one hundred dollars, I was in my seven-by-ten room to figure out my next move. It came furnished with a twin bed, the headboard at one wall and the foot of the bed butted up to my jimmy-rigged pantry shelf. The shared bathroom was right next door to me, so the toilet wasn't far, but the showerhead sucked so I bathed in another floor's bathroom.

The location was perfect. I could walk to the State Career Center or the public library in under ten minutes. A laundromat and my morning AA meeting were a little farther away, but doable. Fred Meyer's was the nearest grocery store, which wasn't so close. The closest thing to me was a convenience store, which I used to stayed stocked in beer to supplement my pruno. I became a regular at the library where I checked out DVDs so I could take a break from my *Lost* reruns.

Express finally called me one afternoon at 2:00. "Can you be on assignment at five?"

With a tall beer already in me and my constant pleas for them to put me to work, I was not going to turn it down. It was for two nights, dinner shifts, washing dishes at the hospital.

Mid-shift on the second night, the kitchen supervisor asked

me to join him in his office. Even his office seemed bigger than my apartment. He grabbed a dish towel and wiped away a bead of sweat from his forehead where dreadlocks fell forward. His dark brown eyes captured my attention. He said, "Thank you for coming in on such short notice. Our regular guy is out sick, and we can't go without a dishwasher."

I said, "You're welcome. I'm glad Express called me to help you."

He tossed the dish cloth in a dirty rags bin. "Most people could care less about washing dishes."

"It feels good to work," I said.

"I see that," he said as he sat down on his desk. "You're handling those pots and pans without any complaining."

"I've been looking everywhere for work. I've got a college degree, but I can't even get a fast food place to hire me," I said.

"Yeah, in this town, sometimes it's a matter of knowing the right person. If you didn't go to school here or aren't in someone's hood, then people don't know you," he said.

"Working tonight is a nice change from looking for work," I said.

"Check in at our personnel office. I haven't heard of any openings at all, but if there is something, they've got my word that you're a good worker."

"Thank you. I was in here last week, and a month ago. You all have a hiring freeze."

He grabbed a binder and a pen and got up off his desk. As he walked me out of his office, he added, "Yeah, that's the recession for you. Keep up the good work. I've got a meeting to catch."

♦ ❖ ♦

My two nights of washing pans paid off. Two days later Express had me on another assignment. It was a production line position at a nearby greenhouse nursery, set to last until the end of their current season, or about a month or two. The job offered day hours at nearly full time, which left no time to look for permanent work. But on the plus side, it was an income, but again at minimum wage.

Each morning, I dressed in long johns under my jeans, alternating days for my two pairs of jeans. I'd wear a long john shirt under a long sleeve shirt and top it off with a heavy sweater. Snow boots, coat, hat, and cheap gloves gave me extra warmth on my thirty-minute walk to work. Sidewalks were not common on the way to the industrial area, and my boots often sunk ankle-deep in the snow-covered grass.

Once at work, only my coat and gloves came off. Inside an aluminum warehouse, I stood with others at a wooden work table. The garage-style doors stayed shut all day, but opened a crack, which caused snow to drift inside. The inside perimeter was eight inches high in snow in some places. No sunlight came in.

I was a drone among other drones. We each counted out either three or five seeds for each pod, pod after pod, after pod. To pass time, I counted hour by hour how many more dollars would be on my paycheck. Some coworkers talked to pass time, but I didn't seem to fit in, and like in Las Cruces, English was a secondary language. One day, I got an opportunity to do something different when my lead coworker called out, "Hola, Sower Number Five, follow me."

That's what they always called me, *Sower Number Five*. When still inside my first week, I had told them countless times to call me by my name, but absolutely no one did. I was Sower Number Five. I carefully put my handful of seeds back in a shared paper cup. My lead person repeated herself, "Sower Number Five, follow me."

I followed her outside to another work area. We walked into a real greenhouse. Sun beat down through the green window panes from above us. I took my knit hat off and put it in my back left pocket. When in the warehouse, I had worked beside women. Here, I was handed over to two guys. My lead said, "Stan and Roberto, this is Sower Number Five. She's going to help you get rows set up. We need every table you can give us. We have a lot of pod trays to transplant."

I was their gopher. But my time in the warmth of the greenhouse was short-lived. My next task, which lasted days, was to work with them outside in snow-covered dirt. Stan brought me pallets. I used a hammer to pull nails out of the pallets. Roberto loaded my pallets on a forklift. I tried to get all the nails out for them, but if I missed one, I'd hear Stan say, "Hey, Sower Number Five, you gotta get all the nails out. Here, like this."

And then he'd show me his method, expecting me to understand the fine art of nail pulling. At least he was fluent in English, although it might have been more tolerable if he hadn't been. I reported to work as Sower Number Five each day, but kept my coat and hat on. No matter how much I worked up a sweat pulling those nails out, it was cold outside. And the pallets were rough on my hands. My gloves were always getting holes in them, and then crusty with dirt and snowflakes. The convenience store where I bought my nightly beer sold basic brown work gloves for a dollar, and every few days I had to buy another pair.

After work each evening, I'd step into my tiny room, walk six feet across my wooden floor, and plop into my green canvas camping chair, the same chair I had hauled out of the trailer. The five o'clock night sky was not yet dark as rush hour traffic took over the downtown street through my window view.

I took the beer out of its paper sack and dropped the sack in my plastic trash can, chair-side. On the other side of me, I set one can of beer next to my ashtray on my makeshift table, which wasn't anything more than two cardboard boxes, one on top of the other, with an orange cloth draped over it. Orange was still my favorite color.

I had yet to warm up from the frigid day, but had no qualms about holding my beer, also cold, freshly pulled from the store freezer. I tapped the top of the can and pulled back its tab. I took a big gulp, and felt its icy liquid warm my blood. I struck a match from my matchbook, lit my smoke, and took another drink, but only a sip, to conserve my gulps. Smoke filled my lungs, superseding my need for a big swallow.

I stared out at the boring city of parking lots. People had some sort of meaning in their life. I stared at them, wondering what it was. As Sower Number Five, I didn't have purpose. I had fallen short of Nana's ideals of my worth as a bright young woman.

I was occasionally distracted from that nightly routine when Eve visited me, but this soon died off. Words weren't needed to tell me what brought her into town—she never stopped in unless she was on a pot run. I didn't care. It was the easiest way to let our friendship die off.

I was earning money, but only enough to survive in my precarious poverty-stricken homelife. I couldn't fathom working my way into a better apartment. Hating my job didn't matter. What mattered was it would end soon, at the end of this growing season.

How many more nails will Sower Number Five have to pull?

Not many. About a week later, my run as Sower Number Five ended. Life picked up where it had left off before that venture, but not exactly. Oh, the job hunting and pleading with Express was the same, but the motivation and hope behind these actions were things of the past. Money ran out fast. All my paychecks put together weren't going to cut it. The money from unemployment comp wasn't enough to keep covering rent.

It had been close to a year since I had left Seattle. Six months of that year I was in Klamath Falls. I'd once believed that no matter where I relocated, it was up to me to make a meaningful and purposeful life, and as long as I did the footwork, it could happen. As I sat in my canvas chair, window-side, I realized I had been misled by whoever had told me that, whether it was Nana or some other wise person.

I was not living the life I had envisioned for myself. I was not in a warm climate with friends and a job I looked forward to each day. I knew I couldn't make it work in Klamath Falls. I had tried, only to fail. The thought crossed my mind to pack up and hitchhike out, perhaps to Medford, the nearest big city. But the last time I had hitchhiked was a long time ago. Times had changed. It was dangerous for a woman to hitchhike. Besides, where would I go once I landed in Medford?

As much as I had hated being Sower Number Five, I wished I was still that person. Then I could pay rent. As much as I had loved being Sam', it had become an impossible feat to find happiness again. Nor was I Kym anymore. That, too, was a long time gone. And I had once been Ellie, but certainly not by choice.

Who am I? No matter, how am I to survive?

I popped open my second can of beer and took a gulp. I called Don to ask if I could stay with him until I got back on my feet. After all, he was still my husband, even if legally separated and in Wichita. I hadn't given any thought whatsoever as to how I'd get to Kansas from Oregon, only that I needed to get somewhere other than where I was. Don said, "You know I care about you, but it's not a good idea. It will hurt the Social Security and other benefits I'm getting. If they found out you were living with me, I could lose everything I get."

I hadn't thought of that either. He was right, and I understood. Then I called Bud. I had sworn to myself on the day I left Springfield, Missouri that I'd never return nor contact anyone there. He said, "Well, I'm not in good shape right now. It's been awhile since I've been sober. If you think you can live with me, you can, but you know how I am as a drunk."

I knew, and I didn't want to return to that, and I especially didn't want to return to Springfield, and besides, I had no way to get there. The only person left to call was Krista, my old AA sponsor from Seattle. I couldn't do that. It would mean I had failed in my search for a good life after college.

I lit a smoke and looked around. My home, if I could call it that, was tiny. A fire escape was right outside my window. That's where I kept my perishables. My jar of mayo looked sad. It was probably frozen solid again. I took a gulp of beer.

Better slow down, I told myself. *Too many gulps and this beer will be gone.*

I counted the cash in my pocket.

Damn. I'll survive, but not here in Klamath Falls. The people have proven there is no work for me here. I must get out of this town and try again somewhere else. I don't want to depend on welfare or any-one else. I need to do more than just survive. I must fix my dismal life. Life must change. I must make that change. I must do whatever it takes to make that change, even if I hate myself for what I have to do.

Surrendering, I made the call I had to make. Mike answered. He said, "I'll come get you. Where are you?"

CHAPTER 23

ELLIE, II

From my window view, I saw Mike get out of a vehicle I'd never seen before. He walked toward the front of my building with the normal limp in his walk from his bad knee. His head bobbed up, scanning the windows, and Manny, his dog, tagged along after him. I swished some toothpaste in my mouth to hide my beer breath. We had agreed on a firm rule of no alcohol.

He'd been living in Oroville, California, only a four-hour drive away, and didn't have the trailer anymore. Before leaving Klamath Falls, another rule we agreed on was to put an ID collar on Manny. The last stop we made before leaving town was at a pet store. There, we had a tag engraved with Manny's name and both of our cell phone numbers.

Traveling in a used van that we lived out of, our first week was spent under a downpour of rain. Had I stayed in Klamath Falls, I would have faced nothing but snow and no shelter. At that time, Klamath Falls didn't have shelters for women—only men. There was no way my money could have kept me afloat, and I'd already learned social service agencies couldn't help.

Fear of homelessness without even a van to live in kept me at his side. At least we were talking again, although I had to pretend to like him and brush off any condescending remarks he made. My hatred for him intensified with his outspoken opinions of people. When he talked bad about me, my inner thoughts of self-love blocked his penetrating words. When he talked bad about others, it left scars in me that I'd fight long afterward. In a grocery store parking lot, a black man passed by us and then spit on the pavement. Mike looked at me and said, "Black people spit when they see white people because they don't like us."

Another time, we saw two men together who exchanged words of affection, and Mike said, "Gross."

Nights were my only relief from his constant backstabbing words. As we drifted off to sleep, it was more like, "Get your foot out of my face." Or, "No, don't roll over."

The van was much too small to accommodate a bed bigger than a twin. We slept with our heads at opposite ends. Bright orange paint buckets from a hardware store were packed tight with any stuff we didn't need every day, like my ceramic fish from Krista. Those four buckets were the pillars that held up the four corners of a sheet of thick plywood. On top of the plywood board was our flexible twin mattress, not quite the full size of a standard twin.

I was small in stature, but in that confined van, I had a big, heavy, 260-pound man I hated with whom I had to share my bed.

As much as I liked to escape into sleep, it was fitful sleep that lasted all night. Even Manny wouldn't sleep with us, preferring a blanket on top of the ice chest that held our perishable foods.

Come daytime, and when I could, I'd look in front of me, daydreaming of disappearing. Mike's hovering often kept me from my imagination. The only place he couldn't follow me was into public restrooms, and those didn't have back doors or open windows to crawl through. I couldn't even pee without him standing guard right outside the door.

If I could have walked off, I'd have walked toward the center of whatever town we were in to seek out guidance. I knew from experience to find a government building, whether it was a post office, Social Security Office, or police station to get help. Government workers, unlike private companies, are responsible when approached for help, even if it's only to tell someone where to find help.

Fear of the unknown, of failing again and losing my possessions, kept me in place. My love and concern for Manny strengthened my need to stay put. If I disappeared, Mike would have an excuse to get drunk. That would put Manny at risk. Fear of what outcome Manny might face was what I couldn't overcome. My daydreams were fantasy.

By mid-May, our travels took us farther than we had ever gone together before. It had been a little more than a year since we had left Seattle. A quick drive through Oklahoma put us safely out of tornado warnings, then to the beaches along I-10. It was May 2012 and the week of my forty-fifth birthday.

Meandering through coastal towns in Louisiana, Mississippi, and Alabama, the ocean water was warm with a grey murkiness that overshadowed any hints of the beautiful blues and greens in its rumbling waves. Old plastic soda bottles, used paper plates, and shredded clothing littered the edge of the gulf and caused putrid bubbles to surface, but the local townsfolk seemed to enjoy it. Ample public areas and parking causeways provided easy access to several beachfronts on which to play with Manny.

Again, I didn't get a birthday gift. There was also no birthday cake or Corona beers, unlike the year before. We were sticking to our agreement of no alcohol. It was the only way to control Mike's volatile nature.

The sprawl of the small towns, one after another, businesses and shopping centers housed in historic buildings, reminded me of the northwest corner of Oregon where Astoria and Seaside were located. If only the water were prettier and the weather calm, I could have easily pictured myself relocating there. Its layout was pleasant, and the air was easy to breathe, free from industrialized pollution.

But when it rained, which was often, it hailed baseball-sized pellets. The horrible weather won out as we continued our wayward journey. On the interstate northward, traffic slowed to about ten miles per hour. Nobody could see in that hail to drive.

Countless camping trips took up the month of June and then, our next weekly stay was well off our beaten path, as if we even had a road we were sticking to. On the interstate northward, Mike suddenly turned west. We ended up at his aunt's place for the Fourth of July. She was the first family contact he had made back in Salt Lake when early out of Seattle.

Aunt Celeste lived way out in the country, right smack in the middle of Texas. Staying at a hotel in town paid for by her, we visited daily. A few days into our stay, I reminded Mike, "Let's keep going. I don't think Texas is a good place to settle down and we need to get somewhere. And I don't mean camping, either. We need a good home."

Mike leaned on the wooden fence, crossing his arms. His aunt had a huge sprawl of land with different parts of it fenced off. As he watched Manny play freely, Mike said, "You'll just run off again."

"No, I won't."

"I don't know why you ran off in the first place. Manny missed you. Don't you care about Manny?"

I looked at Mike and answered him. "Yes, and he needs a good home with both of us to take care of him."

Mike kicked the fence. "How are you going to take care of him, when you can't even take care of yourself? You think you are so smart, with a college degree and all, and you are stupid for running off." He looked at me. "You better not run off again. No one can take care of you like I can. You won't leave us again, will you?"

I answered, "No, of course not. We're family."

"Got that right. Manny and I are your family. We'll take care of you."

◆ ❖ ◆

Thursday morning, the day after the Fourth of July, we said our goodbyes to his aunt and continued on to parts unknown. By then, summer heat had made van life stifling and uncomfortable. It didn't have air-conditioning. We drove during morning and evening hours to stay cool. Midday, we hung out at city parks to get out of the steam oven of that van. Nights, we often slept with the passenger window rolled down a bit to let some air in but had to use caution. One night, someone tried to break in, only to be surprised when Manny barked, and Mike jumped out of bed and scared him off.

To escape the unrelenting summer heat, we checked into a cheap monthly motel in Fort Smith, Arkansas. There, we lived in air-conditioned bliss with cable TV, jigsaw puzzles, and Scrabble games. We'd go days without leaving the motel, save for taking Manny on bathroom walks. Outside, it hovered in the upper nineties with a humidity index much hotter. Stocking up on groceries or visiting the public library were the only things that got us out of the motel.

We also visited the University of Arkansas. Mike stayed by my side while I inquired about their bachelor programs. College enrollment would come with Federal Financial Aid. I saw that as a viable income. Any monies left over after tuition were given for living expenses.

Their degree programs didn't fit my needs. My wants had to be set aside in favor of something relevant to my professional credentials so that Mike would believe college advancement was important. Although I didn't settle for that school, I was determined in my research, seeking the perfect answer.

And then I found it. I got off the public computer at the library to join Mike in the parking lot. His distaste for people kept him out of the library, and it was too hot to leave Manny alone in the van. Outside, Mike would play with Manny while impatiently waiting for whatever it was I felt was important.

With the first smile in a long time on my face, I beamed as I told Mike, "Elizabethtown, Kentucky has a technical college that offers a one-year certificate program complementary to my degree. That will help me get a professional job. Kentucky's not far from here. We could go there to settle down, so I can go to college. Sound good?"

Mike said, "Yeah, Kentucky. Like the movie with the Hatfields and the McCoys. They were from Kentucky. The land is beautiful there. I lived in Radcliff back in the seventies and it was fine."

"I think we'll like it. I could go to college and Manny could have a bigger place to live."

Mike said, "Let's get out the map and look."

The admission application had to be done by mail, so we stayed holed up in the Fort Smith motel another month until I got my acceptance letter. In the meantime, I used library computers to complete the application process for the Financial Federal Aid end of it. By early August, all was confirmed for my start date in mid-September. We packed our bags and resigned ourselves to another round of living out of the van, and headed for Elizabethtown, Kentucky, or E-town for short, as we'd soon learn.

♦ ❖ ♦

Elizabethtown proved favorable with a long main drag full of month-to-month motels, much like the Fort Smith one. We wouldn't want to live out of a motel for my two terms of college, but it was a good transitioning point from van to apartment. No landlord was likely in be in favor of a person whose history and creditworthiness came straight from a van. But going from van to motel to apartment could easily work.

After six more weeks of motel living, we landed an ideal apartment, situated one block from the college. In that proximity, I'd demand Mike let me walk to school by myself. Nestled in the Fontainebleau neighborhood, we had neighbors on both sides of us with a shared front courtyard and outdoor walkway. A back door from our bedroom opened to a large lawn that was perfect for Manny, provided he was on a leash.

Hardin County had been dry up until a few months prior, and the stores and restaurants hadn't yet caught up to selling alcohol. Then again, we stayed true to our rule of no alcohol. I sweet-talked Mike into an AA meeting for us, but that was a one-off. He'd have nothing to do with AA, or any people unless he had to. He wouldn't let me go to an AA meeting by myself. But my goal was not to make my life better while under Mike's thumb. My goal was to make my life better by getting rid of my connection to him. My return to college was only the first step toward making that happen. I had more action steps in front of me, and no room to care about non-essentials like AA meetings.

I had two classes, one in medical transcription and the other in medical office procedures. In my early days of campus life, I'd walk its outdoor pathways between buildings and stop to sit on the grass or at a table. I'd pretend to do homework, only to stare off into the unknown. I was weak and alienated as I emerged from a life of homelessness, subordination, failure, and loss. Not only was I socially inept, but as I tried to read lesson plans, my poor vision made it difficult. I hadn't needed to read or write much at all in the prior year, so I hadn't paid attention to how bad my vision had become. I needed reading glasses.

In my free minutes between classes, I had to call home to check in with Mike to appease his insecurities. I also called Don in Wichita to update him that I was in Kentucky for further schooling. Later, I called Don again to probe him for wisdom without telling him my whole story. Same as I had probed Nana when I was younger, I also trusted Don and his genuine care for my well-being.

My admissions counselor arranged a student job for me in the campus library. I showed up for my first day on the job not knowing what to expect or how big the library was. The Library Director, who was an older gray-haired lady, greeted me with a firm handshake. "Hello, I'm Ann Thompson. I understand you know your way around libraries. It's great to have you with us."

I returned the handshake, and without any forethought, the first thing that came out of my mouth was, "I'm Elle Mott."

Up until then, campus staff called me by my full name, Sam-uelle. With my tribulations, I'd lost all touch with the 'Sam' I had once been. I was used to answering to "Ellie" as Mike called me. But when I introduced myself to Ann, I dropped the long "e" sound at the end of my name to professionalize it. With three silent letters, I pronounced it "L."

However, my impromptu change in name was not my first surprise in our shared introduction. An indescribable warm emotion swept through me—appreciation that someone could be so kind. I was not a sower among other sowers or a drone among other drones. In her first words to me, Ann treated me with dignity, as if I was a real, live person, worthy of being human. That was the first time in a long time for me.

I worked five mornings a week with Ann and four other librarians. Aside from support duties, I was given responsibility for a long-term project in their annexed room of archives. I didn't take my personal challenges into the classrooms, and I tried not to talk about my homelife to the librarians, but they were naturally curious about me. I answered with as few words as possible when asked, "So, what brought you here to Kentucky?"

I took my job seriously and gave my energy in every way possible. In return, I received the librarians' praise and comments like, "Why don't you go for your bachelor's degree to become a librarian? Then you could come back here to do your internship. Kentucky has two great universities for you to think about."

I thought about it and a few days later confided in one of the librarians. I knocked on her open office door one morning, as usual, to give her my daily update on my work. Katie looked up, smiled, and took a folder from me. She took a sip of her canned soda, and without opening the folder, said, "It's amazing the difference you're making with the archives."

I said, "It's the perfect project for me. It takes my mind off my problems."

Pictures of her with her parents sat on her desk, in white frames with pretty flowers. She also had pictures of her cats, in smaller frames, all around her computer. Her diploma was framed too, and hung on the wall behind her in a solid black frame. Katie said, "Tell me what's going on. Are there problems at home?"

"Yes. You remember me saying something about Mike?" I said.

Katie answered, "Yeah, the guy you live with?"

"Yes. I know I never talk about him. I can't stay with Mike. I left him once before, back in Oregon, but couldn't make it on my own. I couldn't afford to live, so we got back together even though I didn't want to. It was the only way I... Oh, I don't know how to talk about this."

Katie laid the folder on her desk. She said, "I had a horrible boyfriend once, too. It was when I was in college."

I continued, "I'm going to apply to NKU and not tell him."

Katie moved her computer screen to the side. "NKU is a good idea. Think about how you're going to get there. You don't have your own car, do you?"

"Oh, no, Mike would never allow that. I have thought about it.

Somehow, I have to convince him I need a car. And I have to figure out where I'm going to live once I get there."

NKU was a three-hour drive away, closer to Cincinnati, Ohio. We were closer to Louisville. I had three months until the semester ended. I had three months to figure it out.

Katie said, "If you need help with anything or if you need to step away to make a call... Whatever you need, you have my support. Chase—he'd get so angry, but that was Chase, always with an attitude."

I replied, "Yes, that's Mike, too."

Katie was a lifeline to me, perhaps more than she ever gave herself credit for. She was there for me, helping me think clearly. Soon, Ann and the other librarians were brought into the pact Katie and I shared, giving me their full support.

One morning as I worked on my project in the archive room, Katie came in and said, "Wow, I know I keep telling you this, but I can't believe how great this room is looking."

I finished putting a trophy in a box and set it on the shelf of the filing cabinet. I said, "I know, you keep telling me."

Katie added, "I don't know why Ann waited so long to have someone come in and organize this mess. People would ask us for something and we knew it was here somewhere but could never find anything."

"I know," I said. "Remember this table here," I said as I patted a short stack of papers on it. "It was piled high to the ceiling and there were papers on the floor under the table. Flags and posters and all kinds of stuff was piled everywhere in this room."

"Wow, it's amazing," she said again. "The reason I came in here wasn't to check on you but to make a suggestion."

"Yes, Katie?"

She leaned on the table and softened her eyes, looking at me. "Will you please take some time out one day this week and call the women's crisis hotline? I have the number for you." She handed me a small piece of paper, folded, with a phone number penciled on it.

"You think I should?" I asked.

Katie answered, "I'd feel better if you did. I thought I could handle Chase when I left him, after all, I knew what he was capable of, but then things got bad when I tried to walk out. You know what Mike's like. You can't control him any more than I could control Chase. It's for everyone's safety. Robin is afraid of what he might do. If he comes in here and causes problems... Well, call, will you please?"

Robin was one of the other librarians. "Okay, I'll call them now. I'm ready for a smoke break."

I stepped out on the loading dock and called. My first words in that call were, "Hi, this isn't an emergency, but my boss suggested I call you to tell you about my situation, just in case something happens."

We talked for about twenty minutes. I told the woman on the other end of the line about when Mike and I were together before

Klamath Falls. I told her about how controlling he was in the campground when the trailer door got broken. I told her how violent and unpredictable he was when we left that campground. I told her we weren't drinking, and that alcohol made him violently stupid.

The lady on the other end gave me suggestions. She said, "Don't tell him your plans. We've seen too many times that when someone has a history of violence, they can erupt if they feel threatened." She also told me, "Arrange your personal items so that when it's time for you to leave, you can take what you need without packing. Make sure you have your identification and important papers in a place that's easy for you to get to."

I assured her, "I keep my ID on me. I don't carry a purse. I know to keep my valuables close to me all the time."

She also told me, "Call nine-one-one any time you feel threatened. I'm making a report of our phone call and will file it with the city police, so they know your situation."

I had often lived in denial that Mike's patterns of control and emotional abuse could escalate. And yet, when we were camping back in Oregon, he had been violent, throwing stuff around. Especially when we ended up on that gravel road, back before I had first left him, I really didn't know if I would live through it. There was a reason I kept my valuables on me, even though I often shrugged off my reasons. Not only did I want a better life, but I realized in that phone call that I had to have a life in which I felt safe.

◆ ❖ ◆

In March, I cajoled Mike into understanding I needed my own car. College would be over soon, and I'd need to get myself to and from work. I didn't want to inconvenience him. He had the van. I needed a car. I got my car in April. As far as he knew, we were staying in E-town and I planned to go to work that summer of 2013.

What he didn't know was that I had applied for and was admitted to the Bachelor of Science Librarian Program at Northern Kentucky University, or NKU. I had also made roommate arrangements with a fellow NKU student who lived in Dayton, Kentucky, close to campus.

What Mike also didn't know, was that in a little over a month's time, I slowly, a few items at a time, rearranged my personal effects and my closet of clothes. I separated items I planned to leave with from items I didn't have to keep. I knew I'd be limited in time to vacate the premises. I moved the items I planned to keep to a spot where they would be easy to grab later on.

I usually got home from work at only a few minutes after 1:00. Mike usually woke up from a nap as I walked in. He'd then take Manny out for a bathroom walk, which lasted about ten minutes. On my last day of work at the library, I planned to use that ten minutes of free time to gather my luggage and run for my car. It didn't happen that way.

Crossing the parking lot to our apartment building, I saw Mike. He was already up from his nap and walking Manny. They were toward the front of the building. On my side, I saw Katie and Laurie, another librarian, pull into the parking lot as we had planned.

Mike had never seen them before and I ignored their arrival. Instead, I kept walking toward the front door, looked Mike's way, and said, "Hi."

Manny was too intent on finding the perfect spot to do his business, and he didn't pay any attention to me. Mike tugged on his leash to urge him to walk to an area away from apartment doors.

I walked in our apartment, opening my bookbag at the same time. From the living room to the kitchen, I grabbed must-keep stuff without stopping as I walked to the bedroom. That's where our back door was. I opened it. As planned, Katie and Laurie were standing in the courtyard, a ways away, but still in listening distance.

Some stuff from my grabbing got dropped in my bag. Other stuff was in my arms. With one hand, I turned the laundry basket in the bathroom over, dumping it and letting the stuff in my arms fall in. Next, I swept my arm across the shelf above, letting my keepers drop into the basket. I carried the basket to the bedroom and set it on the bed. The double-wide closet was shut. I slid one half open and started gathering my to-go pile.

Mike came through the open back doorway. "Why's the door open?"

"Fresh air," I said. I didn't stop to look at him. I kept grabbing stuff.

Mike asked, "What are you doing?"

I was still at the closet, reaching in for things. "I'm leaving."

Mike punched the wall that was between the closet and the other door. He yelled, "You can't leave. This is your home. Manny and I are your family."

I twisted around with an armful of clothes, raised my voice and said, "I'm leaving."

Mike stood in front of me and stretched his arms out, putting one hand on each end of the closet. "No. I'm telling you. You're not leaving."

His breath reeked of spicy Doritos. Raising my voice louder than before, I said, "I'm leaving."

Raising my voice was my cue for Katie to call the police. That was our plan. And that part of our plan went well.

I next yelled, "Get out of my way!"

Mike screamed back, "Think about Manny. You'll break his heart. This is your home. You can't!"

I yelled, "Move!"

I was stuck between the closet and Mike. I couldn't go any deeper into the closet. There was nowhere for me to go. I was blocked.

We stood there in a stalemate, Mike with his arms outstretched, and me repeating myself, "I'm leaving."

A heavy knock sounded on the bedroom door, which was still open and facing the backyard area. I bent down to reach for a bag at my feet. From my view under Mike's arm, I saw a uniformed city cop standing just outside on our back porch. Tall and stout, he looked in at us.

Mike didn't move.

The cop said, "Sir, step away from her."

Mike turned his head to see who had knocked but didn't let go of the closet doors.

Another officer appeared beside the first cop. He said, "Ma'am, we need to come in. We're coming in, okay."

I didn't know if he meant it as a question or a statement, but they came in. The same officer told Mike, "Sir, I need you to step away."

That officer escorted Mike out of the bedroom and toward the living room. The first cop stayed with me. I said, "I filed a report with the women's crisis line. They gave me a report number for you. I'm leaving."

❖

PART SIX

CHAPTER 24

ELLE

I pulled over to the side of the street and looked through my passenger window at the house. It sat high up on a hill. It was the same as I remembered from the pictures Cayla had sent me in her emails. I turned my car off. I was here, at the end of a street, at the east end of the tiny town of Dayton, Kentucky.

Fifteen steps at a steep incline led me to her door. There was a drizzle in the air; it would probably bring rain later. For now, clouds seemed far off. Her door opened, and a huge dog leapt at me. "Kano down," a bubbly gal with blonde hair said.

I hugged her dog before letting him go to obey her. A tiny Pomeranian teased at my ankles while the bigger dog backed off and ran to the yard to play. "Hi, you must be Elle. Come in. I'll show you around."

In my emails to her, I had used the name Elle, same as I had introduced myself as "Elle" to Ann, back on day one of my E-town library job. "Sam'" seemed so far in the past. As I stepped inside, the Pomeranian barked with spunk. The tiny dog was as spunky as a lion, but as quiet as a kitten's meow.

I followed my new landlady and roommate through a jam-packed hallway, and then up the stairwell to her place. Her cousin lived on the ground level below us. Four stories high in all, they'd bought the house from their grandma, since deceased. That's what Cayla's emails had told me.

Sunlight through the window in the hallway behind us was the only light as we went into her dark living room. She stepped over a pile of clothes and a hairdryer, then pulled back heavy burgundy drapes. She said, "We have a wonderful view of the Ohio River. You can take that street there," she said, pointing to a side street, "and it's just a four-block walk to the river."

We turned toward the kitchen and she pushed some fallen books farther back on their shelf as we passed. "I'll do the dishes before I leave today. I'm going on an overnight trip, but you get settled in while I'm gone. And help yourself to anything you need in here." The microwave door was open. She shut it and said, "Let me show you your room."

I followed Cayla up a stairwell. "I think you'll like it here. It's quiet and neighbors are nice and friendly. I might be gone this weekend, too. It's Mother's Day, you know? You got plans then?"

Each step had a pile of stuff on it. I had to either sidestep or skip a step to keep going. "No, no Mother's Day plans. But my birthday is next week, so maybe then."

Her emails had told me she was a bit messy. Messy was an understatement. But I couldn't recoil. Anything was better than the nightmare I had pulled myself from.

She grabbed a vacuum which was leaning against the stairwell wall and set it upright in the empty bedroom. "Sorry, I didn't have time to vacuum, but you can use mine. Rent is three-twenty-five a month for your share, plus half of the electric bill."

I recalled it as $235 a month, but didn't want to stir up trouble. She was offering me a safe place to stay and my own private room. Money seemed irrelevant. I'd never be able to make a dent in paying back all I'd ever received or taken. I could handle the "new" dollar figure and gave her the cash to cover me through the end of June, a month-and-a-half out.

Cayla left for her trip, foregoing washing her dishes. I took a big gulp from a twelve-ounce bottle of beer and started unpacking. It was one of several beers left over from the night before. Although Cayla's place was under a four-hour drive from E-town, I had stopped at a motel. It had been my midway point, not only in driving, but also between leaving a nightmare and starting a new life. I deserved a beer, or two. I had to have a beer or two to unwind. Klamath Falls was a year behind me, but my surrender to Mike over that failure was less than twenty-four hours in the past.

I set about unpacking, finishing my beer. My coffee mug and other dishes even found a place in my room. In every step I took, my two new tail-wagging friends followed. I had to hope if Mike stayed put and sober back in the E-town apartment, Manny would be fine.

◆ ❖ ◆

Job searching and getting settled into college were the priorities ahead of me. And by early June I was back in AA. Also in June, I made my second trip ever into Cincinnati, the big city across the river and the state line. It was only a ten-minute drive, but one I had put off. That trip was for an interview with the public library, one of the top libraries in the country.

When I had completed the job application and testing online, I hadn't pictured how big the place was. It took up two city blocks, with a sky bridge connecting two buildings. Waiting in the lobby of the personnel department, I thumbed through my resume, running over answers in my head. I was self-assured in my skills, but also gun-shy. Klamath Falls had made its indelible mark on me. Anything could go wrong at any time. With no guarantees in life, it was up to me to build my foundation. The results of this interview would test the faith in my courage.

The office door into the lobby opened and a tall slender woman in a pantsuit looked my way. She smiled and asked, "Samuelle?"

I closed my attaché, smiled back and answered, "Yes."

She said, "Hi Samuelle, I'm Andrea, the Personnel Manager. Please come in."

I tugged at my suit jacket to make sure it hung just right with my slacks. "Thank you."

The interview proceeded well, and when Andrea asked for my references, I handed her my list, saying, "My references are excited to talk to you. They know about my interview and are as enthused as I am that I'm here."

My references were Ann and Katie from the library back in E-town. They had truly helped me become confident in my professional attributes. I had kept in contact with Katie, however, her texts later died off. Andrea informed me they'd make their decision soon, letting me know within two weeks if I was hired. Two weeks came and went without a word.

Before summer's end, Cayla threw me a curveball. "I don't know how to tell you this, but this house was owned by my granny, and when she died I inherited it."

I knew that much from back when she advertised the room for rent. Cayla continued, "I don't have the title to the house and now the bank wants it back."

Come to find out, we could stay if we had money to get ourselves out of the legal entanglement, but that was not an option she was looking at. She let me know she'd find a two-bedroom apartment for us close to the NKU campus. At least she was taking me along in this change of plans. Through an AA contact, I left Cayla's idea behind and moved into a spacious loft apartment, also in Dayton.

Moving was planned for the last weekend of July, and it couldn't have been better timing when Andrea from the library in Cincinnati called me. "We'd like to hire you. Can you start the first week in August?"

Wow. Gee, can I. It was a permanent job at the state government level. *Nana would be proud of me, same as she was proud of me when*

I worked with the Social Security Office. The job was part time, with afternoon hours in their processing department getting brand-new books ready for circulation.

Two AA friends helped me move my belongings down the three flights of stairs at Cayla's place, then up the two flights of stairs to my apartment. Heather was young and strong, but my other friend, Lorene, was an older woman, spry but short-winded. After we carried the first load downstairs, we made the following trips easier. I threw my stuff out my bedroom window to the lawn below while Heather and Lorene loaded my car.

Once we got everything to my new place, I thanked Heather as she left. Lorene stayed to help me unpack. The room I had at Cayla's place came with a mattress and box springs. Here, my bedding on the carpeted floor would have to do. I opened a window to let in summer breezes. Coconut and tanning oil smells drifted up from my landlady's salon below.

Lorene emptied another box and asked, "Elle, honey, where do you want these books?"

I didn't have any furniture. The kitchen and bathroom had built-in shelves, but those were small and not good for books. I looked around my loft. It was one big open space. Tall skyscraper windows, three in all, lined one wall. I answered, "Turn the box over. I'll use it as a nightstand by my bed. We can put the books on that."

It didn't take long to get me settled in, save for my clothes. Those stayed bagged for the time being. "Sit, let's take a break," I told Lorene.

We sat on my carpeted floor, looked at my bags of clothes,

looked around my apartment, then back at my clothes. I drifted into memories of Nana's huge walk-in closet. It was shortly after Grandpa died when she had the house remodeled. That was when Nana got her walk-in closet and dressing room. Her clothes always hung organized by color. Nana had often told me, "Remember, Kym, red, white, and blue always go together."

Blue had been Nana's favorite color. Blue was her must-have color. Nana was gone now, and so was Kym. Shoot, even Sam' was gone.

Lorene interrupted my thoughts, but I didn't mind. It was time to let go. Lorene asked me, "Where's your hammer, Elle?"

I handed her the hammer.

"And I need nails."

I handed her the box of nails.

Lorene was originally from the hollers of Hazard, Kentucky. She often had her own way of doing things, which city folks found different. In no time, Lorene had my place artistically homey. On the walls that cornered my sleeping space, she hammered in nails, but not all the way in. She then put my clothes on hangers and hung the hangers on the nails on the walls. Jeans and shorts remained folded and in a designated spot on the carpet, but all my shirts and jackets and dress clothes hung beautifully. I didn't need to be in any hurry to hang art. I already had a masterpiece from Lorene's handiwork.

August was an equally busy month for me. It began with my first day on the job at the library, and ended with my first day in online classes with NKU. Every free weekend, I scoured yard sales to furnish my place. AA meetings and time with friends also filled my life. Of all the friends I made, Lorene was my strongest ally.

Tracie was one gal who caused me to test the waters of friendship. My first impression of her was great. My last impression, far from great. The same age as me, we met in the social hour after an AA meeting on the last Friday in September. The next morning, we met for coffee. Then, a few days later, she called me. "I don't know what to do. I can't stay here."

Tracie had been staying with a friend. I didn't exactly know her story, other than she was facing the risk of homelessness. Over the past few days, I had shared with her what had worked for me. And here she was on the phone, confused and sad.

"Come spend the night at my place," I told her.

I later told her it was temporary, and I couldn't do a roommate situation. My landlady would frown on that idea, I explained. The story about my landlady was a cover. I wasn't going to give up my independence. That could jeopardize my stability. I saw Tracie's situation as an emergency, and as such, was compassionately drawn to help. After my immediate reaction of trying to rescue her, it dawned on me I didn't even know her last name.

During my afternoon at work, I realized she could rob me blind while I was away. I knew nothing about her other than what she told me. If I had once invented an alias life, certainly I wasn't the only one who could. My renter's insurance appeased my worry. At only ten dollars a month, I could afford to protect myself from yet another apartment fire or any other misfortune. In past times, to come up with ten dollars for insurance was impossible, but I could afford it with the part-time library job and school monies I received.

As I watched Tracie meander in her second morning on my couch, I couldn't wrap my head around the fact that she had stayed in my apartment all day the previous day. In my dire moments, I had refused to sit still. When in Klamath Falls, I pounded the pavement every day in search of answers. Yet Tracie was complacent, as if she wasn't willing to fight her way out.

She opened her eyes and watched me as I was getting dressed for work. Not moving from the couch, she said, "I promise I'll do something today."

The morning was getting late, and I had to leave for work by noon. When I returned home from work, she told me about some phone calls she had made. "And I went out for a walk," she added. She tossed the book she was reading on my coffee table. "I needed cigarettes."

Early in her third morning, I said, "Let's get up. Let's go. I have to work this afternoon."

Tracie asked me, "Where are we going? I don't have anywhere to go."

I answered, "Well, you can't stay here."

"Fine. You don't have a TV anyway. How can you live without a TV?" she said.

I watched frickin' reruns of Lost on a tiny portable DVD player when I was too poor for TV, let alone cigarettes.

With my pulling and prodding, she got up off the couch, then showered and dressed. I drove her to a social service agency and stayed by her side until processed. Tracie was admitted into a women's transitional housing unit. I thought that would be the end of her neediness, and as she got her life put back together we'd stay friends. And we did remain friends for a short while, but as my hopes for her failed, our friendship also died.

Andrea from the library called me one morning a week later. I could hear that smile of hers in her voice. She always sounded like she was smiling, even when she wasn't. After exchanging good morning pleasantries, Andrea said, "In response to your background check, we received a letter from the Ohio Attorney General Civilian Identification Service, saying you may not meet employment conditions. Now, not to worry, we just need to go a step further by requesting your FBI rap sheet. So, there's more paperwork for you to complete, and then you will need to mail those to the FBI. They will not release information to us, only to you. But when you receive their report and show it to us, that should get your background search satisfactorily finalized."

I did as Andrea instructed with the paperwork and understood it could take up to four weeks to receive a reply. I was willing to fulfill any responsibilities to keep my job, although I had no guarantee of job security once Andrea discovered my twenty-one past felony convictions. In the meantime, I was free to continue working as normal.

More than twenty years had passed since my convictions, so I hadn't revealed any of that in my library job application process. Online, I investigated all I could to find out what might show up on this FBI rap sheet. I was used to my legal name changes, far too many to count, showing up any time a deep search was done on me. That sometimes happened with job applications. I figured my trail of name changes might have triggered the questionable response from the state of Ohio.

My research attested that anything I had ever been fingerprinted for would be on my rap sheet, convictions included, as well as my employment with the SSA and IRS back in the 1980s. Luckily, I didn't recall being fingerprinted during my security hold at the Susanville jail.

As I waited out the month, I acted as if everything was normal to my boss and coworkers. My job responsibilities gave me purpose, and the comradeship among coworkers gave me self-esteem. I wasn't a putz among putzes. I wasn't Sower Number Five.

I also readied myself to fight for my job with all the gumption I had. I gathered documentation concerning employee rights, received pro bono advice from an attorney, and prepared like a paralegal prepares for a murder trial. I also had to be ready to accept the outcome if I lost this battle. Financially, I'd be okay living off my school monies. I knew how to live under the poverty line and come out alive. I could do it again if I had to. The thought of struggling, though, exhausted me. I needed my job.

When my FBI Rap Sheet arrived in the mail, I scheduled an appointment with Andrea. Stepping into her office, Andrea smiled and waved her arm toward the chair across from her. "Hi Elle, come in, sit."

I sat down and started to pull my papers out. Andrea tilted her computer monitor to the side, away from us, then sat back and relaxed in her chair. It rocked back then forward again. She said, "I see you have some papers for me."

I leaned forward and kept my eyes on my FBI rap sheet as I handed it over. "I didn't reveal my prior convictions in my initial hiring paperwork. It was such a long time ago. I was real young then and I've since turned my life around."

I looked up at her, away from the papers as she took them from me. She smiled at me and said, "Tell me, Elle, how is your new job? Are you enjoying it?"

We talked with a good rapport, even as we shifted our discussion to the information in my FBI rap sheet. Andrea remained kind about the whole matter. In the end, she informed me she needed to file my FBI rap sheet with my employee records. Andrea added, "As long as we are aware of your past, I see no reason to let you go. After all, as you say, it was a long time ago. Your supervisor often speaks highly of you. I think you'll do just fine working here at the library."

At the cusp of losing my friendship with Tracie and retaining my work with the library, I received a phone call late one winter evening. It was 11:00 and I had laid a book down, having finished the chapter. I reached for my lamp to turn the light off when my phone rang. I didn't recognize the out-of-state number, so I let it go to voicemail. It wasn't unusual for me to get wrong-number calls. I was still using the phone I had in Klamath Falls, Oregon.

I left my light on and listened to the message. "Hi, I'm in Elko and I just found your dog... He just walked up to me and my friend at Weavers... We're gonna, what are we gonna do with him? We're goin' to take him to our car and warm him up a bit because he's so cold. If you could please, give us a call back."

Of course, "your dog" meant Manny. And Manny's ID tag had both my phone number and Mike's engraved on it. My phone call from Elko, Nevada meant Mike had left E-town, Kentucky to return home to his folks in Elko. I immediately called her back. "My heart goes out to Manny, but I'm in Kentucky. Could you please call the other phone number listed? Please let me know if you have any problems."

A few minutes later she called me back and said, "I got ahold of a woman at the other number who told me she is Mike's girlfriend. She's on her way to pick him up."

Later, I received another call from the woman who had found Manny. She said, "Mike's girlfriend seems to be drunk, but at least the dog, Manny, is safely on his way home with her."

I said, "I know, it's scary. It's sad. I don't know what else to do or say, but thank you. I'm at a loss for how to protect Manny when I'm here in Kentucky."

"We're at a loss too in this, but at least Manny is safely going home now."

I texted Mike but got no text or call back. I then turned my laptop computer on and looked online to find the publicly listed phone number for his elderly parents. I called. Mike's mom answered the phone, but in confusion, she handed the phone to her granddaughter. She told me, "Uncle Mike's in jail for DUI. I'll call my mom to see about going to Mike's place to get Manny."

When she said "my mom," she meant Mike's sister, Melanie. I thanked her and mistakenly felt that was the extent of what I could do long distance. The next morning, at 8:00 a.m. Elko, Nevada time, I received a call from Mike's number. I answered. It was his girlfriend. "I still have Manny. But look, Mike's bail is three hundred and fifty dollars, and I can't afford that. Maybe you could pay it. We don't even live together, and Manny can't stay here, but I just fed him."

Ignoring the girlfriend's plea, I gave her the phone number to Mike's family. Later, she called me again, and said, "Mike's sister, Melanie, is on her way to get Manny." In her simple, dumbed-down words, this girlfriend kept talking. I let her talk about her frustration over Mike. She then giggled and added, "He's a good guy."

In my fight for Manny's survival, I bit my tongue rather than argue with her. I replied, "Hopefully this DUI will be a wakeup call to him that he needs help for his drinking. Hopefully, he can get back into AA."

She said, "Oh, I hope so. I'll go to AA with him."

Talking down to her level, I replied, "Oh good. Please talk with him about that, and please call me if you have any problems at all with Manny being picked up. Call me if any problems come up later with Manny."

She agreed, and I felt assured I had done all I could.

I began spring semester classes with a degree change to Creative Writing. The library degree would only lead to a librarian position. That involved face-to-face customer service. The speech impediment I had acquired in the summer of 1998 still troubled me when faced with such responsibilities. The support duties I had in my current library position gave me plenty of self-worth, and I had little difficulty in speaking clearly as needed. No longer going after what I needed, I was now pursuing a degree in something that truly interested me.

More "lost dog" calls came in. Those calls seemed to come in spurts. At times, weeks could go by without my concern. At other times, I was hounded with calls, but never turned them away. At first, Mike's sister was willing to house Manny, but then she no longer could.

I enlisted help from Karen Walther, manager of the local animal shelter. Over several months, Karen stayed in close contact with me as her staff stayed in contact with Mike. Several times Manny landed in their overnight shelter. Unfortunately, Mike retained ownership rights, but Karen worked with him to encourage him to relinquish his rights. Manny needed to be placed in a safe home. Mike never allowed that. Being in control was his m.o.

I wrote letters to the Elko City Police Department, informing them of Mike's in-depth criminal history with my plea to turn Manny over to Ms. Walther during any response calls. I furthermore wrote the municipal judge, pleading with him to consider Mike's full history whenever he appeared in his courtroom. My letter also appeared in an open and public online forum.

At one point, and all in one week's time, I received several phone calls from Ms. Walther with the animal shelter, two from their city dog pound, and three calls from city police officers. I could care less about Mike, but I had to do all I could to get Manny safe. The only reasonable action left to do, which wasn't feasible or financially possible for me, was to literally travel to Elko, Nevada and snatch Manny to find him a good home. I was assured that everyone who needed to be aware of Manny's needs was well informed.

Spring semester classes closed with my application for transfer to another college, Southern New Hampshire University (SNHU). It offered a bachelor's degree in creative writing completely online. However, I received disappointing news from my SNHU advisor, who informed me I was at the edge of my lifetime limit for Federal Financial Aid Awards.

My hodge-podge of college credits had put me over the limit and didn't fit neatly into any degree at either NKU or SNHU. I never could seem to do anything only once. I'd attended four high schools when younger. Now, it was three colleges and too many credits to keep going on Federal Financial Aid. I could stay in college if I wanted, but at my own expense. I couldn't afford that on my part-time income. College was over for me.

My income covered my rent, but little else. Other departments offered me extra hours in supporting duties. This gave me not only more money, but a greater exposure to the library and the people who made the library great.

"Lost dog" phone calls continued to pour in, each in an unexpected moment to pull me away from online classes or work. If I needed to thank Mike for something, it was that he kept Manny's ID tag on his collar, complete with both his phone number and mine. Any time my cell phone's caller ID showed a Nevada prefix, I dropped what I was doing to answer.

In mid-December 2014 I received one such call. A year and a half had passed since I had arrived in Dayton, Kentucky, but those calls kept coming in. At the sound of my female voice, "Hello, this is Elle," the caller said, "Your poor dog is tied to a newspaper stand. I saw some guy tie him up, then go into the bar. Can you come get him?"

"Oh no—not again," I answered. "I'm in Kentucky, but I'm so glad you called."

She raised her voice. "You're in Kentucky?"

"Yes, I had to get away and it's his dog, not mine, so I couldn't bring him with me, but I care about him so much—"

The lady on the phone interjected, "We're in downtown Elko,

Nevada. It's four o'clock, almost dark, and snowing hard. We've had wind gusts and several inches of snow all week. It's too cold out here for a dog and he's such a tiny little fellow."

I said, "Let me give you an Elko phone number. It's to Karen Walther, manager of the local animal shelter. She knows what's going on—unfortunately, this happens often. Karen can get Manny in out of the cold. That's his name, Manny."

She said, "I saw that on his tag. I can call the number if you want, but listen, if this happens a lot, why not let me help you. I have a friend who'd love to have another small dog."

I jumped at her offer. We talked a few more minutes until she hung up to rescue Manny. Two hours later, she called me back. "My husband and I brought him to my friend Ginger's house. She fed him a big bowl of food and gave him fresh water. He was hungry like he hadn't eaten in a long time. Now that he's eaten, he's running around the house playing with her two little dogs. He's happy here, and warm. Oh, his tail is wagging. Ginger wants to keep him if it's okay with you."

"Okay? Yes, please," I exclaimed. "I've been trying so long to get Manny into a safe place. Thank you so much."

A week later, I called her back for a follow-up. She said Manny was well and gave me Ginger's phone number. I called Ginger who told me, "Oh, Manny is doing fine. He's happy here and we are so happy to have him. I gave him a good bath and threw away his ratty dog tag with your ex's phone number. He deserves better. I put a new collar and tag on but kept your phone number."

I didn't bother to clarify our relationship when she called Mike "my ex." Manny was all that mattered to me. During our talk I asked Ginger, "Can I send you dog food or any money for him, to say thank you?"

Ginger answered, "Oh no, honey, that's not necessary. We're happy to help. We have a big house and are fine on money. Manny is in good hands here."

As I write this, I understand Mike is no longer with us. He died in 2015, at fifty-eight years old. His sister, Melanie, has since contacted me online. Her message was short. It read, "My brother Mike drank himself to death. It's painful and I don't want to talk about it."

No ties to Manny existed anymore. Some folks in AA chalked it up to a "God thing." That concept made no sense to me. No matter who or what higher being, if any, resolved this dilemma, sitting still in prayer couldn't have saved Manny's life. My action steps saved his life.

That's when I met Quinn, in the fall of 2014. She, too, was in AA, and like me, was trying to stay sober no matter who or what, if anything, was behind our spiritual well-being. We sought out meetings that were relaxed in their religiosity. Unsuccessful, we connected with four others in AA, who in their like-mindedness, joined us for a steering committee to start a new AA group.

Alcoholics Anonymous has a level of autonomy that makes it successful as a recovery program. After a month of hashing out the logistics, the six of us opened our first meeting of the All Shades of Belief Group in the oldest AA clubhouse in America, in Cincinnati, Ohio. We took our name from the AA pamphlet addressed to the newcomer in AA, which says there is room in AA for people of all shades of belief.

Many AA meetings open and close with a prayer. Instead, we opened with the AA Preamble, which defines the AA program. Following that, we shared our Group Preamble, which we wrote. This spoken statement explains our autonomy. It includes a description of our group. More importantly, it states that the intention of our group is to promote recovery from the disease of alcoholism without having to accept anyone else's beliefs or having to deny our own.

Although I'm a charter member, our group's growth is in the hands of the whole group. Our AA meetings and fellowship give me a foundation for living. Focusing on life, rather than questioning who or what made life, my spirituality can flourish.

Only one question remained for me. *How did it all begin? My life, that is.*

I came into this world as Kimberly Louise and knew my mother existed. Who my father was, though, left me guessing. Other than his name, Robert Frank Wells, and his Little Rock address, my birth certificate was vague. An age without a birthdate, his race, and his occupation as laborer were the last remaining clues on my state certified document.

I dug deep into the internet and strung clues together until I hit the jackpot. It was his current address, in Tulsa, Oklahoma of all the unlikeliest places. To write him a letter was the most respectful and least intrusive way to make contact. I mailed it certified, his signature required for delivery. According to the post office, he got my handwritten letter.

CONCLUSION

CHAPTER 25

WHO I AM

My letter began: "The reason for my letter is to discover who my birth father is as a person, but respecting you, who I feel is my father. Enclosed is a photocopy of my birth certificate from 1967, along with supporting documentation from legal name changes. Today, people call me *Elle*. If I'm mistaken in understanding you are my father, please disregard my anticipation and expressions. If you agree you are this man, please read on."

In part, it ended with, "I've been living in northern Kentucky for a little over a year. I was raised in the then-sleepy community of Salem, Oregon, but haven't been with those folks or back since 1993. I grew up knowing little about you, even being denied the use of your last name. If you'd like to consider getting to know each other, or opening the possibility of a relationship, please reach out to me. If you feel any awkwardness in this, know you are not alone, and maybe together we could patch up the past, following an initial step of saying hello."

He never replied to my letter.

◆ ❖ ◆

In October 2015, after a yearlong unsuccessful succession of interviews for a full-time position, the manager in another department of the library hired me. It was also a support position as a library page. My office was still in the basement, but unlike before, I wasn't stuck in the basement. My new duties and responsibilities took me all over the library, which spanned two city blocks.

Not more than two weeks into my new job, I stepped outside on my late-afternoon break and checked my cell phone. Someone with an out-of-the-area phone number had left me a voicemail. I was puzzled. The Manny situation was long over. My friends were here in Cincinnati and northern Kentucky. I listened to my voicemail. "This is Sharon. I was a friend of Bob, your dad, Bob. Please call me back."

I replayed the message. I wanted to call, but oh, I was caught off guard. It had been more than a year since I sent my letter to him. I had long ago accepted that my life was not about finding out where I came from.

Overhead, birds were fluttering in trees. How carefree they must be, without the same kind of emotions us humans have. I had less than two hours until I was off work. I reasoned to myself that I would wait and call from home. I returned to work. I still had so much more to learn on the job, but my attention wavered in what little was left of my working day.

As soon as I got home and shut the door behind me, I called

her back. She introduced herself again as Sharon, his friend. She then said, "I've got something important to tell you. Your dad died last week."

I sat down in my easy chair. "Oh no."

Sharon said, "Yes, I'm so sorry to have to tell you, he's gone. He thought of you often and had your letter close to him when he died."

As we talked, she added, "He loved you, and oh how I wish he would have called you, but your dad, your dad was so stubborn. I never could get him to call. I don't know why."

I said, "I didn't want to call in case he was married or settled with a family. But since he never called, I surmised he didn't want me to interrupt his life."

"Oh no, not at all," Sharon explained. "I think it was more of a surprise to get your letter all these years later. He thought you were long gone. He didn't think he'd ever see you again. Then, he got your letter."

I wanted to know so much more. "Did he have other children?"

Sharon answered, "No. No, other kids. And he never remarried. Your parents were so young when you came along. They were just kids. And then she took you and was gone. He figured you were gone forever."

I said, "I was always told he was in prison when I was born."

Sharon said, "Oh, I don't know anything about that. Maybe. I don't know. He was in the navy."

"The navy?" I asked.

"Yes," Sharon answered. "He retired from the navy."

Damn, I don't know whether to be mad at him for not reaching out to me, or to slow down and be thankful for Sharon's concern.

I shifted in my chair and didn't know what to say. After thinking about Sharon's side of it, I said, "I'm sorry for your loss. I wish I had known him."

Sharon explained more to me. "Bob was sick for about a year now, and finally went into the veterans hospital. Problems with his lungs. That's when he died. He had vision problems too. Couldn't see much of anything out of one eye. Oh, I wish you two had gotten to know each other. He wanted to, but he was so stubborn. You should get yourself an attorney. He has money in the bank, and I'd hate for the state to take it."

"Do you have any pictures of him? That's what I'd like."

"I'll have to see if I can find some. I can send you some of his things. He was such a pack rat, your dad was. He hated doing laundry, so he'd just go buy new clothes instead of washing the old. But, that's Bob for you. He was such a funny dud, set in his own ways. The VA hospital, I don't know what they'll do with his clothes he had when he went in. I had to go into his apartment and clean it out, back when he went into the VA."

We talked a little longer and promised to keep in contact.

Within days, I received a small box by mail from my father's friend Sharon, which held documents and a jewelry case. A tiny latch secured his leather trinket box. I unlatched it and lifted the smooth round top. Its hinges opened a world never before known to me.

Several tie tacks were grouped together, one of a stallion, and another with a square blue stone. I slipped his high school ring on. Raised gold lettering that read "LRHS 1965" rubbed against my ring finger, rolling around my middle finger, a finger comparatively tiny to the man who'd worn it. I became astir with a warmness that resonated from my heartbeat as I felt closer to him than I had ever thought possible.

That's when I saw it. Eight bronze coins were in the upper left compartment. I let the ring drop off my finger and back into his box as I swooped up one coin. It was an AA medallion. The Roman numeral XVIII was engraved on it, commemorating eighteen years of sobriety. A teardrop fell from me, and I felt a consequential sniffle coming on.

I looked at the other bronze coins. The father I never knew was just like me, sober with a rich history in AA. With the Serenity Prayer on one side, I lingered to rub each medallion, each deserving of its own respect and recognition. I allowed my tear to have a mind of its own, as it evolved into a sweet puddle and flowed over my cheekbone. I put all but one medallion back in its place, in its respective compartment. I pocketed his twenty-five-year medallion and wondered if he'd mind if I kept it close to me, to feel his love bravely.

Returning to his box, I let my fingers run along his possessions, each item deserving merit. Nowhere in his case or in my entire care package of his belongings did I find a religious momentum.

No cross, no token in observance of a saint, and no bookmarks or personal writings to infer ties to religion. Other than the spiritual message on his AA coins, I was given no indication he observed or even accepted religion. Not only did we have our source of spirituality in common, we also held our lack of religious observation in common. The father I never knew was just like me.

My heart muscles tightened as a flood of clues poured through me. I was just like my father. Same round face and vision problems too, same personality flaws, same driving forces. It was as if I were finally home, but without anyone to greet me.

In mid-summer 2016, probate closed, and out of his monies I paid over a hundred dollars in postage for his cremated remains. Having been without a vehicle for a while, I bought a cheap used pickup truck. I also bought a good pair of brand-new shoes. With all the highways I'd walked in our great big country, my feet were more than ready to be pampered.

There was nothing else I needed, other than a place to call home, one that wasn't a rented apartment. And no more tents for me. House hunting with a lady friend and real estate agent, Alvena, we stuck to my limited budget.

I was adamant about not taking on a mortgage. Even if, and who knows why this would happen, but even if I lost my income and went broke, I'd still have a roof over my head, and not a canvas roof. His probate monies wouldn't cover the price of a suburban higher-end property. It would cover the cost of a junk house in a bad neighborhood.

The third house we looked at was perfect for me, although not perfect as a safe dwelling. It came with a problem, which plummeted its price. Tucked safely in a suburban neighborhood with a river-front view, I took it.

Before moving a single thing into my new home, I turned the house over to biohazard professional contractors. All carpet got ripped out in this process, revealing beautiful hardwood floors. My purchase price and the expense to make the house safe and clean came to a small fraction of the going prices for houses in this neighborhood.

As soon as the contractors were finished with their work, my friends, Mary Kay, Janet, and I repainted and made other cosmetic changes. A plumber replaced the toilet and I got a new water heater. My sweat and toil went into making this house my dream home. It is a small house, described by many as a doll house. I only have my pet birds and me, so the one bedroom and open floor layout accommodates us quite well.

I was twenty-five years old when sleeping under an overpass was normal for me. Twenty-five years later, I found a place to call home and have good friends. At a half-century old, I walk into a dessert and coffee bar one afternoon with a friend, Kim. I'm wearing a princess tiara. It's not a real tiara, but one of those plastic ones from the store where no matter what you buy, it's only a dollar. Kim grabs my hand, giggles, and pulls me to tag along. She's forty years old yet giggling like a four-year-old.

As thick-skinned as her dark black skin, Kim has become my confidante, the one person with whom I can share openly. In return, she tells me honestly what she thinks and how I could think differently. Her boldness lets me love her as a dear bosom friend.

Kim is tall at nearly six feet tall. I stay close to her in excitement as we make our way to the party table. The smell of brewing coffee wafts through the air. I love my coffee. We pass by a dessert counter with fancy designed cakes, each small enough for one person. At the back of the restaurant we join others. Janet, who helped me paint my house, stands up from our booth and gives me a bear hug. "Happy birthday, Elle."

Lorene is with us. She's been by my side since those early days here in northern Kentucky, when she helped me set up my apartment, hammering nails into my walls to hold my clothes. Wise, smart, and true to herself, living life with utmost honesty is a trait I admire in Lorene. Alvena joins us after the party starts. As sweet as her never-ending smile, she was a perfect real estate agent for me.

Kim fiddles with the tiara on my head. "You are fifty years old now."

No real rubies on the tiara I wear, but I am as happy as a princess. It's who I am that reveals my happiness. No longer traversing cross-country in wanderlust, my life today is about being who I am, and not questioning who I am.

It's about an inner peace from liking me and liking you. It's about coming together, you and me, to make our world a better place for everyone. Far removed from secrets that had a strong hold on me, I've seized my life with complete trust in myself for how my life will continue to unfold.

Today, when I walk into my house, the first thing I see is my credenza where my college diploma, pictures, and other items that I had safeguarded in my transiency are prominently on display. My father's boxed ashes are also on my credenza.

Hanging on the wall to the side of this credenza, I have the deed to my house, framed. Next to my deed is my father's picture, also framed. Another framed picture on this wall is one of me receiving an award. It's an award for Community Service Leader of the Year 2017, presented by a community organization with which I am an active member.

My transformation is about being a positive contributor to community progress, enhancing friendships, commitment to my employer, and gratitude for my home, with love for my pet finches. I remember Nana's love, not for what she expected me to do, but for the courage, resilience, and fortitude she instilled in me. In living by her example to aim big, I also remember to share my kind-heartedness for others, as Grandpa showed me.

With no memories of my father, I carry his medallion in my left pocket every day, letting it clink next to my own medallion.

Just like him, I am accepting of life's challenges, brave enough to make change, and in awe of our phenomenal existence in our vast universe.

THE END

April 1994

December 2017

ACKNOWLEDGMENTS

I would like to express my gratitude to the many people who walked beside me in support of this book, and to all those who talked things over, read drafts, offered comments, and assisted me in editing and proofreading through many revisions. Kim Armstrong and Brad Hudepohl, your loyal friendship and support have been invaluable. Lorene, Mary Kay, and Janet—your ears, always available to hear my ideas, and your hugs have kept me sane.

Thanks to another friend, Tommy Hughley, who like me, has risen above homelessness and chaos. Our shared talks are my reminder that life is great today. You help me stay spiritually balanced and understand what it means to be grateful.

I'd like to thank Johnboy Walker and Stacey Johnson for their mentorship. Johnboy, your suggestions regarding the writing craft, along with your humor, got me started on the right foot when beginning my journey to write this memoir. Stacey, your professional guidance as an acquisitions specialist has helped me make informed decisions throughout the publication process.

Thank you to Covington Writers Group. Jenny, the unabashed

encouragement and critiques that you and others so graciously give me have helped me immensely, strengthening my writing capabilities. Thank you also to the online writing communities and groups that I hang out in—your camaraderie and collaboration has meant the world to me.

A special thank you goes out to Don Birran, who lives in Wichita, Kansas. Since the day I met you, nearly twenty years ago, you have believed in me, ever reminding me that I can do anything—even write a book.

> *There is only one way to avoid criticism:*
> *do nothing, say nothing, and be nothing.*
>
> —Aristotle

ABOUT THE AUTHOR

Elle Mott has called northern Kentucky her home since May 2013. She writes about homelessness, recovery, activism, and spirituality and humanitarianism. Her writing is published in literary journals, anthologies, and a national news magazine.

Elle works as a page with the public library in downtown Cincinnati, Ohio. She volunteers often with community places that help those in need. Elle was recognized for her efforts when named Community Service Leader of the Year 2017, receiving this award from an area non-profit organization.

Visit Elle's website at: www.ellemottauthor.com.

A NOTE FROM ELLE

I would love to hear your feedback! When you're finished reading
Out of Chaos will you please leave an honest review on the website
where you purchased this book or on Goodreads.com?
Visit this page on my website to find links to leave a review on all
of the most popular websites:

ellemottauthor.com/reviews

Made in the USA
Middletown, DE
11 October 2018